Civil Societies and Social

Civil Societies and Social Movements examines and contributes to debates surrounding social capital, social movements and the role of civil society in emerging forms of governance.

The authors adopt a broad range of research approaches, from testing hypotheses drawn from rational choice theory against available statistics on associations, to ethnographic study of emerging attempts at participant/deliberative democracy. The book is divided into three clear sections, which focus on the following core aspects of civil society:

- The position of civic organizations between state and society in emerging forms of governance.
- The geographical scales of social movement mobilizations and actions from the local to the global.
- The patterns of public trust and civic engagement that fall under the rubric of social capital.

The volume draws on case studies from a wide range of countries, including Russia, Ukraine, Britain, Greece, Spain, Germany, Argentina and new Asian democracies.

Presenting current research on the key dimensions of civil society, this book will appeal to those researching and studying in the fields of political science, sociology and social policy.

Derrick Purdue is Senior Research Fellow in the Cities Research Centre of the University of the West of England, Bristol, UK.

Routledge/ECPR studies in European political science
Edited by Thomas Poguntke
University of Birmingham, UK on behalf of the European Consortium for Political Research

The Routledge/ECPR Studies in European Political Science series is published in association with the European Consortium for Political Research – the leading organization concerned with the growth and development of political science in Europe. The series presents high-quality edited volumes on topics at the leading edge of current interest in political science and related fields, with contributions from European scholars and others who have presented work at ECPR workshops or research groups.

1 **Regionalist Parties in Western Europe**
Edited by Lieven de Winter and Huri Türsan

2 **Comparing Party System Change**
Edited by Jan-Erik Lane and Paul Pennings

3 **Political Theory and European Union**
Edited by Albert Weale and Michael Nentwich

4 **Politics of Sexuality**
Edited by Terrell Carver and Véronique Mottier

5 **Autonomous Policy Making by International Organizations**
Edited by Bob Reinalda and Bertjan Verbeek

6 **Social Capital and European Democracy**
Edited by Jan van Deth, Marco Maraffi, Ken Newton and Paul Whiteley

7 **Party Elites in Divided Societies**
Edited by Kurt Richard Luther and Kris Deschouwer

8 **Citizenship and Welfare State Reform in Europe**
Edited by Jet Bussemaker

9 **Democratic Governance and New Technology**
Technologically mediated innovations in political practice in Western Europe
Edited by Ivan Horrocks, Jens Hoff and Pieter Tops

10 **Democracy without Borders**
Transnationalisation and conditionality in new democracies
Edited by Jean Grugel

Also available from Routledge in association with the ECPR:

Sex Equality Policy in Western Europe, *Edited by Frances Gardiner*; **Democracy and Green Political Thought**, *Edited by Brian Doherty and Marius de Geus*; **The New Politics of Unemployment**, *Edited by Hugh Compston*; **Citizenship, Democracy and Justice in the New Europe**, *Edited by Percy B. Lehning and Albert Weale*; **Private Groups and Public Life**, *Edited by Jan W. van Deth*; **The Political Context of Collective Action**, *Edited by Ricca Edmondson*; **Theories of Secession**, *Edited by Percy Lehning*; **Regionalism Across the North/South Divide**, *Edited by Jean Grugel and Wil Hout.*

Civil Societies and Social Movements

Potentials and problems

Edited by Derrick Purdue

LONDON AND NEW YORK

First published 2007
by Routledge
2 Park Square, Milton Park, Abingdon, Oxon OX14 4RN

Simultaneously published in the USA and Canada
by Routledge
270 Madison Ave, New York, NY 10016

Routledge is an imprint of the Taylor & Francis Group, an informa business

Transferred to Digital Printing 2010

© 2007 Selection and editorial matter Derrick Purdue; individual chapters,
the contributors

Typeset in Times by Wearset Ltd, Boldon, Tyne and Wear

British Library Cataloguing in Publication Data
A catalogue record for this book is available from the British Library

Library of Congress Cataloging in Publication Data
A catalog record for this book has been requested

ISBN10: 0-415-39933-5 (hbk)
ISBN10: 0-415-58675-5 (pbk)
ISBN10: 0-203-96189-7 (ebk)

ISBN13: 978-0-415-39933-3 (hbk)
ISBN13: 978-0-415-58675-7 (pbk)
ISBN13: 978-0-203-96189-6 (ebk)

Contents

Contributors

Moses A. Boudourides is Associate Professor at the Department of Mathematics of the University of Patras in Greece. His work in mathematics is on dynamical systems (chaos, fractals and complexity) and on mathematical sociology, in particular in the areas of social networks, social movements, social choice, Internet research and science and technology studies.

Iosif Botetzagias is a Lecturer of Environmental Politics and Policy at the University of the Aegean, Department of Environment. His research interests include environmental politics, environmental NGOs, new social movements and social networks analysis. His recent publications include 'The Greek Environmental Movement' in Kayla M. (ed., 2005), *Environmental Education* while he was guest editor of the *Journal of Southern Europe and the Balkans*.

Manlio Cinalli is the main researcher of the French team of the LOCALMULTIDEM project. He is currently Charge de Recherche FNSP at the Centre de Recherches Politiques de Sciences Po (Paris, France). He is author of several research reports for British funding bodies and the European Commission. His comparative research focuses cross-nationally on political participation and networks, with particular attention to issues of ethnicity, integration and exclusion.

Luigi Curini is a researcher in political science at the Department of Social and Political Studies (University of Milan) where he teaches political science. His major interests are linked to the problems of collective action within loosely institutionalized contexts, including the relationship between deliberative processes and game theory. He has published in *Rivista Italiana di Scienza Politica* and *Quaderni di Scienza Politica*.

John Diamond is based in the Centre for Local Policy Studies at Edge Hill University, Lancashire, UK. He is the co-author of *Management of Regeneration*, Routledge (2005) and co-editor of *Managing the City*, Routledge (2007). He is on the management committee of the Association of Research into the Voluntary and Community Sectors.

Sebastian Haunss is senior researcher at the Institute for Political Science at the University of Hamburg. He is currently working on his habilitation on knowledge governance and on a research project on the European conflict around software patents. He has published mainly on the issue of social movements, collective identity and visual protest repertoires.

Ji-Young Kim is Assistant Professor in the Department of Journalism and Communication Studies at Sungkyunkwan University in South Korea, and formerly Hallsworth Research Fellow at the University of Manchester in the UK where she received her PhD. Her research interests include civic journalism, social capital and e-governance in a comparative perspective. Her earlier works have been published in leading scholarly journals including the *International Political Science Review* and *Information Polity*.

Darcy K. Leach is Visiting Assistant Professor of Sociology at Boston College.

Kateryna Pishchikova is a researcher at the University of Amsterdam. She lectures in political science and international relations at the University of Amsterdam and at the International School for Humanities and Social Sciences. She studied linguistics at the Kharkiv National University (Ukraine) and completed her Master's degree in gender studies at the Central European University (Budapest).

Derrick Purdue is Senior Research Fellow in the Cities Research Centre of the University of the West of England, Bristol. His research interests include social movements, community engagement and urban governance. He is author of *Anti-Genetix*, Ashgate (2000) and has had articles published in several academic journals, including *Urban Studies, Sociological Review, Environment and Planning* and the *Community Development Journal*.

Suvi Salmenniemi is a sociologist specializing in Russian and gender studies. She works as a researcher in Aleksanteri Institute (Finnish Centre for Russian and East European Studies), University of Helsinki. Her fields of interest include civic activism, citizenship, democratization and feminist theory. She is the author of 'Civic Activity – Feminine Activity? Gender, Civil Society and Citizenship in Post-Soviet Russia' published in *Sociology*.

Julien D. Talpin is a PhD student at the European University Institute. He currently works on participatory democracy in Europe; his research tries to evaluate the individual effects of deliberation in the construction of civic competence.

Rafael Vázquez García is an Associate Professor in the Department of Political Science and Administration at the University of Granada, Spain, where he teaches. His major research interests focus on civil society, political culture, public opinion, leadership and theory of democracy.

Joris Verhulst is a PhD student at the department of political science of the

University of Antwerp. He works and publishes on social movements and mobilization.

Stefaan Walgrave is Professor of political science at the University of Antwerp. His research interests are social movements and political participation, political communication and electoral behaviour.

Acknowledgements

Thanks are due to the ECPR for supporting the proposal for a workshop on 'The Changing Structure of Civil Society', at the ECPR Joint Sessions, in Uppsala in 2004. The chapters of the book are drawn from a selection of the papers presented to that workshop. Thanks to the participants for their lively discussion of the papers that now make up this book. Particular thanks to Mario Diani, who co-directed the workshop and provided the inspiration and initial advice for attempting to develop this book. Thanks also to the ECPR Routledge series editor, Thomas Poguntke, and three anonymous referees, for their helpful comments on the proposal for this book. Finally thanks are due to the Faculty of the Built Environment at the University of West of England in Bristol, who funded my work in editing the book, and of course to the authors, who have contributed chapters to the book.

Derrick Purdue

1 Introduction

Dimensions of civil society

Derrick Purdue

This volume brings together current research on three analytical dimensions of civil society – the position of civic organizations between state and society in emerging forms of governance; the geographical scales of social movement mobilizations and actions from the local to the global; and the patterns of public trust and civic engagement that falls under the rubric of social capital. The book aims to advance theory in each of these areas, which are topical themes within political science and sociology, as well as policy and practice literatures. The research underpinning the book has been conducted in a wide range of countries within and beyond Europe, and applies and develops a range of quantitative and qualitative methodologies.

Over the past decade and a half, civil society has been acknowledged to be of increasing significance within political science, social research and policy making. Civil society is broadly considered to be the cradle of democracy, yet it remains a highly contested concept. The concept of civil society has a complex genealogy of shifting meanings, according to the rhetorical needs of the day. In contrast to community (which is concerned with familiarity), civil society indicates the ability to deal with strangers without using force, and so is ideally suited to examining cities, the places where strangers meet. Civil society thus implies a level of mutual trust between strangers, who may therefore pass among each other in the physical space of cities and trade with one another. For these reasons civil society was seen as underpinning the functioning of the emerging capitalist market by the economists and philosophers of eighteenth-century Scotland (Seligman in Taylor 2003). Civil society was later viewed as playing a similar role in nation states and liberal democracies. Hegel, writing in early nineteenth-century Germany, used the state–civil society couplet to contrast the historic collective project of the Prussian state to the sphere of egoist impulses in civil society, in which he included the emerging capitalist economy. Tocqueville, exploring the nature of democracy in America in the mid-nineteenth century, excluded the economy from civil society, and focused his interest on the right to free association and the presence of informal organizations (Keane 1988).

After a period of abeyance, the concept of civil society re-emerged in the early 1990s to describe the transition to liberal democracy of former communist regimes in Eastern Europe (Walzer 1995) and of former military dictatorships in Latin America. In contrast to state monopolies, civil society was posed as representing a more complex social fabric, consisting of a diverse set of organizations, with more active participation by a greater number of citizens, and hence the cradle of democracy. Similarly, more recent debates about global civil society also draw attention to a 'democratic deficit', this time to the domination of global politics by unelected bodies such as the World Trade Organization (WTO) and the International Monetary Fund (IMF). However, confounding this neat distinction, Keane (2003) argues that global civil society comprises all non-state cross-border transactions and so is prone to intense inequalities of both wealth and opportunity to engage. Global civil society is also threatened by uses of the new civil freedoms for criminal purposes, or for religious and ideological oppression. Even at a local level civil society is always a sphere of conflict and dispute, where individuals and groups pursue their interests as well as a sphere of agreed civil rights (Tester 1992). Civil society is nevertheless seen as a crucial component of liberal democracy, and associational life complements the representative organs of the state (Warren 2001).

Whether civil society is one side of a state–civil society dichotomy (Hegel), or one part of a three-way division between state, economy and civil society (Tocqueville), is an ongoing debate. Broadly speaking those on the political Right identify the flowering of civil society with market freedom, while those on the Left prefer to see civil society as a counter-balance to the powers of large-scale economic actors, such as international corporations, as well as to the powers of states (Jenkins and Smith 2001).

Leaving aside the ambiguity of whether or not it includes the market, it is still difficult to define the limits of civil society. Civil society clearly lacks the physical coercive power of the military or any other repressive uses of state power for the direct control of bodies. Thus a significant aspect of civil society is that it functions as a realm of free association, guaranteed by the state through civil rights, but not directly controlled by the state. Yet many institutions straddle the divide. Political parties bring together individuals into free associations in civil society, yet also participate in government within the state. On the frontier of the market, pubs, clubs or shopping malls may belong to large commercial companies, but provide meeting space for a range of social groups and civic organizations. Civil society is often seen as an intermediate layer between private life and institutionalized politics, hence one definition of civil society is the 'network of institutions through which groups in society in general represent themselves – both to each other and to the state' (Shaw 1994: 647). Civil society is therefore the terrain of social movements.

Yet representation within civil society has traditionally been selective in the established democracies, favouring white, upper and middle class males. Successive waves of social movements have struggled for a place in civil society, guaranteed by civil rights. Since the 1960s civil society within the liberal democracies has had to accommodate a range of new social groups – black and minority ethnic people, women, gays and lesbians, environmentalists, disabled people, as well as hippies, punks, clubbers and skateboarders.

In addition to free association, civil society is underpinned by inter-personal civility. Civility is a 'game without agreed rules' which depends on the ability to make appropriate moves and anticipate responses in a changing context – the skill of dealing with strangers (Bauman 2000). Yet civility depends upon the production of codes of behaviour, manners and physical deportment, through which bodies are disciplined (Jowers *et al.* 1999). Each social movement therefore struggles not only over access to civil society as a space of free association, but also against the colonization of civil society by dominant forms of civility. For example, feminism has broken down the wall between public and private life, family and civil society, and challenged sexist behaviour in public. This has led some writers to a more diffuse sociological conception of civil society (Hegedus 1989), in which civil society falls closer to everyday life, as opposed to the more political definition given above. However, civil society cannot be identified with a single point of view, it is a competitive realm, where individuals and organizations compete to win hearts and minds for their ideas and life-style choices.

Civil societies have been reshaped by globalization, which undermines the nation-state as the sole reference point of civil society. Everyday life practices are often oriented to global issues – campaigns against international wars, or charitable support for Third World development projects – and hence participation in global civil society. However, even global processes – migration of people, or disputes over conflicting ideas – have to happen in a locality. Cities are in many ways areas of interaction and forums for civic argument and so have always been closely connected to ideas of citizenship which have their base in civil society.

There are a number of research strands that deal with civil society in different ways, and this book is organized around three analytical dimensions of civil society that accord with three of these strands. The first is that civil society is always defined in relation to the state and new patterns of governance represent a shifting boundary between state and civil society. The roles that civic organizations play and their positioning are shaped by this dynamic relationship between state and civil society in emerging forms of governance. The second is that civil society is always a space of contention, but the geographical scale of that space is increasingly open to question. While civil society has traditionally been conceived of in relation to the nation-state, processes of globalization have precipitated the development of global civil society, yet the role of nations, cities and local milieux remain important in transformed forms, having important impacts on how social movements mobilize and appear on the ground. The third dimension is civil society 'from within' – matters of civic virtues and public trust, social interaction and networks – which have crystallized around the concept of social capital. An important claim within the social capital debate has been that public trust is an important bridge from civil society to the state through democratic politics (Putnam 1993).

Civic organizations between state and society in emerging forms of governance

The dominant idea in contemporary discussions of the relations between state and civil society is the transition from Government to governance. That is, from a system where a single organization, the state, governs territory, at any particular level from national to local, to more complex forms of governance involving a number of governing organizations, and structures through which they collaborate. These may include partnerships, within which government retains a reduced but still significant strategic role (Allen and Cars 2001). Key issues in the governance debates include first, whether governance significantly disperses the power previously concentrated in government, or whether power remains where it was, only less obviously so; and second, whether the expanded opportunities for civic organizations to engage in the new governance structures outweigh the loss of autonomy they undergo through integration and institutionalization.

Thus in Part I of the book the representation of civil society is explored within the shifting sands of the new governance, through the medium of civic organizations. Civic organizations are a core element of civil society acting as hubs of social networks and social capital, elements of social movements and points of integration into governance. More formalized civic organizations tend to be analysed as 'public interest groups' in national politics, or as 'NGOs' in the international and development literature (Princen and Finger 1994). Social policy circles in Britain refer to these civic organizations as 'the voluntary sector', which has been described as a force field located between state, market and community (Evers 1996). Voluntary organizations tend to focus on a specific remit of service delivery, but to a lesser degree also campaigning around a particular issue or constituency. These civic organizations can be the result of the institutionalization of social movements, and they may continue to articulate new social issues and identities (e.g. HIV+), forming focal points for communities of interest within a locality while delivering services.

The less formal civic organizations and networks at the local level (city wide or neighbourhood) are usually understood in terms of community politics. While community studies and debates over the nature of community and its relation to neighbourhood stretch back to the Chicago School of the 1920s, 'communities' are today predominantly discussed in terms of policy (Taylor 2003) and their place in local governance. Intervention in local communities in Britain has consisted of open-ended community development, often claiming a radical heritage of community activism (related to social movements). However, government programmes now sponsor more strategic community capacity-building activity, geared to encourage local community engagement with the webs of multi-sector partnerships that play a crucial role in governance at a local level (Banks and Shenton 2001).

The whole revival of thinking about civil society has in part been inspired by the collapse of the statist Soviet system and the rise of civil society activity that preceded it. In the reconstruction/transition period that followed the collapse of the Soviet system a predominant view from the West has been that civic organizations have a major role to play in the emerging forms of governance, and that this role could be facilitated by Western donors, who themselves became powerful governance actors. However, the role that is now demanded of them is much less that of democratic renewal than as service delivery agents, able to respond to change far quicker than the state, especially as the state is perceived as the problem in the first place. In a perhaps less stark fashion than in Eastern Europe, the paradigm shift from Fordist to post-Fordist economy in Western Europe has meant new relationships between state and civil society and new roles for civic organizations in local governance.

The key theme of unequal power relations in governance and struggles to maintain the autonomy of civic organizations in relation to more powerful actors runs across the three chapters in this section, which provide an East–West European comparison, with two chapters on countries of the former Soviet Union and the third on Britain. Policy shifts in all three countries indicate that the opening up of governance structures to civic organizations was perhaps a brief policy window, which is closing again as civic organizations move through a cycle from democratic innovators to service delivery agents and then are tied into tighter forms of control by government and international donors, either as more incorporated service agents or returned to a marginal place in local politics under the banner of civic activism.

In a case study of the provincial town of Tver in Central Russia, Salmenniemi explores the increasing domination of civic organizations by the Russian state. As Russia moves towards 'managed democracy' the independence of civil society is endangered. Civil society in Russia is shaped in part by regional variation, but there has also been a shift from civic activism during perestroika, in the form of informal clubs and loose social movements, to professionalized civic organizations. The discourse of 'civil society' has been replaced by that of 'social partnership' or the 'third sector' where civic organizations have been granted a service delivery role in the social policy domains that the state has abandoned – a fact which is not unconnected to the high profile of women in the civic organizations. During the Putin era, public discursive space and room for action by civic organizations have decreased and critical voices are no longer welcome in the public sphere. The central point here is that there has been considerable political change in Russia but that the process of opening up governance to civil society as a favourable political opportunity structure (POS) has moved into closure, and as the term 'managed democracy' denotes, civil society is expected to play a purely symbolic role, as power is concentrated back into the hands of the state. State power remains central in spite of new forms of governance.

Pishchikova provides a complementary approach, exploring the dynamic between international funders (mainly USAID) and civic organizations in Ukraine. Here the second side of this triangular relationship between state, civic organizations and external funders is problematized and includes a critique of the generalized 'transition paradigm'. Shifts in the analysis of 'transition' are embodied in the reformulation of funding programmes and their priorities. Three successive discourses were embodied in the programmes, the first focused on building democratic institutions. As interest among the local population in reform and civic participation appeared to be flagging, USAID shifted emphasis to an empowerment discourse to build capacity for action through empowering individuals and organizations, which in turn was to raise expectations and revitalize interest in reform and civil society. An emerging discourse of civic activism then shifted the emphasis from civic organizations as service deliverers back to advocacy and making demands of local and national government. The rapid growth in civic organizations in Ukraine is in part at least dependent on the engagement of international donors in provision of social programmes and encouraging new expressions of civil society. These donors have therefore become important, if ambivalent, players in governance at local and regional levels, as is local government, where many of the 'paper NGOs' reside. Thus a three-cornered dynamic is apparent in the construction of a space for civil society, between the civic organizations themselves and the local power holder in local government and the external funders.

Diamond picks up the story of civil society–state dynamics in Britain, where the engagement of civic organizations in governance and service delivery has been the most developed in Western Europe. Again the chapter reveals tensions organized around a triangular dynamic. After a decade of engaging civic organizations in neighbourhood and sometimes city-wide partnerships dealing with a plethora of policy issues, government policy has extended to larger Local Strategic Partnerships and to funding correspondingly larger Community Empowerment Networks to facilitate a stronger engagement between the sectors. Again, however, a triangular power relation is revealed between central government-funded initiatives, existing power bases of local government and civic organizations. Community activists tend to see the arrival of new government initiatives in their neighbourhoods in the context of a long sequence of interventions in a highly differentiated micro-geography of neighbourhood. This contrasts with the views of many professionals, who see the initiatives as working on a clean slate with no history and a universally applicable geography. For many local government officers working in partnership with civic organizations is a distraction from their mainstream service delivery and their own internal targets.

Civil societies and social movements from local to global: arenas for mobilization and action

Social movements are a key element of civil society. New social movements theory started to appear in the late 1960s and 1970s to explain new waves of political activism – student protests, feminism, peace and environmentalism. Unlike political parties, new social movements have a loose network structure and often use direct action as a campaigning tool. On the other hand, what distinguishes a social movement from social networks more generally is that a movement has a purpose beyond sociability, in that it is engaged in social change.

The origins of social movement theory in the USA go back to the attempts by the Chicago School to make sense of informal social action by understanding the rationality of the actors themselves. The political process model derived from the historical research (Tilly *et al.* 1975) suggests that modern social movements appeared after the French Revolution as local actions against individuals (for example landlords) were replaced by national movements to change state policy.

Social movements rise and fall through cycles of protest, in which some movements act as 'early risers', while others follow as 'late comers'. In the course of a protest cycle social movements develop action repertoires which are understood by their opponents. Since the nineteenth century Tarrow argues a modular action repertoire has come into being, to which particular modules are added in each new cycle of protest. Action repertoires tend to focus on convention (lobbying government, press work and so on) or contention (protest, particularly direct action) (Tarrow 1994). The context of collective action is the political opportunity structure (POS). Like civil societies and social movements, the POS was conceived of in terms of the national government. The political opportunities open to social movements can increase when the state is opening up to give greater access to power or when divisions emerge between ruling elites (Tarrow 1994). An open POS may encourage social movements to engage in conventional action repertoires, whereas a closed POS may encourage a more contentious action repertoire of direct action. Conflicting political opportunities may, however, appear at the local, national and global levels.

Social movements must mobilize their resources of membership, money and expertise. This involves forming organizations and building networks between organizations. Movement leaders need to provide a strategy that links up these resources in the most effective way and that makes participation most attractive to their potential supporters. Yet strategy needs to be put in the context of a movement culture. Social movement leaders present their actions in terms of collective action frames. Several authors have distilled specific framing tasks they see as essential for any successful social movement – Gamson (1995) offers three such frames. An injustice frame defines what's wrong – the social issue at stake. An identity frame defines who 'we' the social movement are and who the adversaries are. An agency frame defines what 'we' can do – viable methods of social change. The alignment of these frames among key actors and organizations and their diffusion to wider publics is then a key process of establishing a social movement.

Contemporary social movements do not simply mobilize existing challenging groups against power holders, they create new values and identities (such as feminists and environmentalists) (Melucci 1989). In emphasizing culture and emerging identities as the main product of social movements, Melucci encouraged students of social movements to look beyond visible mobilizations, to the submerged cultural networks of social movements in everyday life, which act as 'cultural laboratories' experimenting with new identities (Melucci 1989). Thus festivals and protest actions began to merge in the 'DIY Culture' of the late 1990s (Purdue *et al.* 1997; Jowers *et al.* 1999).

At the turn of the millennium, the radical environmental movements took a distinctly global turn and connected with social justice issues. Both governance and civil society now operate at a number of geographical scales. Not only has global governance become far more significant in itself, but has also become evermore the focus of global civil society and social movement mobilization activity (Purdue 2000), as events in Seattle, Prague and Genoa have demonstrated. Since then global financial and trade organizations have been a focus for a series of actions, mobilizing a wide range of participants, using and innovating a mixture of conventional and contentious action repertoires, combining global and cultural politics (Chesters and Welsh 2005). The heightened tensions of international politics since 2001 have caused recurrent waves of peace mobilizations against wars and threats of war. Yet it has remained unclear whether radical elements are able to combine with broader sections of civil society to sustain a social movement dynamic in which alliances are not purely instrumental, but are strongly backed by shared identity (Della Porta and Diani 1999). While the nation-state still remains a central focus for politics, global issues are central to current social movements (Purdue *et al.* 2004). However, even the most global social movements recruit, mobilize and act much of the time in particular localities, as is evident, for example, in the differing patterns of social movement mobilization in Glasgow and Bristol (Purdue *et al.* 2004).

The four chapters in Part II of the book cover a range of geographical scales on which social movement mobilization and action occurs and the interaction between these levels. Haunss and Leach explore the territory of collective identity and cultural experimentation, introducing a novel concept of 'social movement scene' to describe mobilization and connection between a movement and other elements of a broader civil society at a local level, even where the issues are global. They explore the fluid meeting point of movements and wider civil society and argue that the robustness of social movement scenes are an important measure of civil society that reaches beyond the institutional and organizational contexts where we are more accustomed to examining civil society. Scenes are both symbolic and physical places – particular neighbourhoods where activists, supporters and life-style aficionados concentrate and more specifically particular bars, cafes and community centres where they congregate. Using the 'autonomous movement' in Germany as a case study, the authors argue that scenes are part-time life-style oriented social structures, often more accessible and less demanding than social movements, and so allow individuals to join and leave movements easily. Movements scenes are clearly regions of civil society with high densities of bonding social capital permeating the everyday life of the participants, as well as allowing a degree of bridging to more diffuse regions of civil society.

Social movements at all geographic levels accumulate social capital – bonding capital internal to the movement and bridging capital in connections with wider civil society. They also have relationships of some sort, positive or negative, with governance structures, and where these are positive relations, they accumulate linking capital. Cinalli demonstrates the connections between social movements, social capital and governance at the national level (Britain), by comparing the impact of social movements on two policy domains (unemployment and asylum), and exploring the relative importance of horizontal connections within civil society and vertical links into governance structures. Significant differences were found between the two movements – pro-asylum networks were strong horizontally and weak vertically, whereas pro-unemployed networks were weak horizontally and strong vertically. These differences in network structure can be explained by the contrasting political opportunity structures each movement faced. Asylum seekers face legal exclusion and require support in everyday life issues, while pro-asylum organizations have little access to government in a politically charged policy domain; whereas unemployed people have greater access to welfare resources and pro-unemployed organizations have greater political access to the Labour administration. In other words, unemployment is a policy field with a more open POS where access to national governance structures is somewhat easier than asylum.

Movements concerned with power, politics and governance at one geographic level are likely to have to mobilize at other larger or smaller geographic scales, and encounter difficulties specific to those scales. In their case study of local and national mobilizations in Greece, against war and globalization, Boudourides and Botetzagias explore the persistent importance of national organizational and ideological cleavages, through the concept of 'anti-participation' in networks. The key contribution of this chapter is that it broadens the focus from positive network ties between organizations, which will appear together at the same events, to include negative repulsions, where organizations will avoid each others' demonstration and work in parallel. Using both positive and negative ties allows the construction of structurally equivalent blocks of organizations and the relations between them. They find two distinct coalitions at the national level running through the protests against war and global economic processes. These two coalitions start from different organizational bases and have distinctive priorities. Although they display greater overlap on protest issues during the period of hottest protest action, they still remain in distinct blocks, demonstrating again the significance of national cleavages to social movement mobilizations at the global level.

Verhulst and Walgrave take up the same general theme of national influences on mobilization over global issues. By comparing the mobilizations in seven European countries and the USA in an international day of action against the Iraq War on 15 February 2003, they again reveal national differences in who was mobilized in each country and what their motives were likely to be, in spite of the global nature of the issue. While the POS for any movement or action may have a global dimension, national factors shape a distinctive POS, which interacts with existing national protest cycles. Thus in terms of the global anti-war demonstrations an obvious factor was the position of the national government on the war – whether initiating, supporting or opposing the war. Thus protestors could be directing the protest mainly against their own governments where they wished their government to change its decision to support the war, but in countries where governments opposed the war, the protest had a mainly global target in the hegemonic power of the USA. The complexion of the government (Left or Right) was also significant, with Spanish protestors, for example, standing out as having a distinctively labour movement profile with a much higher percentage of manual workers than elsewhere. In a similar way, Italian protestors were a product of a much more developed protest cycle, and consequently were prepared to use a more confrontational action repertoire than in other countries. While overall there is a long-term trend for the socio-economic profiles of demonstrators to become more diverse and closer to the overall population, national variations were important. In the USA protestors were oldest, two-thirds women and mostly professionals and most closely followed the demographic for a new social movement. Mobilization structures also varied from country to country, with more organizationally based recruitment in Italy, also drawing on a higher level of far left voters than elsewhere. These findings are significant, as the more diverse demonstrating populations become, the wider the range of civil society is engaged in social movement actions.

Social capital and trust within different democratic systems

Social capital indicates the more internal relationship individuals have with civil society and the civic trust they put in the ability of states to provide good governance. As traditional social groupings break down in favour of individualization and globalization (Beck 1992), trust has emerged as the crucial element in maintaining viable social relations and is the core issue of civil society. Trust embedded in networks is commonly portrayed as 'social glue' (bonding social capital) or 'social oil' (bridging social capital) or a 'hook' into institutions (linking social capital) (Renewal.net). These three types of social capital correspond to different aspects of civil society: bonding to communities or movements; bridging to wider civil society; and linking to governance.

The concept of social capital emerged from a line of thinking that claimed that development depends not only on money (financial capital) and natural resources, but also education and skills (human capital) and trust between individuals in functioning social networks (social capital). This line of thought has been applied to economic innovation (Granovetter 1985) and flourishing democracy (Putnam 1993), as well as local communities and neighbourhoods (Coleman 1988). Social capital in a community or neighbourhood has been defined as networks of mutual obligations for outstanding favours, flows of information and enforceable shared norms, residing in relationships between individuals or families in communities (Coleman 1988). In this approach social capital is a flow that binds people together. Coleman suggests that the more outstanding favours there are, the greater the social capital, since more people are engaged in social networks. However, these social networks need to be regarded as mutual, so that individuals meet their communal obligations. Norms of behaviour need to be shared in order to underpin what Coleman calls closed social networks. So where people have a broadly shared outlook and have common problems to face they can trust each other and develop a system of reciprocal support for their mutual benefit. The resulting web of obligations ties the community together and increases overall trust. In this version of social capital, it is equated with community cohesion and is used to indicate the need to build horizontal connections between community members in excluded neighbourhoods to overcome individual isolation.

A problem with applying social capital in this way even to a single neighbourhood is that it is clear that there may be many distinct communities in one neighbourhood. Community action on a particular problem or to secure a community facility such as a community centre may be ineffective unless activists are able to bridge the divisions in the neighbourhood. This depends on the 'strength of weak ties' (Granovetter 1985) – connections with others that are not part of your immediate circle. These more extended networks are 'bridging' social capital as opposed to the 'bonding' social capital of close knit groups or single interest groups (Putnam 2000).

Equally, however, social capital can be viewed in the context of a stratified social system, where each social class has more money, power and status than the class below. Bourdieu (1986) argues that three types of capital are relevant to this status hierarchy – money (economic capital), cultural taste or privileged knowledge (cultural capital) and membership of a prestigious group (social capital). Possessing social capital (i.e. good networks) allows one to gain access to others who have considerable stocks of economic and/or cultural capital. In this version, social capital is a means of maintaining or improving your social standing by accessing resources.

While these two versions of social capital seem contradictory, they can also be seen as complementary. A series of writers have pointed to different dimensions of social capital pertaining to either the links within a group or those extending out from the group to institutions and power holders. A distinction has been made between social capital as 'internal' bonds within a social movement or 'external' links to governing elites (Diani 1997); as 'integration' of a community or 'linkage' which includes the ability of individual community members engaged in bottom-up development to make links with big players such as local authorities, banks, private companies and funding bodies (Woolcock 1998). This sort of 'linking' social capital (Renewal.net) connects civil society to key institutions in governance. Just as civic organizations need to have the capacity to engage with institutions, so too do institutions need to develop the capacity to engage, both with each other and with communities. Woolcock (1998) breaks this institutional social capital down into 'synergy', the ability of local government, for example, to work in effective partnerships with the private sector, and 'organizational integrity', the capacity of government to deliver on its promises to citizens. That is, whether the government can get the voters to trust it.

Part III of the book contains four chapters on social capital, three dealing with more recent democracies. The authors question whether the existence of one type of social capital leads to another, and whether the social benefits claimed for social capital are, in fact, lost when no distinctions are made between these types of social capital. Curini poses the social capital question in the most general terms: whether high levels of membership of civic organizations deliver the collective good of generalized trust, which it has been claimed may have numerous positive outcomes such as increased political engagement, effective economy and lower levels of crime. The question has two parts: whether people learn to cooperate through active (or inactive) membership of associations; and whether a high level of associations in a region can lead to a generalized trust being diffused to non-members as well. Using data from the World Values Survey, he runs a multi-level model analysing data at both the level of the citizen and at the European regional level. He finds that in regions with a high density of associations, active membership does correlate with higher generalized trust, but that for inactive members in the same regions the impact of associational density depends on the kinds of associations involved. Only in those associations which have a wider social base (bridging associations) do inactive members experience heightened trust. In interest based associations (bonding associations) there is no spillover effect. There appears to be no spillover effect of heightened trust for non-members at all.

Vázquez García takes up the issue of trust in historical form. He traces the low performance of Spain on indicators of associational strength back to the lack of democracy in the country's relatively recent past, which limited the development of civil society. The analysis of membership and participation of voluntary associations in Spain shows that they remain relatively low compared with most other Western nations, as do political interest and social trust. Institutional change and democratic politics may promote the creation of social capital in some degree, but are not necessarily enough to break a situation of low intensity equilibrium. The development of new democratic institutions does not per se create social capital beyond this level; something more than formal institutions and an established democratic system are required to drive change in civil society.

Kim takes forward the relationship of social capital to trust in the political system by reviewing the relationship between civil society and social capital. She examines Putnam's claim that social capital embodied in voluntary associations is good for democracy and whether or not it is valid outside 'core democracies'. She presents two orientations of civil society: one is that of support to the state and systems of governance, which is implicit in Putnam's approach; and on the other hand, civil society as critical counterweight to the state (Foley and Edwards 1996). She then argues that 'political capital', or trust in political institutions, is distinct from more amorphous social capital. This political capital is then dependent on citizens' assessment of government performance and on their own political viewpoints. Analysis of membership of voluntary associations and political participation in South Korea and Taiwan leads to the finding that membership of voluntary organizations often correlates with scepticism about the state and political engagement in these two countries. This suggests a more nuanced view of social capital and politics is in order. Trust and networks within a social group (bonding capital) cannot necessarily be expected to generate wider engagement with politics and governance, especially where there is a high level of conflict. This idea of low political capital resonates with the post-Soviet politics explored by Salmenniemi and Pishchikova in earlier chapters where democratic reform has stumbled and political cynicism is rife.

Talpin connects several of the themes running through this book, through an ethnographic study of popular neighbourhood assemblies in Argentina, which were set up out of distrust and rejection of the national government and ruling elites. Thus Talpin's chapter is concerned with local social movement mobilizations, and their ability to bridge into wider civil society at the neighbourhood level. However, Talpin analyses the local experience not in terms of social movements, but instead through theories of social capital and theories of deliberative democracy, both of which stress the value of associations as schools of democracy teaching democratic skills and civic virtues, and evaluates whether deliberative democracy generates social capital. The popular assemblies drew together heterogeneous groups in neighbourhood based forums, and participants interviewed claim that their participation led them to change towards more tolerance and solidarity with others in their neighbourhood. However, this real life experiment in deliberative democracy showed up some of the weaknesses in the theory. Differential power led to domination and marginalization within the formally open discursive practice of deliberation. Furthermore, changes in the participants may have been determined more by mutual participation than the deliberative process per se. While bonding social capital appeared to increase with the appearance of tighter collective identities, bridging social capital fared less well, as particular groups and styles came to dominate the forums, causing others to exit. Conflict and corruption can therefore produce bonding social capital that works against engagement with mainstream politics rather than in favour of it, while linking capital was very weak due to the high level of distrust of established politics. Indeed, distrust of political institutions and elites is accepted in the social movement literature as a force in social movement mobilization (Flam 2005).

Methodologies

A variety of methodologies have been developed within the social movement literature making conflicting claims about the appropriate quantitative and qualitative research methods and data sources for researching social movements, with a similar variety in the field of organizational (and inter-organizational) studies. These methodologies fall in line with three broad paradigms in social research. The first is more inclined to collect mainly quantitative data in order to determine patterns of behaviour, the second mainly collects qualitative data in order to understand the world views and experience of the research subjects. Third is a set of interventionist methods including evaluation and action research, which attempt to produce some change in the research subjects' behaviour or learning, while gathering data. While these paradigms frequently blur into each other in practice, for example through multi-method case studies, each section of the book draws on at least two of these paradigms, allowing some triangulation of the findings.

In Part I, the first chapter relies on a combination of qualitative interviewing of civic activists and local authorities and participant observation in civic organizations, as well as quantitative survey data from civic organizations and discourse analysis of documents produced by government (Salmenniemi), the second is based on interviews with civic participants and discourse analysis of documents produced by funding agencies (Pishchikova), while the third is based on an evaluation of a partnership, with interviews conducted with both governmental and civic actors (Diamond). Thus the perspectives of the civic participants are set in a wider context.

Two chapters later in the book also use an interpretive qualitative approach. Haunss and Leach conducted an ethnographic study of the 'movement scene' in two urban neighbourhoods in Germany to explore how movement activists interact in their everyday lives with each other and with looser forms of civil society. The pattern of civility revealed is closely connected to actor self-perception of themselves as participants in a critical movement. Talpin also used ethnographic participation in neighbourhood forums in Buenos Aires to explore the finer grain of the experience of being an activist in a social movement. Participants' reflections on their experience are used to trace the interaction between deliberative politics and the types of social capital that effectively develop (or not) under these circumstances.

Cinalli uses both qualitative and quantitative analysis, based on 80 in-depth semi-structured interviews, conducted with core policy-makers, political party representatives and civil society organizations, pro-beneficiary groups and movements, to provide maps of the networks in the pro-asylum and unemployed people's movements, across civil society and into national governance.

The remaining two social movement studies use purely quantitative approaches. Boudourides and Botetzagias use social network analysis to analyse newspaper representations of anti-war, anti-globalization or anti-international summit protests in Greece, which allowed them to discover systematic cleavages in the global protest networks in Greece. Verhulst and Walgrave provide a comparative study of the global anti-war demonstrations of 15 February 2003, with a survey of participants on the protest marches in Belgium, the Netherlands, Switzerland, Germany, Italy, Spain, the UK and the USA. This allowed them to relate the pattern of mobilization to the POS and protest cycle in each country.

Part III on social capital contains a further three studies based on statistics drawn from the World Values Survey, alongside the ethnographic study. Curini tests a game theoretic model based on a rational choice theory of social capital against World Values Survey data for European regions. He is able to use both regional and individual data to explore the wider social impacts of high levels of civil society organization, both bonding and bridging in nature.

Vázquez García uses survey data, most of which come from World Values Survey, European Social Survey and Spanish Centro de Investigaciones Sociológicas, to conduct an analysis of membership and participation of voluntary associations in Spain. Kim, too, draws on World Values Survey data, to explore the links, real or imagined, between social capital and political trust and voting in South Korea and Taiwan.

The quantitative and qualitative methods used complement each other, as the wider scope of quantitative analysis, for example, on social trust and political cynicism, support the narrower but deeper findings of the qualitative approaches in a variety of countries. Similarly the quantitative analyses of mobilization are consistent with the qualitative accounts. This diversity of methods allows the authors to build up an overall picture through the book of these live topics within the studies of civil societies.

The conclusion will summarize the key findings of each section and aims to develop the key ideas of civil society and social movements in the light of these findings and four themes are pursued. First is the ambiguous position civic organizations occupy between civil society and the state and their role in governance or governmentality and the creation of governable subjects. Second is the paradoxical interaction between local, national and global factors and their impacts on social movement mobilization, as well as on the relationships of social movements to wider civil societies. The third theme concerns the balance of different types of social capital which develop in different situations and the forms of trust that underpin them in relation to movements, civil societies and states. Finally we consider the conception of civil society as the supportive cradle of the democratic state or the apparently opposing orientation of civil society as a critical and challenging counterweight to the state, and explore the possible dialectic between these positions.

References

Allen, J. and Cars, G. (2001) Multiculturalism and Governing Neighbourhoods, *Urban Studies*, 38 (12): 2195–2209.
Banks, S. and Shenton, F. (2001) Regenerating Neighbourhoods: a Critical Look at the Role of Capacity Building, *Local Economy*, 16 (4): 286–298.
Bauman, Z. (2000) *Liquid Modernity*, Cambridge: Polity.
Beck, U. (1992) *Risk Society: Towards a New Modernity*, London: Sage.
Bourdieu, P. (1986) The Forms of Capital, in J. Richardson (ed.), *Handbook of Theory and Research for the Sociology of Education*, Westport, CT: Greenwood Press.
Chesters, G. and Welsh, I. (2005) *Complexity and Social Movements: Multitudes at the Edge of Chaos*, London: Routledge.
Coleman, J. (1988) Social Capital in the Creation of Human Capital, *American Journal of Sociology*, 94: S94–S120.
Della Porta, D. and Diani, M. (1999) *Social Movements: An Introduction*, Oxford: Blackwell.
Diani, M. (1997) Social Movements and Social Capital: A Network Perspective on Movement Outcome, *Mobilization: An International Journal*, 2 (2): 129–147.
Evers, A. (1996) Part of the Welfare Mix: the Third Sector as an Intermediate Area, *Voluntas – International Journal of Voluntary and Non-profit Organisations*, 6 (2): 159–182.
Flam, H. (2005) Emotions' Map: a Research Agenda, in H. Flam and D. King (eds), *Emotions and Social Movements*, London: Routledge.

Foley, M. and Edwards, B. (1996) The Paradox of Civil Society, *Journal of Democracy*, 7 (3): 38–52.

Gamson, W. (1995) Constructing Social Protest, in H. Johnston and B. Klandermans (eds), *Social Movements and Culture*, London: UCL.

Granovetter, M. (1985) Economic Action and Social Structure: The Problem of Embeddedness, *American Journal of Sociology*, 91 (3): 481–510.

Hegedus, Z. (1989) Social Movements and Social Change in Self-Creative Society: New Civil Initiatives in the International Arena, *International Sociology*, 4 (1): 19–36.

Jenkins, P. and Smith, H. (2001) The State, the Market and the Community: an Analytical Framework for Community Self-development, in M. Carley, P. Jenkins and H. Smith (eds), *Urban Development and Civil Society: The Role of Communities in Sustainable Development*, London: Earthscan.

Jowers, P., Dürrschmidt, J., O'Doherty, R. and Purdue, D. (1999) Affective and Aesthetic Dimensions of Contemporary Social Movements in South West England, *Innovation*, 12 (1): 99–118.

Keane, J. (1988) Introduction, in J. Keane (ed.), *Civil Society and the State: New European Perspectives*, London: Verso.

Keane, J. (2003) *Global Civil Society*, Cambridge: CUP.

Melucci, A. (1989) *Nomads of the Present: Social Movements and Individual Needs in Contemporary Society*, London: Hutchinson Radius.

Princen, T. and Finger, M. (1994) *Environmental NGOs in World Politics: Linking the Local and the Global*, London: Routledge.

Purdue, D. (2000) *Anti-Genetix: The Emergence of a Global Movement against GM Food*, London: Ashgate.

Purdue, D., Diani, M. and Lindsay, I. (2004) Civic Networks in Bristol and Glasgow, *Community Development Journal*, 39 (3): 277–288.

Purdue, D., Dürrschmidt, J., Jowers, P. and O'Doherty, R. (1997) DIY Culture and Extended Milieux: LETS, Veggie Boxes and Festivals, *Sociological Review*, 45 (4): 645–667.

Putnam, R. (1993) *Making Democracy Work: Civic Traditions in Modern Italy*, Princeton, NJ: Princeton University Press.

Putnam, R. (2000) *Bowling Alone*, New York: Simon and Schuster.

Renewal.net, Building Social Capital, www.renewal.net.

Shaw, M. (1994) Civil Society and Global Politics: Beyond a Social Movements Approach, *Millennium*, 23 (3): 647–667.

Tarrow, S. (1994) *Power in Movement: Social Movements, Collective Action and Politics*, Cambridge: Cambridge University Press.

Taylor, M. (2003) *Public Policy in the Community*, Basingstoke: Palgrave Macmillan.

Tester, K. (1992) *Civil Society*, London: Routledge.

Tilly, C., Tilly, L. and Tilly, R. (1975) *The Rebellious Century: 1830–1930*, Cambridge, MA: Harvard University Press.

Warren, M. (2001) *Democracy and Association*, Princeton: Princeton University Press.

Walzer, M. (1995) Introduction in M. Walzer (ed.), *Toward a Global Civil Society*, Providence: Bergham Books.

Woolcock, M. (1998) Social Capital and Economic Development: Towards a Theoretical Synthesis and Policy Framework, *Theory and Society*, 27: 151–208.

Part I

Civic organizations between state and society in emerging forms of governance

2 Civic organizations and the state in Putin's Russia

Co-operation, co-optation, confrontation

Suvi Salmenniemi

Introduction

Nastia, a civic activist from Tver', Russia, sent me an e-mail in November 2004. She had set up an art club with her friends that received financial support from the regional governmental committee of youth affairs. The club published a journal and had recently prepared an issue on nationalism in Russia. However, this issue was censored by the authorities with the words 'now is no time to write about nationalism'. Nastia wrote to me saying:

> Here everyone is afraid of their position, afraid to tell the truth. We tried [with our journal] but we were silenced. . . . Here in Russia everything is much more complicated than it seems. People are not inactive, but they are not allowed to be active; their mouths are shut, everything is decided by those who have power!

A strikingly different picture of the relationships between authorities and civic organizations was presented by President Putin a few years earlier in the Civic Forum. This Forum was initiated by the presidential administration and it gathered together representatives of state institutions and the civic sector. Putin addressed the audience as follows:

> Without a true relationship of partnership between the state and society there can be neither a strong state nor a prosperous and happy society. What is needed is an equal dialogue. And we are aware that the effectiveness of the dialogue depends on us to a great extent, on the representatives of power. . . . We are ready to listen attentively and to hear what you propose. I believe that now that the time of truly great opportunities has come for Russia and its citizens such cooperation can become highly productive. . . . It is our duty together to use the historical chance presented to us. Otherwise, we may again find ourselves in the 'backyard of civilization'.

These examples illustrate the contradictory and ambivalent relationships between the state and civic organizations in today's Russia. The analysis of the role of state for the development of civic activity in Russia has been neglected until recently, although, as the examples above suggest, the state's participation in determining the boundaries of and opportunities for civic activity is of crucial importance. Much of the existing scholarly investigation into Russian civic activity has concentrated either on discussing theories of civil society in the post-Soviet context or on exploring the characteristics of the emerging NGO sector and, in particular, its relations to foreign donor agencies. However, as Marc Howard has argued, the strengthening of civil society in post-socialist societies essentially involves a reappraisal of the state: 'A convincing body of literature has demonstrated that in the older democracies, the state has played a crucial role in enabling, facilitating and encouraging the existence and flourishing of civil society organizations' (Howard 2002, 168).

This chapter seeks to unravel the dynamics and logics of interaction between the state and civic organizations and the implications for governance by examining where and how civic organizations encounter the state, and under what conditions and power constellations this takes place. The analysis is based on a case study conducted in the city of Tver' during 2001–2004.[1] The main locus of civic activity in Russia is the local community and hence a case study from the grassroots level can shed important light on the prerequisites for and patterns of interaction between the state and organizations. The case of Tver' will be also discussed in relation to trends and practices in interaction at the federal level and in other Russian regions, and in relation to global trends, such as the neoliberal vision of development. The chapter, thus, aims at placing local socio-political dynamics in a dialogue with national and global developments.

The chapter draws on two sets of data. First, the organizations' relationships with governmental structures are illustrated by two civic organizations: the Tver' branch of the Trade Union of Medical Workers (TUMW), a successor of the Soviet trade union, and the Centre for Women's History and Gender Studies (CGS), founded in 1998.[2] The CGS is a grassroots feminist group that organizes courses and carries out research in gender studies. The TUMW can be defined as an interest group, whilst the CGS is best characterized as a social movement organization (SMO), a part of the women's movement. The aim is to illustrate how these two organizations which differ substantially in terms of their raison d'être, history, organizational form and financial base have negotiated relations with the state. Second, this article draws on a quantitative survey ($n = 105$) conducted in registered civic organizations in Tver'. It provides statistically generalizable information about the local organizational field.[3]

By 'civic organization', I refer here to organized socio-political activity, such as voluntary associations, clubs and labour unions. Civic organizations offer an arena for practising political citizenship. Political citizenship refers not only to a set of formally defined rights, such as suffrage, but also to individuals' opportunities to participate in and influence socio-political processes and struggles regarding meanings and values in society. Organizations provide forums for individuals collectively to (re)negotiate conditions of citizenship and to rework citizen identities. The 'state', for its part, is here divided in terms of functions –

legislative and executive power – and of territory – federal (Moscow), regional (federal subjects) and municipal power (towns and villages).[4] Thus, the state is not a monolith, but rather 'an abstraction that refers to ensembles of institutions and practises with powerful cultural consequences' (Schild 1998, 97).

I begin by discussing the general characteristics of Russian civic activity. In the next section, I examine public discourses on civic activity. I discuss how they have changed and are related to the structuring of the relations between the state and civic organizations. I also analyse the interpretations of the activists in Tver' and how they are linked with these public discourses. After that, I examine practices and features of interaction between the state and civic organizations and trace how they have changed over the last few years. Finally, I explore those strategies of resistance that civic organizations practice vis-à-vis the tightening of state control over the civic sector.

Characteristics of Russian civic activity

Since perestroika and the disintegration of the Soviet system, the field of civic activity has undergone a series of structural changes: institutionalization, localization and professionalization. The institutionalization of the civic sector has manifested itself in the process of 'NGOization', i.e. the informal clubs and loosely defined social movements of the perestroika period have evolved into more structured organizations. It has been estimated that there are about 500,000 civic organizations in Russia today (Zdravomyslova 2005). Simultaneously with this formalization of civic activity there has been a decline in mass socio-political mobilization.

Although some of the Soviet All-Union organizations continue to exist today and some of the large civic organizations have subdivisions throughout the Russian regions, the main arena for civic activity is the local community (see Yanitsky 2000, 6). Localization can be seen as a result of the regionalization process of the Yeltsin era (1991–1999) and as a counter-reaction to the Soviet Moscow-centred and hierarchical organizational culture. In the trade union movement, this localization has manifested itself in the fact that the union's work has largely shifted from the federal to the regional level. This has produced new tensions between the centre and the local level. For example, the leader of the Tver' TUMW perceives that its Central Committee in Moscow has distanced itself from the regional situation and does not understand the harsh reality in which medical workers and unions have to work in the province.

Civic organizations have also become more professional. Professionalization does not, however, apply with equal strength to the whole field of civic organizations, nor to all Russian regions. It pertains in particular to urban centres and organizations that receive foreign funding, such as environmental, human rights and women's groups. Professionalization has turned civic activity into a privileged site of the educated classes. According to the survey in Tver', 89 per cent of the organization leaders have higher education and Zdravomyslova (2005) has estimated that about 60 per cent of those involved in civic groups have academic degrees. The Russian intelligentsia has thus been able to make use of the cultural capital it acquired during the Soviet era to enter the civic sphere. It has been able to find in civic activity a way to obtain and maintain professional qualifications and acquire a livelihood in new circumstances.

Civic activity can be seen in this sense as a social practice that contributes to producing new and, in part, reproducing old social hierarchies and inequalities by offering the educated class access to social mobility, power and resources (see Hemment 2004b; Sampson 1996). This illustrates how the formation of the civic sphere is intimately linked with the construction of a new class structure. The changes in the relative weight and convertibility of different types of capitals (Bourdieu 1984) has opened and excluded different strategies of socio-political participation for different social groups. This professionalization may exclude from the public sphere social groups that lack cultural and social capital, and thus, prune public discourse. It also runs the risk of widening the gap between civic organizations and their constituencies, a highly acute and problematic issue in Russia at present.

Another manifestation of the link between intelligentsia and civic activity is that a number of civic organizations operate under the auspices of various educational institutions, such as universities and research institutes. These institutions operated as important nests of social movements and organizations also in the perestroika era (see Hosking 1992; Urban 1997). The CGS, for example, is both a civic organization and an educational unit incorporated with the Tver' State University, combining both governmental and non-governmental resources. The leader of the CGS interprets that this incorporation makes the CGS's activities more sustainable in two ways. First, the institutionalized status at the university decreases the group's dependence on foreign funding, and second, it reduces the tendency to associate the CGS with its leader rather than with its activities. Obviously the close co-operation with the university also poses its own risks. One CGS activist expressed the fear that if the CGS ceased to receive grants, the university administration could pressure it to close down. The CGS has prepared itself for this scenario by having its members 'infiltrate' decision-making positions at the university.

Socio-political activity in Russia is also a gendered field.[5] Political mobilization and the democratic movement during perestroika was associated with, and led by, men who often came from academic and dissident circles (see Hosking 1992). Women were also participants in political mobilization, but they were less visible publicly and rarely represented in the leadership. During the 1990s this gender constellation in socio-political activity changed. Weigle (2002, 120) points out that many (male) activists in the democratic movement quickly moved from civic activity into formal politics and the emerging private business sector. This shift from civic to political activism opened a window and created a demand for women's civic activism. Today, women participate actively in civic organizations (see Henderson 2003, 19; Sperling 1999); for example, according to the survey in Tver', 56 per cent of the registered civic organizations have a female-dominated membership. The survey, however, also revealed that women and men tend to be involved in different kinds of associational activities. Women dominate the traditionally femininely marked territories of social welfare, health care, education and culture, whereas men participate more in military-patriotic groups and sport and leisure organizations.

At the same time with this increase in women's participation in civic organizations, women's representation in formal politics has fallen significantly. In the current Federal Parliament (*Duma*), only 9.8 per cent[6] of the deputies are women and institutional politics tend to be associated with masculinity (Salmenniemi 2005; Hemment 2004b). However, this male dominance of politics is not only a post-Soviet phenomenon, for the higher echelons of political power were in the hands of men also in the Soviet Union. Thus, democracy has meant not a removal of, but a reconfiguration of, gendered power structures.

Conceptual shifts

Public discourses on civic activity in Russia have undergone recontextualizations and reframings over the last decade. Key participants in the (re)formulation of these discourses have been state actors, international organizations – in particular donor agencies – civic practitioners, politicians and scholars.

The discussion on civil society (*grazhdanskoe obshchestvo*) began in Russia in the 1980s. During perestroika and the early 1990s, civil society was a key notion in political imagery and functioned as a central political tool in reconceptualizing the relationship between the state and citizens. Civil society was interpreted as referring to independent and autonomous civic organizations acting as a counterforce to the state (see Zdravomyslova 1996, 19; Pursiainen 2004). However, in the mid-1990s competing notions, such as 'third sector' (*tretii sektor*) and 'social partnership' (*sotsial'noe partnerstvo*) emerged, which provided a different articulation of the relations between the state, economy and society. Social partnership and third sector are more practically oriented notions than civil society. They emphasize social problems as the main arena of civic activity and co-operation between different sectors of society. By contrast, the notion of civil society tends to underline the political aspect of civic activity and the potentially conflictual relations between civic activity and the state. Thus, these notions are embedded in different symbolic and material orders, underpinning and legitimizing different social practices.

Liborakina, Fliamer and Iakimets (1996), among others, have elaborated the concept of social partnership as a way to challenge the Soviet organization of social relations. They define social partnership as a 'constructive co-operation between two or three sectors – the state, market, non-profit sector – in resolving social problems' (ibid., 3). The stress on the necessity of co-operation between different sectors marks a break from the Soviet state monopoly in solving societal problems.

According to Ashwin and Clarke (2003), in the central organization of the Russian trade union movement, FNPR, social partnership has achieved considerable popularity as a way of rethinking the relationship between the state and trade unions in the post-Soviet era. Social partnership has been considerably influenced by social dialogue, a practice promoted by the International Labour Organization (ILO). In the Russian trade union context, social partnership refers to collective tripartite agreements between the state, employers and employees, and aims at social peace with an emphasis on negotiation and collaboration instead of confrontation. Ashwin and Clarke (ibid.) note that the FNPR leadership considers the social partnership model as a shift away from the Soviet tradition because it emphasizes equality between the partners. In reality, however, social partnership has often been turned into a tool to incorporate trade unions into state structures and to undermine the unions' position as opponents. For example, the Tver' TUMW includes in its membership all the three partners involved – employees, employers and health care administrators – which in effect waters down the whole partnership constellation.

The Russian state has also adopted the notion of social partnership and has reinterpreted it for its own purposes. According to Zdravomyslova (2005), social partnership has become the official discourse of the Russian state vis-à-vis civic organizations and it has started to mark 'selective corporatism'. The authorities divide organizations into collaborative or contentious ones and include into the corporatist framework collaborative organizations that are concerned in particular with social problems and do not question state authority. By contrast, the authorities distance themselves from critical and contentious organizations, such as political, human rights and environmental groups, which they frequently regard as adversaries of the state. The authorities have also attempted to manipulate civic activity by establishing quasi-civic organizations under the auspices of state structures, which can be seen as an attempt to co-opt the civic sphere into state structures. Thus, in this context, social partnership means that the state aims to turn independent organizations into Soviet-type 'transmission belts', which would mobilize masses to support and implement governmental policies. This would also facilitate state control over civic activity.

The conceptual home of the 'third sector' can be located in the United States (see Etzioni 1973). The third sector model builds on neoliberal thought (Raik 2004, 222) and encompasses the idea of non-profit organizations that take care of those tasks that neither the state nor the market are able or willing to deal with (Pursiainen 2000, 20). Julie Hemment (2004a, 216) argues that international donors were the first to introduce the term to Russia. Because Western, and in particular US funding, has played a pivotal role in the formation of the Russian civic sector, we can conclude that donor agencies have played a crucial part in promoting the understanding and structuring of civic activity as a third sector.

Thus, the notion of civil society, implying potentially contentious relations with the state, has been, to some extent, outstripped by the more socially and collaboratively oriented integration into governance through notions of social partnership and the third sector. Pursiainen (2004), who has studied shifts in public Russian political and scholarly discourses, argues that the dominant discourse on civil society in Russia since the end of the 1990s has been based on the idea of a strong paternalistic state and formal democracy with a third-sector type of civil society mobilizing society to help the state. Thus, there has been a discursive shift from 'civil society against the state' towards 'third sector as a helpmate of the state'.

Although the concept of civil society has lost ground somewhat, it still has a certain currency in Russian political discourse. For example, President Putin has made numerous references to it in his speeches. During the Putin era, the concepts of 'managed' (*upravliaemaia*) and 'Eastern' (*vostochnaia*) democracy have been introduced, which entail a strengthening of the 'verticals of power' and increased state control over society. This type of democracy also seems to presume a 'managed civil society'. Thus, both democracy and civil society are currently under redefinition: they have been co-opted to the Putin administration's 'discourse of management', losing in this discourse their critical and emancipatory dimension.

The emphasis on the third sector and social partnership has meant that the political dimension of civic organizations has, to some degree, become blurred. Of course, the social is also profoundly political: for example, disabled people's organizations have questioned prevailing definitions of disability by promoting a conception of disabled people not as objects of care, but as subjects and experts on their own issues. However, this type of political dimension tends to disappear in the third sector and social partnership frameworks. The resonance of social partnership and the third sector in contemporary Russia stems from the dislocation of the social welfare system. The state has withdrawn from its previous social obligations and the family, social networks and civic organizations have started to shoulder more responsibility for welfare than before. A large majority of Russian civic organizations operate in the social welfare sector (Iakimets 2002; Henderson 2003). Many civic organizations have been established precisely in order to produce those social services that the state and private businesses cannot or do not want to provide anymore.

This also highlights how the formation of the Russian civic sphere is linked to and affected by global political, social and economic changes, most notably the rise of neoliberalism, which shapes how the relations between the public and private spheres and between the state and society are organized. Russian socio-economic development has been directed, for example, by the guidelines of the World Bank and the IMF. Alvarez *et al.* (1998, 1–22; see also Hemment 2004a, 820–821) in their analysis of Latin American development argue that neoliberalism has promoted a minimalist conception of the state and engendered a service-oriented NGO sector. Similar tendencies can be detected also in Russia. Yúdice has questioned whether civic organizations have increasingly started to 'buttress a public sector evacuated by the state and at the same time making it possible for the state to steer clear of what was once seen as its responsibility' (quoted in Alvarez *et al.* 1998, 17).

Local interpretations

How do the concepts of civil society, social partnership and the third sector figure at the local level, in the accounts of the activists in Tver'? The survey revealed that 25 per cent of the leaders of civic organizations, mainly representing education, culture and social welfare, associated their organization with the notion of 'civil society'. This means that civil society is a meaningful and relevant framework of self-understanding for a number of practitioners. By contrast, only eight out of 105 surveyed leaders identified their group with the concept of the third sector. Somewhat surprisingly, three political parties described themselves with this term, whilst none of the social welfare organizations, conventionally considered as the main agent of the third sector, associated themselves with it. This indicates that the third sector has different shades of meaning in Russia than it does in Western societies. Although the third sector model has been actively promoted by foreign donors, it does not seem to have permeated the civic sector, at least in the Russian province. None of the organization leaders associated their activities with the notion of social partnership.

Interestingly enough, although the social partnership model is an important framework for the Russian trade union movement at the federal level, the activists of the Tver' TUMW did not employ this concept in their interviews or meetings. They did, however, refer to collective tripartite agreements, which in practice form the backbone of social partnership. The concept of civil society was unfamiliar to almost all TUMW activists and neither did they employ the term third sector. This allows the conclusion that these three notions are not meaningful discursive frames for articulating the TUMW's identity and relationships with the state. Instead, the TUMW activists continue to make sense of and define the union's position with a culturally strong and symbolically loaded Russian discursive formation of *vlast'/narod*, rulers versus the people. This discourse constructs a hierarchical relationship and opposition between the ruling elite and ordinary people, the union being identified with the latter. The union activists narrate the people, 'us', as a victim and object of the indifference of the state, but at the same time they associate it with supreme moral strength. They construct health care workers as altruistic and moral actors by contrasting them to the self-seeking political elite.

As for the CGS, the concept of civil society operates for most members as an important framework of self-definition and articulates the group's relationship to the state. Civil society is a notion with which the CGS members distance themselves from both the Soviet party-state and the current political power that, according to them, increasingly resembles the Soviet regime. Civil society is a term employed to denote a certain utopia, an ideal society; it is a concept with which the activists imagine and envision new forms of citizenship and a new social order.

By contrast, the notions of the third sector and social partnership were employed only once in the interviews with the CGS members, by the leader of the group. Thus, these concepts do not have much relevance in the discursive practices of the CGS. The leader of the CGS wished to make a clear distinction between the third sector and civil society:

Regrettably, over the past few years in Russia there is now less talk about civil society. When perestroika began – the law-governed state (*pravovoe gosudarstvo*), civil society – those notions were introduced. . . . Then all that began to vanish somehow. One started to talk about the verticals of power (*vertikali vlasti*). . . . Or one tries to reduce the notion of the civil society to the notion of the third sector. . . . The third sector means grants, foundations – which is different. . . . Civil society is far broader, not just the third sector, not only activities related to fund-raising for one's projects. [It means] people's capacity for self-organization.

The concept of social partnership was employed by the leader of the CGS in the context of renegotiation of welfare obligations. She alluded to this notion in questioning the state monopoly in service delivery and in advocating a partnership between organizations and the state in provision of social protection, in a similar vein as Liborakina *et al.* (1996) have suggested.

Collaboration and contention

Iakimets (2002) and Brygalina and Temkina (2004) have suggested that the relations between the state and civic organizations moved to a qualitatively new phase at the turn of the millennium, as the parties started to approach each other and search for collaboration. Civic organizations in Tver' and in Russia in general have established more frequent and functional co-operation with the local authorities, and, more specifically, with the local executive power, whereas co-operation with the federal structures and legislative power is perceived as unsatisfying and sporadic (see Iakimets 2002; Sevortyan and Barchukova 2002). This interest in co-operation is presumably connected with conceptual shifts in understanding the relationship between the state and civic organizations. The introduction of the third sector and social partnership has encouraged the state and organizations to co-operate, whilst the rise of 'managed democracy' has, for its part, brought corporatist features and state control to this co-operation.

At the national level, one of the most salient and, at the same time, ambivalent attempts to establish co-operation between the state and civic groups was the Civic Forum held in Moscow in 2001. The aim of the Forum was to engender a dialogue between the state and society. The Forum was received ambiguously among civic activists. Some interpreted it as a genuine gesture of good will by the state towards civic organizations, whereas others criticized it for paying only lip service to the idea without any real attempt to empower civic organizations. In the worst scenario, it was regarded as an attempt to co-opt organizations into state structures (see Nikitin and Buchanan 2002; Weigle 2002).

At the local level, we can distinguish four main mechanisms of co-operation between the authorities and civic organizations. First, the local government often announces competitions to civic organizations for realizing socially significant projects with government funding. Second, governmental structures may offer organizations benefits in kind, such as free premises. Third, co-operation can acquire a more institutionalized form, as, for example, in Tver' where the women's group *Zhenskii Svet* founded a women's crisis centre in co-operation with the town administration. The administration paid the salaries for four employees and gave the centre free premises. Otherwise the centre functioned on a voluntary basis. Fourth, in many localities special co-operation organs have been established where representatives of civic organizations, the local government and business life meet and discuss topical questions. Several such co-operation councils functioned in Tver' until 2003. The most important of them was the Social Council under the auspices of the mayor, which gathered together representatives from well-established civic organizations and state bodies. These co-operation councils were embryonic institutionalized channels for public participation and provided, at least to some degree, opportunities for civic organizations to voice their opinions and utilize their expertise in addressing public issues. On the one hand, these councils could be seen as a way to improve governance by increasing state accountability and citizens' participation, but on the other hand, they could also turn into vehicles of selective corporatism, involving only loyal and obedient organizations.

Financial resources affect the strategies and positions civic organizations adopt vis-à-vis the state. On the one hand, foreign funding can be seen to have contributed to a tendency to damp down conflicts and promote the search for 'constructive' co-operation between the state and organizations. Yanitsky (2000, 78) has argued that foreign donors have facilitated the taming of the Russian environmental movement, because they have preferred to finance moderate organizations that deal with environmental education, but not more radical protest groups. The representative of the British Council I interviewed stated that the Council does not finance organizations that openly challenge the authorities, but rather organizations that are willing to engage in co-operation with them. On the other hand, foreign funding has also enabled independent civic activism. In the case of the CGS, co-operation with foreign donors and the transnational women's movement has provided it with access to symbolic and material resources, which in turn give the centre autonomy and authority vis-à-vis the local government and the state university.

Organizations' funding affects also the ways the authorities view organizations. Foreign assistance to civic groups has been regarded with suspicion by the state. For example, the federal security service chief Nikolai Patrushev has accused civic organizations of operating as a cover for Western spies in Russia, and President Putin has warned that his government will not tolerate any foreign support to political activities of Russian civic organizations.

There is considerable regional diversity in the ways civic organizations have forged relations with governmental structures, due to many local social forces and power relations (see Iakimets 2002; Sevortyan and Barchukova 2002). As a result of Soviet economic policies there are still a number of localities that are dominated by a single production plant wielding considerable political power. In such localities independent civic activity can be very difficult (see Rautio 2003), as is the case in regions with an authoritarian leadership (Sundstrom 2002, 221). Tver' illustrates well the ambivalence involved in some regional locations. For several reasons, the scope of action for civic organizations has been relatively broad in Tver' until recently. First, there are no monopolistic production plants located in the area that could dominate the socio-political landscape. Second, there have not been any strong competing interest groups in the region and the political elite is quite poor in terms of resources (see Ovchinnikov 2000). Third, the relative poverty of the Tver' region, in comparison with many other Russian regions, has motivated civic activity, in particular, in the social sector and has also encouraged the local government to search for points of contact with these organizations. On the other hand, Tver' has traditionally been dependent politically and economically on Moscow, which also shapes local civic activism. The Putin administration's regime of managed democracy, for example, was quickly felt in Tver'. In contrast, some of the geographically more remote areas and areas with strong regional political and economic elites and rich in resources have more autonomy and are less subject to political fluctuations in Moscow.

The TUMW combines both partnership and contentious orientations in its interaction with the local authorities. In the words of the president of the TUMW, 'We are both diplomats and extortionists'. The partnership orientation is manifested in the TUMW's active collaboration with local government and in its striving for consensus, whilst the contentious element may be seen in its public protests. The TUMW also positions itself occasionally as an ally of the local government against the federal power. The TUMW, representing public sector workers, and the local government, struggling with insufficient resources, can find a common enemy in the federal power in Moscow. It is in the interests of both the TUMW and the local authorities to seek to win as many resources as possible to distribute at the local level. However, in the local corporatist framework of redistribution, the TUMW positions itself as an interest group vis-à-vis the authorities, trying to lobby and secure resources for the medical workers. This illustrates how the organizations can position themselves in different ways in relation to different levels of the state power.

By contrast, the CGS's relationship with the local government is characterized by a 'strategy of involvement' (*strategiia vovlecheniia*). The leader of the CGS summarizes the idea as follows:

> We use them [authorities] for our goals. We involve these people in our projects and then they start to consider these projects as theirs. Thus, it will be difficult for them to refuse to help when they are themselves participants.

The strategy of involvement takes place at the level of the leader of the CGS and the mayor of Tver' and his assistant. Co-operation is, therefore, based on personal relations: it is interpersonal, not inter-institutional. The CGS activists assess this strategy as a useful and necessary one for advancing the CGS's goals, because they do not believe that the authorities listen to political and civic *groups*, but only to specific, well-known *individuals*. Unlike the TUMW, the CGS does not position itself as a contentious group vis-à-vis the authorities, but rather wishes to avoid confrontation with them and practises tactical collaboration. Conflicts with the authorities are seen not to advance the CGS's goals.

In general, these types of personal connections and networks play a key role in the co-operation between the authorities and civic organizations in Russia (see Yanitsky 2000, 143; Sevortyan and Barchukova 2002). The importance of connections is linked to the weakness and uninstitutionalized nature of the co-operation. The legislation regulating it is still inadequate and regionally diverse, and in general well-established rules of the game for this co-operation have not been developed. This means that changes in the administrative staff can significantly alter co-operation relations, making collaboration fragile in the face of shifting political allegiances. This emphasis on interpersonal over inter-institutional relations indicates the personalization of public relations and patron–client mechanisms, i.e. asymmetric but mutually beneficial transactions that are based on differential control by social actors over the access and flow of resources (Roniger 1998, 72). As a result, governance is based on personalized and particularistic patterns instead of generalized and universal rules. The persistence of patronage mechanisms in post-Soviet conditions is hardly surprising considering their pervasiveness in the Soviet system (see Fitzpatrick 1999).

A major stumbling block for the development of democracy in Russia is the absence of links between political parties and civic groups. Parties in Russia are not, in general, grounded in grassroots activities, but are rather established around a leader and not based on a political ideology or on social identities and interests (see McAuley 1997). Civic activists in Tver' frequently associated politics with self-interest and corruption and perceived political parties only to tend to use civic organizations for their own selfish purposes. Lack of co-operation and trust between parties and civic groups hinders the latter's capacity to function as a mediator between the political power and citizens, i.e. to channel citizens' demands to decision-making bodies.

The concentration of power in the hands of the so-called party of power, the pro-President United Russia (*Edinaia Rossiia*), has also restructured the relations between the state, political parties and civic organizations. It is evident that United Russia has become the centre of a new political, economical and administrative elite – a new *nomenklatura*. The leader of a disabled people's organization whom I interviewed in 2004 said that she had applied for membership in United Russia, because she hoped that it would open new opportunities for her to extract resources for her organization, as all 'important people' are members of this party.

Power and resistance

Relations between the state and civic organizations in Russia have recently become more contradictory, as the Putin administration has increased state regulation and control over the civic sphere. The Interior Ministry's proposal to assign police liaison officers to all human rights groups, in order to 'enhance co-operation' between them and law enforcement bodies, is one alarming example of this. Human rights activists interpreted this as an attempt to place them under police surveillance. Furthermore, Putin, in his 'state of the nation' speech in May 2004, accused civic organizations of serving 'dubious groups and commercial interests' and of ignoring the problems of citizens. He also criticized organizations for being more interested in obtaining funding from international donors than defending 'the real interests of people'.

The state has also impeded the activities of civic organizations by legislative means. According to Dzhibladze, many civic organizations are in dire financial straits because they are not guaranteed tax exemptions. Furthermore, tax legislation is so complicated that it is practically impossible for organizations to abide by it. This makes organizations vulnerable vis-à-vis the state, because they can be prosecuted on the basis of so-called tax irregularities. This can result in organizations moderating their criticism and practising self-censorship. (Dzhibladze 2005). The state also controls corporate philanthropy by offering tax concessions only for contributions that are given to organizations that the government supports and/or finances (Liborakina 2004).

The plight of civic organizations due to the pressures of managed democracy was tangible also in Tver' when I visited there in May 2004. A telling diagnosis of the current conditions of civic activity was presented by the leader of the CGS: 'If it continues like this, we'll soon become a dissident organization'. Another member of the group commented in a similar vein: 'As soon as all [foreign] foundations leave here, when the [state] policy becomes clear, civic organizations will probably cease to exist. Or they will go underground, or talk to each other in the kitchen, like Soviet dissidents'.

Those seeds of civic activity that had developed during the 1990s were now increasingly being weeded out. The newly elected mayor of Tver' had decided to disband the co-operation councils and cut funding to the women's crisis centre, which was forced to close down its activities. According to CGS activists, these decisions were not, however, so much politically motivated, as connected with the deteriorating economic situation. They interpreted that it was easy for authorities to cut funding first from civic activities that they perceived as 'alien' anyway.

The co-operation framework between the authorities and civic organizations in Tver' experienced severe setbacks and disintegrated in many respects as a result of the appointments of a new mayor and governor for Tver' in 2003 and the subsequent changes in their administrations. The TUMW, for example, had a long history of personal contacts and co-operation with the local government, but these administrative changes dismantled, to some degree, those previous ties. The CGS's strategy of involvement also ended up in trouble, as its two key 'involved' allies in the local government, the mayor and his assistant, were replaced by the new leadership. This illustrates the limits of the strategy of involvement based on patron–client relationships, because the involvement, which was based on interpersonal instead of inter-institutional ties, proved fragile in the face of political changes.

It is, however, important to acknowledge the insistent resistance that organizations present vis-à-vis managed democracy and state-centred form of governance. The leader of the TUMW noted in 2004 that the political situation in the country had pushed the union to forge links with other civic organizations more actively and to seek to build larger coalitions in order to advocate their interests. The CGS, for its part, has added a course on civil society again to its curriculum as a way to protest the ubiquitous discourse of 'verticals of power' and correspondingly, the attenuation of discussion on civil society, or its abuse in the hands of the powers that be. The CGS has also sought to continue the work of the women's crisis centre in the framework of the CGS by inviting former crisis centre employees to deliver lectures on gendered violence. We can also interpret the references to underground and dissident activity in the CGS as signs of protest. Invoking these associations in the current context implies that although it might become impossible to practise the CGS's work publicly, the work will not cease, but only shift again to the semi-public sphere of kitchens as in the Soviet times.

Finally, one CGS activist summarized still another strategy of resistance as follows:

> The work of the CGS is like growing flowers in the frost. It's unpleasant to go out of the greenhouse, that is the CGS, and end up in a freezing wind, that is, in our Russian life, which doesn't have mercy on anybody. It is, however, a question of a citizen's stand – that you won't bow. Because usually, the more you bow, the more the pressure grows.

Notes

1 Located in the vicinity of Moscow, Tver' is a city of 454,000 inhabitants and the centre of the Tver' region. Tver' is an economically deprived region; its GNP in 2000 fell well below the average of the Russian regions (Finnish–Russian Chamber of Commerce 2004). Tver' has several institutions of higher and secondary education and consequently relatively strong intellectual resources.

2 The data include participant observation and ten one-to-one and group interviews in both organizations, conducted by the author together with Marina Manevich and Ekaterina Ryzhkova.

3 The survey was conducted by the author together with a researcher team from the Tver' State University. In choosing the sample, stratified sampling was used in order to ensure that different sectors of civic organizations would be included in the study. The survey was conducted through personal interviews with the organization leaders. The data have been analysed with the help of the SPSS statistical program. I wish to thank Dmitrii Borodin, Anna Borodina, Igor' Emel'ianov, Nastia Milaia, Aleksanda Zimina and Oleg Belousov for their help in conducting the survey.

4 According to Russian legislation, municipal power is not formally part of the state power. However, municipal power is here dealt with in connection with the state power, because it is in many ways dependent on and intertwined with regional and federal powers. Putin, since his rise to power, has also established one more territorial-administrative category, federal districts (*okrugi*), which encompass federal subjects.

5 The gendered meanings of socio-political activity in Russia are analysed in more detail in Salmenniemi (2005).

6 In the Soviet legislature, women's representation was 33 per cent, due to the quota system.

References

Alvarez, S., Dagnino, E. and Escobar, A. (1998) Introduction: The Cultural and the Political in Latin American Social Movements, in S. Alvarez, E. Dagnino and A. Escobar. (eds) *Cultures of Politics, Politics of Cultures: Re-visioning Latin American Social Movements*, Westview Press: Boulder, 1–31.

Ashwin, S. and Clarke, S. (2003) *Russian Trade Unions and Industrial Relations in Transition*, Palgrave: Basingstoke.

Bourdieu, P. (1984) *Distinction: A Social Critique of the Judgement of Taste*, Routledge: New York.

Brygalina, J. and Temkina, A. (2004) The Development of Feminist Organisations in St Petersburg 1985–2003, in A-M. Castrén, M. Lonkila and M. Peltonen (eds) *Between Sociology and History*, SKS: Helsinki, 207–226.

Dzhibladze, Y. (2005) Kansalaisaktivismi vahvan valtion puristuksessa, in A. Leppänen (ed.) *Kansalaisyhteiskunta liikkeessä yli rajojen*, Palmenia-kustannus: Helsinki, 171–190.

Etzioni, A. (1973) The Third Sector and Domestic Missions. *Public Administration Review*, 33 (4) 314–323.

Finnish–Russian Chamber of Commerce. www.finruscc.fi/g/200205p/perustiedot-alueista.htm (consulted on 7.1.2004).

Fitzpatrick, S. (1999) *Everyday Stalinism: Ordinary Life in Extraordinary Times*, Oxford University Press: New York.

Hemment, J. (2004a) Global Civil Society and the Local Costs of Belonging: Defining Violence against Women, *Signs*, 29 (3) 816–840.

Hemment, J. (2004b) The Riddle of the Third Sector: Civil Society, International Aid, and NGOs in Russia, *Anthropological Quarterly*, 77 (2) 215–241.

Henderson, S. (2003) *Building Democracy in Contemporary Russia: Western Support to Grassroots Organizations*, Cornell University Press: Ithaca.

Hosking, G. (1992) The Beginnings of Independent Political Activity, in G. Hosking, J. Aves and P. Duncan (eds) *The Road to Post-Communism: Independent Political Movements in the Soviet Union, 1985–1991*, Pinter Publishers: London, 1–28.

Howard, M. (2002) The Weakness of Postcommunist Civil Society, *Journal of Democracy*, 13 (1) 157–169.

Iakimets, V. (2002) Mekhanizmy mezhsektornogo vzaimodeistviia: Tipy, regional'nye primery, problemy razvitiia. Presentation in a seminar '*Formirovanie grazhdanskogo obshchestva v Rossii*', St Petersburg, 21–23.2.2002.

Liborakina, M. (2004) Do 'New Russians' Care about Society? Corporate Social Responsibility in Russia, presentation at the Collegium of Advanced Studies, Helsinki, 27.9.2004.

Liborakina, M., Fliamer, M. and Iakimets, V. (1996) *Sotsial'noe partnerstvo: Zametki o formirovanii grazhdanskogo obshchestva v Rossii*. Izdatel'stvo 'Shkola kul'turnoi politiki', Moskva.

McAuley, M. (1997) *Russia's Politics of Uncertainty*, Cambridge University Press: Cambridge.

Nikitin, A. and Buchanan, J. (2002) The Kremlin's Civic Forum: Co-operation or Co-Optation for Civil Society in Russia, *Demokratizatsiya*, 10 (2) 147–165.

Ovchinnikov, B. (2000) Tverskaia oblast': protopolitika, in V. Gel'man, S. Ryzhenkov and M. Bri (eds) *Rossiia regionov: Transformatsiia politicheskikh rezhimov*, Izdatel'stvo 'Ves' Mir''': Moskva, 294–330.

Pursiainen, C. (2000) Trends and Structures in Russian State/Society Relation, in H. Patomäki (ed.) *Politics of Civil Society: A Global Perspective on Democratisation*, NIGD Publications: Helsinki, 19–28.

Pursiainen, C. (2004) Russian Civil Society Discourses and Practises, presentation in Aleksanteri Institute, University of Helsinki, 6.1.2004.

Raik, K. (2004) Civil Society and EU Integration of Estonia, in R. Alapuro, I. Liikanen and M. Lonkila (eds) *Beyond Post-Soviet Transition*, Kikimora: Helsinki.

Rautio, V. (2003) *The Potential for Community Restructuring: Mining Towns in Pechenga*, Kikimora: Helsinki.

Roniger, L. (1998) Civil Society, Patronage, and Democracy, in J. Alexander (ed.) *Real Civil Societies: Dilemmas of Institutionalisation*, Sage: London, 66–83.

Salmenniemi, S. (2005) Civic Activity: Feminine Activity? Gender, Civil Society and Citizenship in post-Soviet Russia, *Sociology* 39 (4) 735–753.

Sampson, S. (1996) The Social Life of Projects: Importing Civil Society to Albania, in C. Hann, and E. Dunn (eds) *Civil Society: Challenging Western Models*, Routledge: London, 121–142.

Schild, V. (1998) New Subjects of Rights? Women's Movements and the Construction of Citizenship in the 'New Democracies', in S. Alvarez, E. Dagnino and A. Escobar (eds) *Cultures of Politics, Politics of Cultures: Re-visioning Latin American Social Movements*, Westview Press: Boulder, 93–117.

Sevortyan, A. and Barchukova, N. (2002) *Nekommercheskii sektor i vlast' v regionakh Rossii. Puti sotrudnichestva*, CAF Russia: Moskva.

Sperling, V. (1999) *Organizing Women in Contemporary Russia, Engendering Transition*, Cambridge University Press: Cambridge.

Sundstrom, Lisa McIntosh (2002) Women's NGOs in Russia: Struggling from the Margins, *Demokratizatsiya*, 10 (2) 207–229.

Urban, M. (with Igrunov, V. and Mitrokhin, S.) (1997) *The Rebirth of Politics in Russia*, Cambridge University Press: Cambridge.

Weigle, M. (2002) On the Road to the Civic Forum: State and Civil Society from Yeltsin to Putin, *Demokratizatsiya*, 10 (2) 117–146.

Yanitsky, O. (2000) *Russian Greens in a Risk Society*, Kikimora Publications: Helsinki.

Zdravomyslova, E. (2005) Venäjän kansalaisjärjestöt ja kansalaisaktiivisuus Venäjällä, in A. Leppänen (ed.) *Kansalaisyhteiskunta liikkeessä yli rajojen*, Palmenia-kustannus: Helsinki, 204–214.

Zdravomyslova, J. (1996) Kansalaisyhteiskuntakeskustelu Venäjällä, in I. Liikanen and P. Stranius (eds) *Matkalla kansalaisyhteiskuntaan?* Publications of the University of Joensuu No 115, Joensuu, 17–26.

3 What happened after the 'end of history'?

Foreign aid and civic organizations in Ukraine

Kateryna Pishchikova

Introduction

The title of this chapter is meant as a reference to the famous argument by Francis Fukuyama that after the collapse of communism in different places around the world we are witnessing 'the end of history' in a sense that history itself resolved the biggest twentieth-century dispute about the best political system and capitalist democracy proved to be the only alternative for the future. As far as the analysis of post-Cold War developments in the former Soviet Union is concerned, the 'end of history' argument is everyone's favourite straw man, so rigid it seems and so strongly reminiscent of the Cold War paradigm. And yet, I show in this chapter that its impact on the domain of international assistance in the post-Cold War period is substantial. I focus on a particular component of this envisioned 'post-historical' world – the emergence and development of civil society that is actively supported by foreign donors. My argument is that assistance is largely responsible for the rapid growth and further institutionalization of particular types of civic organizations in the former Soviet Union. In this sense, assistance itself became an important governance player in the former socialist space.

In this chapter I show how the 'end of history' thinking translated into particular goals, time frames and organizational designs set for the local civil society from the outside. I argue that the most important implication of the 'end of history' thinking was that it justified the non-reflexive transplantation of norms, values and institutions onto the new assistance settings. It also provided for intellectual blindness towards local political contexts, forms of agency and ownership. This meant large-scale promotion of institutional forms that did not necessarily resonate with the local context, as was the example of many civic organizations created for their own sake. I draw my findings from the case study of the United States Agency for International Development (USAID) civil society assistance programmes to Ukraine.[1]

I start by describing the 'end of history' as a particular rationale that translated into a project to build civil societies in the former communist space with assistance from the outside. Assistance is thereby understood as a means to facilitate an emergence of particular governance structures that are believed to exist in the home countries of assistance donors. In this 'package' civil society is given a prominent place. Next, I provide an overview of USAID assistance effort in Ukraine, which shows the relative importance attributed by USAID to civil society promotion. I also show that in fact the idea of promoting democracy is not entirely new to US assistance. Instead, the post-Cold War civil society assistance is a mixture of new and old ideas, approaches and institutions. Often old approaches were simply put under new headings. I argue that such continuity is possible thanks to the 'end of history' thinking. This thinking implies that the countries that are already democratic do not have to change anything since they are already at a higher stage of development, whereas the post-communist world has to catch up. I further give a detailed account of the conception of civil society that was developed by USAID for its assistance programmes to civic organizations in Ukraine. I show that this conception is based on three core notions of 'institutional capacity building', 'empowerment' and 'sustainability'. I conclude by elaborating on the implications that this particular conception of civil society has for the development of civil society in Ukraine. I further argue that these findings are largely illustrative of civil society development as it has been impacted by foreign assistance in the former Soviet Union in general.

The 'end of history'

Even though in the policy realm the 'end of history' enthusiasm prevailed, the question of what exactly should be done in order to facilitate democratic governance in post-socialist countries was and remains far from obvious. An agreement had to be reached as to what kind of institutions should be built and how, as well as whose agency and ownership should make a difference. In the policy community, however, very little time was dedicated to the deliberation of this kind. Instead, assistance towards democratization was conveniently following the so-called 'transition paradigm' (the term was coined by Thomas Carothers in Carothers 2002). The transition paradigm rests on the key assumption that any country that has been freed from any form of a dictatorial rule is moving towards democracy and thus presents a case of a democratizing country or a country 'in transition to democracy'. According to Carothers: 'in the first half of the 1990s ... numerous policy makers and aid practitioners reflexively labelled any formerly authoritarian country that was attempting some political liberalization as a "transitional country"' (Carothers 2002, 6). Transitional countries are perceived as being on a path towards establishing clearly defined democratic institutions and free market economies. They are being described and evaluated on the basis of the degree of progress made along these lines. The assumption is that all it takes is the desire to abandon communist legacies and to embrace new democratic and capitalist ideals.

After the collapse of communism, the prevailing idea on both sides of the former 'Iron Curtain' was that the West should serve as a model for Eastern European political, economic and cultural revival. The discourse of rebuilding 'the other' part of Europe was organized around the metaphor of a new Marshall

Plan, which stood for the inspiration to remake European countries shattered by the cruel history of communism. The importance of this metaphor at the early stages of American assistance was extensively addressed by Wedel: 'the words "Marshall Plan" became almost a metaphor for America's role as a white knight. They carried a powerful sentimental appeal that called to mind one of America's most celebrated moments of global leadership and enlightened self-interest' (Wedel 2001, 17).

Within assistance, it was also largely accepted that democratic institutions can be built from the outside, at low cost and within a short period of time. Those institutions were largely defined in quantitative and technical terms. The initial understanding of civil society by the agency was that at the time when the assistance programmes began civil society was 'either nascent or nonexistent in most countries in the region [because] most populations lacked the basic rights of a democratic civil society: freedom of expression, the right to organize, to advocate one's interests, to form independent political parties, to hold free and fair elections' (USAID, October 1999, v). In other words, key democratic institutions were not in place, which was true given the (post)totalitarian regimes in those countries. What was interesting, however, was that the absence of those democratic institutions was believed to be a sufficient proof of absence of any kind of civil society. This view seems at best limited, given that those totalitarian regimes did not collapse on their own but through considerable citizen pressure. Given its failure to acknowledge home-grown theories and practices of civil society, the assistance was initially driven by the assumption that civil society had to be built afresh; it reserved for itself the privilege of defining what kind of civil society was to be built and how.

Overall, the 'end of history' thinking precluded posing of questions about the internal coherence or applicability of the winning paradigm. The future trajectory of post-socialist countries was assumed to be clear and self-understood (on both sides of the old Cold War divide even if for different reasons) and no space was created for innovative thinking about solutions for individual countries. Instead, those countries were seen as being on 'the road to democracy' and their political and social life was analysed in terms of following or deviating from this path as well as meeting the expectations of democratization. However, 15 years after the collapse of communism in Eastern Europe the reality seems much more complex and ambivalent than that. For practical and political reasons foreign assistance has become an important actor on the post-Soviet political scene. According to several accounts, civil society in those countries would look different had assistance not been so concerned about supporting it. This does not mean, however, that there would be no civil society at all, rather it points to the impact assistance has had on defining how civil society should look (Cooley 2000; Henderson 2003; McMahon 2001). This is why it is important to analyse in greater detail the particular conception of civil society embedded in assistance. In the following sections I unpack a particular conception of civil society that developed as a result of the 'end of history' thinking by focusing on the USAID civil society programmes in Ukraine, but first I introduce some background information on the USAID assistance effort in Ukraine.

US assistance to Ukraine

With the collapse of the Eastern European communist bloc in the late 1980s and the break up of the Soviet Union in 1991, the USA began its programmes of foreign assistance for transitions towards democracy and free market economy. In 1989 the US Congress passed the 'Support for East European Democracy (SEED) Act' and in 1992 the Freedom for Russia and the Emerging Eurasian Democracies and Open Markets (FREEDOM) Support Act (FSA) to 'support freedom and open markets in the independent states of the former Soviet Union' (US Congress 1992). The overall coordination of the US assistance was placed within the US Department of State. More than half of US government funds are administered by the United States Agency for International Development (USAID), including almost all funds obligated for the support of civil society and democratic reform. The agency claims to be playing a key role in the planning and implementation of programmes to promote economic restructuring and democratic transition, and to address the social dimensions of this transition.

In its programmes to the region USAID always showed special attention to Ukraine. Throughout the 1990s its Regional Mission in Kiev was one of the largest USAID Missions worldwide, and despite some assistance downsizing in the recent years, the US government remains the second biggest donor to Ukraine after the World Bank. US strategic interest in Ukraine is explained as follows:

> The United States has a strong national security interest in Ukraine's successful transition to a stable and independent, democratic, market-oriented, and prosperous state, with good relations with its neighbours and strong links to the West. Its successful transition may assist similar transitions elsewhere in the region. With a population of approximately 50 million and a strategic location between Russia and Central Europe, Ukraine is important for building a secure and undivided Europe.
>
> (US Department of State 2000)

According to the cumulative figures for the financial year 1992–2003 released by the US Department of State, the US government spent a total of about 20 billion dollars on assistance programmes to the 12 countries of the former Soviet Union,[2] out of which almost three billion was spent in Ukraine in support of economic restructuring, democratization and reforms in the health and social sectors; USAID was responsible for expending roughly half of these funds. Although financial institutions, such as the World Bank or the European Bank for Reconstruction and Development (EBRD), account for much larger sums, USAID's impact on the region and on the programmes adopted by other donors should not be underestimated. Capitalizing on its long-standing presence in the region and its networks of regional missions and local offices of US implementing partners, such as Winrock International, the Freedom House, Counterpart International and the US Peace Corps, USAID acts as a major provider of consultation, coordination and assessment in many areas. According to USAID itself:

> Although USAID's financial resources are modest relative to those of the International Financial Institutions, USAID plays an important role as a catalyst, helping to set agendas and leverage multi-lateral, bilateral and private resources. USAID's field presence and ability to make timely technical assistance grants enhances this role ... Through pre-feasibility studies and technical assistance to countries in meeting conditions to multilateral loans, USAID has helped leverage hundreds of millions of dollars, *beyond its own contributions*, for the region.
>
> (USAID, December 1999, 11, emphasis in the original)

The assistance to Central and Eastern Europe and the former Soviet Union was both unique and at the same time bore striking resemblances to the development aid from the previous decades to other parts of the world. One clear difference was that the emphasis was increasingly put not on the economic growth and humanitarian relief, but on political, economic and social restructuring. Aid operations also differed in their high profile and the role played by numerous foreign policy officials and agencies, which reflected the scale of the event and its impact on global politics and economics. However, as some authors argued, since the big aid machines could not be substantially restructured overnight – even if the desire to act differently was strong – similarities in the modes of operation between development aid and assistance to post-communist countries remained prominent (Howell and Pearce 2001; Wedel 2001). Some experts in aid who had previously worked in the Third World were relocated to implement programmes in the new regions, which were designed towards high spending within short timeframes, rather than towards conducting thorough assessments and developing innovative programmes suited to the new conditions.

Programmatically, democracy and civil society were decisively put on the list of priority areas for assistance alongside social and economic assistance and humanitarian aid. Although both the Reagan and Bush administrations had formulated their foreign policy strategies around the notion of democracy, it was the Clinton administration that was believed to have had a particular commitment to democracy and declared a desire to move beyond the Truman doctrine of containment.[3] In doing so, it reinvented the idealist position in American foreign policy, namely the belief that the spread of democracy will lead to higher stability and prosperity in the world. The argument went as follows:

> democratic governments are more likely to advocate and observe international laws and to experience the kind of long-term stability, which leads to sustained development, economic growth, and international trade. Countries that are experiencing economic growth and are actively engaged in trading relationships are less likely to engage in acts of war.
>
> (USAID, November 1998)

The decision to focus on promoting democracy was supported by institutional measures, as for example, by the introduction of civil society specialist positions within various regional bureaus, as well as the foundation of the Centre for Democracy and Governance in 1994. The Centre's role is said to be in providing technical and intellectual leadership to USAID's decentralized, mission-based structure, by developing the tools and methodologies needed to support democratic development (USAID, November 1998, 5). Support for democracy initiatives comprise a variety of areas, such as the political parties and civic organizations, the independent media, the rule of law, (local) governance and public administration. Among these, support to civil society is an important component, in fact, among a variety of donors, USAID stands out for its support of civil society strengthening. Some identify the United States as the biggest 'civil society' donor in the world accounting for around 85 per cent of total aid for civil society projects (Van Rooy 1998, 60). In practice, providing support to civil society effectively meant working with civic organizations on various (often donor-driven) projects as well as creating and sustaining civic organizations for their own sake. In 1995 USAID established a New Partnerships Initiative aimed at empowering civic organizations, creating small business partnerships and fostering democratic local governance. It promised to raise the funding via civic organizations to 40 per cent of the US aid budget, arguing that civic values and a rich variety of voluntary associations that constitute civil society have a critical political and economic potential for conducting democratic and market economy reforms.

One of the reasons for the attractiveness of civil society – now that the aid budget had shrunk in real terms by 50 per cent within the period from the mid-1980s to mid-1990s (Carothers 1999, 61) – is its low cost. Unlike large-scale industry or banking restructuring, or engineering projects, support for civic organizations does not require large inputs of capital. 'Civil society assistance made a virtue out of necessity by providing a theoretical justification for the small-scale assistance dictated by many donor budgets' (Carothers and Ottaway 2000, 8). Working with civic organizations is a cheaper as well as more flexible way of providing assistance; a way which allows for both downsizing and maintaining programmes and influence.

Therefore, one of the important changes that was brought about by the end of the Cold War was the emergence of a new role for foreign donors in the governance of the countries of the former Soviet bloc, through assistance programmes and practices that were, in many respects, different from those of previous decades and other parts of the world. This new pattern of governance required the (re)invention of civil society and civic organizations as one of its main elements. In the following section I investigate the rationale behind this (re)invention and the meanings that were given to civil society and civic organizations in this context.

Building civil society in three steps

'Institutional capacity building'

The idea of 'institutional capacity building' is a cornerstone of assistance to civic organizations and civil society in Ukraine, it captures both the understanding of what was wrong in the country and the method of promoting new democratic institutions. The following quote from an interview with the USAID Deputy Assistance Administrator explains it well:

> I think that what we found in Ukraine was that it didn't need the same kind of things Africa needed, for instance, in Africa it was basic education, immunizing children and things like that. . . . What was missing was something we always had as our high priority, which we call *institutional development*. . . . We found that while the actual types of things we did were different in UA, the *institutional capacity* still needed to be developed. [People] were good technicians but they weren't good managers, had no inventory or budgeting capacity. So we found those sorts of skills were actually quite valuable.
>
> (Turner, 17 August 2004, interview by author, *emphasis added*)

The idea of 'institutional capacity building' stems from understanding assistance in terms of teaching: assistance recipients are seen as 'good students' who have taken the wrong classes. Thus, one of the goals of assistance is to teach new skills and to provide the locals with new information.

'Institutional capacity building' found wide application in civil society assistance. It was based on providing tools and trainings that would make civic organizations resemble their American counterparts in terms of their formal structure. In fact, this kind of know-how transfer between the American and Ukrainian organizations was built into the civil society programmes from early on. As a USAID Deputy Assistant Administrator explained:

> We did have to put most of the money through an American counterpart who then linked with a UA group and helped them establish the ability to have a set of by-laws, to have an accounting process, to open a bank account so they could receive money. That we built in every one of our programs. We said you not only have to deliver services but also strengthen the capacity of local organizations to do these kinds of programs.
>
> (Turner, 17 August 2004, interview by author)

Following the 'institutional capacity building' idea USAID established a New Partnerships Initiative (NPI) in 1995 'to stimulate lasting economic, social, and political developments by building local institutional capacity in non-governmental organizations, competitive small business, and democratic local governments'. The 'NGO empowerment' component was meant to promote 'the active participation of citizens in political and economic decision-making through training and small grants' (USAID/West NIS, 3 June 1996). 'Increased capacity' meant that civic organizations would become more professional and show the formal organizational features characteristic of their American counterparts. NPI was meant to 'strengthen the direct contribution of local organizations to development, and . . . help increase their professionalism, efficiency, accountability, and transparency' (USAID, 21 July 1995).

However, since there were no civic organizations in place whose capacity could be built up according to the USAID scheme, 'institutional capacity building' initially had a component that was captured by a metaphor: 'let a thousand flowers bloom!' Apparently, nobody at the USAID was aware of the controversial origins of the slogan in the Chinese Cultural Revolution, and so it was embraced as an appropriate metaphor for the newly acquired democratic freedoms and democratic pluralism in the former Soviet Union.[4]

> The Europe and Eurasia Bureau (E&E) is very different in respect to civil society from the other regional bureaus; it defines civil society very broadly. When the transition began the E&E said 'our role is to build any kind of associations that are there to appear.' . . . The culture of association as an independent initiative was pretty much crushed by the communist government so the idea was to give people incentives to start working together, organizing themselves one way or the other.
>
> (Hansen, 5 August 2004, interview by author)

The 'thousand flowers' approach was implemented through 'small grants' programmes that were aimed at supporting as many different initiatives as possible. USAID was not investing in long-term relationships but in engaging as many different organizations as possible.

> USAID's goal is to create a large, diverse community of local NGOs capable of promoting sustainable development. . . . NGOs are everywhere a potentially critical vehicle for articulating collective interests and for ensuring citizen participation in the development process.
>
> (USAID, 21 July 1995)

The 'thousand flowers' approach meant that funds were spent to ensure in the shortest possible term there were civic initiatives in place that would resemble non-governmental civic organizations in the US. In this way, the approach was by definition supply-driven, meaning that USAID was supplying funds for particular kinds of flowers to bloom. Questions of how to create civic organizations relevant to the Ukrainian context were never raised. While high levels of technical assistance were put into providing tools and skills, the issue of who exactly would be using those, and for what purposes, was never addressed. So, thousands of Ukrainian activists were taught NGO management skills at rates that were higher than the numbers of civic organizations to be managed. There was a strong belief that civil society assistance should be about putting in place a critical number of 'properly' managed civic organizations. However, the question was never raised whether such organizations would be able to function in the Ukrainian context and to meet the needs of the Ukrainian civil society. In fact, the connection between the growth of professional civic organizations and the institutionalization of a strong civil society was never investigated either. After several years of civil society assistance, USAID could report the former but not the latter as an achievement. Moreover, it had to face a range of criticisms as to the kinds of civic organizations it was promoting.

In response, by the end of the 1990s USAID had to admit that institutionalizing a strong civil society in countries like Ukraine would take longer than was initially expected. On the one hand, the explosive growth of civic organizations was seen as a positive indicator attributed to the success of assistance: 'USAID and other donor assistance has helped fuel the explosive growth of NGO sectors in these countries' (USAID, October 1999, xi). On the other hand, the agency attributed the apparent problems (such as lack of financial viability, poor organizational management, lack of public awareness of NGO activities, failure to serve or represent constituencies and clients effectively) to the nature of the transformation process itself and not to assistance. It argued that the rapid NGO growth was triggered by greater freedom of association, heightened awareness of global issues and 'vigorous response to the opportunities and responsibilities that accompany democracy' (USAID 1999, 10). The donors were positioned not as another influential factor for the growth and its shortcomings but as yet another party overwhelmed by rapid change, almost as a victim. It was the accelerated change that was said to have challenged donors' capacity to be phased and strategic in their programmes and not the problematic design and short-sightedness of those programmes. Here, again the 'thousand flowers' metaphor came in to stress that such flowers do and should grow on their own.

> For donors, the pace of growth has made it difficult to keep abreast of developments in the sector and *to know whether they are working with organizations with a viable, authentic constituency.* . . . In general, accelerated change – coupled with the desire to exert an early positive impact – has challenged donors' capacity to be phased and strategic in their program design, instead, donors have tended to concentrate on the merits of individual projects and the strength of individual organizations.
>
> (USAID, October 1999, 11, *emphasis added*)

Interestingly, the 'thousand flowers' metaphor meant that there were no clearly defined eligibility criteria for the civic organizations and for the projects that were funded to support them – an organization only had to have some formal features of an NGO, and so the notions of a 'viable, authentic constituency' were never part of the civil society assistance discourse to begin with.

The more recent reconsideration of the potential that assistance has for transforming post-Soviet societies points to the fact that assistance has been accommodating particular dynamics it discovered in Ukraine. Even though it has never taken seriously local ideas about forms of civil society, it has made an effort to make its own conception look relevant. The idea of 'empowerment' is one way in which this has been achieved.

'Empowerment'

Throughout its assistance 'career' in Ukraine, the US government constantly had to respond to the harsh social and economic realities and political tensions that resulted from the collapse of the previous socialist system. In 1996 USAID was saying that since 1994,

> there has been considerable progress mixed with significant setbacks. While President Kuchma's commitment to the reform program appears firm, support within the ranks of government has been uneven. The Parliament especially has often proved an obstacle to reform. . .; as long as the quality of life continues to deteriorate for Ukrainian citizens, maintaining political and popular will to see the reform process through will be a constant challenge.
>
> (USAID/West NIS, 3 June 1996, 1)

Uneven local responses to reform and deteriorating conditions were putting the US-supported reform process in danger. In addition, there was always the fear that Russian influence would be resumed. USAID was worried about such tendencies as the 'renewed Russian dominance, compounded by the resurgence of Russian Communism, and the popularity of the Communist Party candidate in the 1996 Russian presidential election' (USAID/West NIS, 3 June 1996, 3). Here another concern comes out clearly – to make sure that hardships in Ukraine do not lead to Ukraine 'falling back' into the sphere of Russian influence.

By the late 1990s the situation in Ukraine was not improving as expected. The years of 1998–1999 were marked by important political and economic events. The shortcomings of the reform process were exacerbated by the Asian financial crisis of 1998, which had a grave impact on both Russia and Ukraine. There was also an apparent rise in support for left-wing parties and movements in Ukraine. In the parliamentary election of 1998 the Communist Party of Ukraine was far ahead of the other parties, taking about 25 per cent of the votes; the other two left-wing parties, the Bloc of the Socialist Party of Ukraine and the Agrarian Party of Ukraine and the Progressive Socialist Party of Ukraine, gained 8.5 and 4 per cent of the votes respectively (CVU 1998). These developments led to the adoption of another important notion of 'empowerment'. The 'empowerment' concept entails three related notions: social transition issues, awareness-raising and information distribution, and mentality change. Assistance not only had a prescriptive claim on what kinds of institutions had to be built, but was also developing a set of responses to the political, social and economic challenges in Ukraine.

The focus on 'social transition issues' was meant to ensure that the critical mass of the Ukrainian population would stay with their heads above water so that poverty and disillusionment would not ignite conflicts or a national crisis. These concerns were voiced from early on:

> Popular support for reform will evaporate unless social benefits and services are maintained..., if affordable methods are not developed to shelter the poor from rapid price increases, falling incomes, and the deterioration of basic public services.
>
> (USAID/West NIS, 3 June 1996)

In 1999 again an increasing emphasis was placed on 'social transition issues'; ten years of economic and political restructuring had led to 'greater poverty and hardship than anticipated at the beginning of the transition' (USAID, December 1999, ii). Fearing that hardship and the disillusionment with reforms would lead to a rise of communism,[5] USAID decided to pay greater attention to improving the quality of life in Ukraine, to mitigate any backlash against the reform process. The worry was that the population was growing cynical about the reform process and apathetic toward participation in citizens' groups in Ukraine (USAID, 29 March 1999, 2). So it was argued that 'USAID has a role to play in bringing the benefits of systemic change to a broader population' (USAID, December 1999, ii).

The agency believed this could be achieved through empowering populations and increasing economic opportunity at the provincial and local levels. Activities at the local level were defined as key for assuring the actual implementation of the nationally adopted reforms. 'Successful transition requires public confidence and acceptance of new ways of operating' (USAID, December 1999, 33). Reaching out to a broader constituency at the grassroots and regional levels was seen as necessary for building an understanding of and a demand for reform and developing a cadre of local leaders for change (USAID, December 1999, 33). Thus, in addition to improving social conditions, there was a perceived need for changing people's attitudes towards reform or, in broader terms, their 'mentality' in order to become suitable subjects for the new governance. The concept of governmentality refers to this aspect of governance, which is concerned with re-shaping the subjects of governance, their mentality, along with the re-shaping of institutions and their capacities (Newman 2005; Lendvai 2005).

People in Ukraine were believed not to be aware of 'the universe of possibilities' for improvement that existed. 'They cannot articulate the changes they want, therefore their advocacy policies are ineffective' (USAID, 29 March 1999, 11). Thus, it was seen as imperative to invest in information campaigns that would explain and popularize the reforms. One of the most expensive civil society projects in Ukraine was UMREP – the Ukraine Market Reform Education Program – established in 1993 as a joint project of the governments of Ukraine and the US through USAID. Its rationale was that:

Increased, better-informed citizens' participation in political and economic decision-making is essential to the development of a viable democracy in Ukraine. USAID's independent media program is enabling Ukrainian citizens to become better informed about current events in general, including issues related to economic reform.

(USAID/West NIS, 3 June 1996, 3)

In addition to informing people about the substance of and the need for the US-supported reforms in Ukraine, this objective also contained a stronger educational claim. It aspired to change what was believed to be the 'wrong' pattern of governmentality inherited by the Ukrainians from their Soviet past. This is, for example, captured by the following quote:

Given the Ukrainian history of top down, political and economic decision-making and service to the state, changing people's expectations and behaviour to accept that the state is responsive to influence by the people is a major transition.

(USAID/West NIS, 3 June 1996, 63)

It is on the basis of these ideas that the discursive centre of 'empowerment' was defined. The key assumption of 'empowerment' was the need to replace the 'wrong' Soviet pattern of governmentality with new liberal values and beliefs in the population. In addition to the task of 'institutional capacity building', the Agency was increasingly speaking of the need to change individual values, attitudes and behaviours: 'the importance of individual attitudes, practices and behaviours for successful transition had been underestimated' (USAID, December 1999, 33). In 2002 the Agency commissioned a multi-party investigation into USAID's civic programming in order to understand how and under what conditions civic education contributes to the development of a more active and informed democratic citizenry and to explore perspectives of integrating civic education components into other assistance programmes. The rationale for engaging with civic education was that 'for a democracy to survive and flourish, a critical mass of its citizens must possess the skills, embody the values, and manifest the behaviours that accord with democracy' (USAID, June 2002).

Individual participation was seen as essential for shaping and deepening the reform process. The goal for the assistance area 'democratic transition' was to 'foster democratic societies and institutions through the empowerment of citizens' (USAID, December 1999, vi). For purposes of 'empowerment' civil society activity was broadly defined as participation in political and economic processes by well-informed and responsible citizens (USAID, March 1999, 31). Across the portfolio, the Agency placed an emphasis on public education, training and exchange programmes as well as selective interventions for curriculum change in schools. In 1999 education was identified as a priority for the future. While the short-term objective remained to push for top-level structural reforms, the long-term goal was seen as 'working to prepare the next generation or perhaps the generation after for coming to power' (USAID, March 1999, 10).

The education approach worked in two ways: it aimed at promoting the so-called 'demonstration effects', on the one hand, and at bringing up a new 'critically thinking' generation of Ukrainians, on the other. The former goal was highly reminiscent of the liberal idealist belief that all it takes is to expose peoples to liberal democratic values and they could not but embrace them eagerly. The educational efforts were related to the idea of a 'wrong' pattern of governmentality in the sense that much blame was directed towards the legacies of communism, which meant that older generations were almost perceived as hopeless for building a new democratic society.

'Empowerment' was defined in terms of individual values and concerns, 'getting people to believe in themselves, to rely less on government to guide their daily lives, and to take control of their destiny through economic opportunities and political choices' (USAID, March 1999, 12). The extent to which 'empowerment' colonized the civil society assistance discourse is striking. On the one hand, this being a question of survival in the first place, it is hard to believe that those people who had the resources (material and physical resources, networks) and belonged to advantaged social and demographic groups at the beginning of transition would not have used the available opportunities to guide their daily lives. On the other hand, according to the Agency's own analysis, the biggest 'losers of transition', such as children, ethnic and religious minorities, women-led households, female pensioners, etc., are the ones who more often oppose the reform or show apathy. These groups are unlikely to benefit from 'demonstration effects' unless provided with structural opportunities and financial means to improve their positions.

On the level of civil society as a whole, its 'empowerment' is seen as connected to its 'sustainability' as a sector. Although very little attempt has been made to incorporate local ideas and forms of activism, the concern with 'sustainability' of the civil society that is built by assistance has been pronounced.

'Sustainability'

Civic organizations had to reach a certain degree of 'sustainability' in a relatively short term by means of increasing their organizational effectiveness and professionalism. The standard of professionalism was set by the American civic organizations implementing programmes in Ukraine. The idea was that the closer Ukrainian civic organizations resembled their American counterparts, the sooner the programmes could be phased out and the activities that constituted them could be relegated to Ukrainian civic organizations. This meant that the 'sustainability' of Ukrainian civic organizations was not defined in terms of their position in Ukrainian society in the after-funding phase, but in terms of how instrumental they could become in facilitating the 'phase out' of assistance. Professional and cost-effective civic organizations were argued to accelerate the 'graduation' from assistance (USAID, 21 July 1995).

USAID's experience with small NGO grants and local development activities is that they are information and staff intensive. However, under NPI, most of these responsibilities will be transferred to USAID's development partners by focusing on *capacity building* of local organizations early in the process and encouraging the development of *intermediary organizations.* . . . USAID's direct management role will be reduced, providing considerable cost savings.

(USAID, 21 July 1995, *emphasis added*)

Thus, the 'sustainability' also meant that local civic organizations would become capable of taking over some of the assistance activities implemented by USAID and its implementing partners, making assistance cheaper for USAID. The idea of 'sustainability' also led civil society assistance to become increasingly similar to such programmes in other parts of the world. Over the past few years, there is no more talk of the 'thousand flowers'; instead, USAID and other democracy programme implementers are increasingly concerned with promoting professional advocacy organizations (Hansen, 5 August 2004, interview by author).

A new Assistance Strategy for Ukraine for financial years 2003–2007 was written up in a much more enthusiastic tone than the previous one due to the improved situation in the country in terms of impressive levels of economic growth and increased social and economic stability. The proposed activities were said to 'fine-tune existing activities building on previous successes' (USAID, June 2002, v). The period was framed as extending 'beyond transition' and into sustainable economic growth. The Agency made a definite claim that the basic institutions were in place and therefore the assistance should focus on increasing their effectiveness and sustainability. Support to civil society was defined under Strategic Objective 3, 'Citizenry increasingly engaged in promoting their interests and rights for a more democratic market-oriented state'. The ultimate goals were (1) to increase the extent to which citizens believe that they can influence the government and (2) to increase civic activism, the former reflecting the notion of 'empowerment', the latter that of 'advocacy'. Advocacy is a relatively new term for the USAID programmes to Ukraine.

As a result of the introduction of the advocacy approach, a distinction was introduced between two types of civic organizations: civil society organizations (CSOs) and NGOs. CSO refers to an organization aimed primarily at influencing public policy. This means that civic organizations working to achieve public rather than private goals (usually referred to as NGOs) are civil society organizations, although all CSOs are civic organizations; NGOs are positioned in a service-delivery role, whereas CSOs are seen as political actors. Although advocacy techniques were mentioned before (more in passing than in a directive sense) in documents for Ukraine, this was the first time that CSOs were singled out as the priority beneficiary under the civil society objective. According to USAID, the strengthening of CSOs was to take place through the building of coalitions, increasing their constituency and membership, financial diversification, information sharing and more sophisticated advocacy. According to the advocacy approach, empowering civil society meant that Ukrainian citizens should be trained to demand transparency and accountability from their government by employing a range of professional advocacy tools.

The introduction of the notion of 'advocacy' marked an almost total abandonment of the 'thousand flowers' idea. Instead of supporting many different civic organizations, the discourse of 'advocacy' privileged a few, well developed, professional, and 'institutionally capable' organizations with good track records. These were the kinds of organizations that would facilitate the 'sustainability'/ 'phase out' idea.

Overall, both 'institutional capacity building' and 'sustainability' highlight the idea that rather than building civil society per se, civil society assistance should be based on a few targeted interventions aimed at creating and developing organizational structures that are professional and effective enough to implement assistance project activities, especially after the 'phase out'. This marked a closure in the conception of civil society, which could have stayed more open had the 'thousand flowers' idea prevailed in its pluralistic meaning. Instead, assistance quickly abandoned its ambitious large-scale project of 'building civil society' and chose to focus on a few targeted interventions. In the short term this means that many of the civic organizations that emerged on the wave brought about by the 'thousand flowers' idea will have to rethink the basis for their existence.

Conclusion

So what do we learn about the conception of civil society embodied in the three steps offered by assistance? 'Institutional capacity building' means enabling the setting up and development of particular organizational structures – civic organizations – and training them in key procedures. Since these kinds of organizations were non-existent at the beginning of assistance, 'capacity building' was defined in terms of reaching out to a wide audience of actual and potential leaders of different organizational forms. This idea of spreading out widely was captured by the metaphor 'let a thousand flowers bloom', which made the initial civil society assistance look different from the civil society assistance programmes implemented in other parts of the world. However, I argue that this initial take was less different from the promotion of civil society elsewhere than it might seem. Importantly, the 'flowers' that were invited to bloom in Ukraine and elsewhere in the region were all of the same kind, and the openness of this discourse did not go beyond allowing anyone to join in the space that was already externally defined. And so, even in the 'thousand flowers' period civil society assistance was not aimed at promoting an open playing field for civic organizations of different kinds and ideologies. Neither had the relevance of the civic 'flowers' for the Ukrainian context been made into an issue to be addressed by assistance. The paternalistic conception of assistance as top-down teaching justified by the 'end of history' thinking implied that the donor reserved the right to decide what had to be taught.

The relationship between the ones who know and the ones who have to be taught was further sustained through the notion of 'empowerment'. The notion of 'empowerment' consisted of three key elements: the notion of 'social transition issues' that defined Ukrainians as being in a dramatic state of disarray because of the social and economic difficulties transition entailed; the information and awareness raising that implied that Ukrainians were disapproving of the reform because they lack information about its virtues; and the 'wrong' pattern of governmentality that Ukrainians were said to have developed during the oppressive Soviet period and that seemed to be in the way of their fully embracing the promise of transition to democracy and market economy. On the basis of these three core notions, 'empowerment' is defined as education towards a new form of governmentality embracing the new ideals offered by governance through 'assistance' and liberation from the legacies of the past that may be in the way. The heavy emphasis on governmentality implied that there was something inherently wrong with the way Ukrainians thought of themselves and of their opportunities and responsibilities, and thus it constructed the demand for being taught. Even more importantly, it downgraded locally grown ideas about civil society and activism as those stemming from the dark communist past. In other words, different forms of activism in Ukraine would be based on a deficient Soviet pattern of governmentality deemed inappropriate for the current period.

The notion of 'sustainability' endorsed the idea that after civic organizations are created they have to be trained to become professional enough to take over the functions fulfilled by their American counterparts. This led to an increase in professional training for civic organizations towards the year 2000. Instead of promoting a 'thousand flowers', USAID is now developing programmes to strengthen think tanks, resource centres and advocacy organizations – all being defined as civic organizations with highly skilled staff that provide technical expertise in the area related to 'assistance'. In the context of a permanent 'phase out', the 'sustainability' of Ukrainian civil society is understood in terms of the capacity of Ukrainian civic organizations to facilitate 'assistance'. This shows that the primary commitment of assistance does not lie with developing its recipient civic organizations but with sustaining the privileged position of foreign donors within the new governance of former Soviet countries.

Altogether, such a conception of civil society by USAID has an important impact on the development of civil society in Ukraine since new definitions of what counts as the 'good' civil society create new boundaries between different kinds of civic organizations. These boundaries are maintained by means of new thematic priorities, eligibility criteria and assistance timeframes.

Notes

1 This case study is part of my PhD research project funded by the Amsterdam School for Social Science Research at the University of Amsterdam. Most of the interviews quoted were conducted during my fieldwork trip to Washington, DC made possible

with the generous support of the Kennan Institute at the Woodrow Wilson International Centre for Scholars.

2 Excluding the three Baltic republics, which were funded together with the countries of Central and Eastern Europe (SEED Act).

3 The Truman Doctrine was announced in 1947 and marked the official reversal of American foreign policy from cooperation with the Soviet Union to containment.

4 Interestingly, the phrase comes from the speech delivered by Chairman Mao Zedong shortly before China's Cultural Revolution. In the original, 'let a hundred flowers bloom, a hundred schools of thought contend' was proclaimed to encourage freedom of expression, debate and independent thinking, and gave rise to the Hundred Flowers movement of 1956–1957. However, shortly afterwards it was twisted to mean that upper-class artists, writers and scientists should have no greater claim than their proletarian counterparts. In fact, it was said, the upper classes had been monopolizing the cultural and scientific spheres for too long. Politically, this translated into the Communist Party of China demarcating a clear line between revolutionaries and counter-revolutionaries. As Lu Ting-Yi, the director of the Propaganda Department of the Central Committee of the Chinese Communist Party, announced: 'no freedom should be extended to counter-revolutionaries: for them we only have a dictatorship. A clear political line must be drawn between friend and foe' (Lu Ting-Yi, 26 May 1956). Within months, the same slogan was used to justify persecution and purges of political opponents.

5 This 'communist phobia' is evident from various assessments of the political process in the former Soviet Union – high levels of support for communist parties are persistently quoted in USAID documents as worrisome tendencies (for example, USAID, June 2002).

References

Carothers, T. (1999). *Aiding Democracy Abroad: The Learning Curve*, Washington, DC: Carnegie Endowment for International Peace.

—— (2002). The End of the Transition Paradigm, *Journal of Democracy* 13 (2): 5–21.

Carothers, T. and Ottaway, M. (eds) (2000). *Funding Virtue: Civil Society Aid and Democracy Promotion*, Washington, DC: Carnegie Endowment for International Peace.

Committee of Voters of Ukraine (CVU). *Returns of 1998 Election to the Ukrainian Parliament* 1998 [cited 10 June 2000]. Available from www.cvu.kiev.ua.

Cooley, A. (2000). International Aid to the Former Soviet States: Agent of Reform or Guardian of the Status Quo? *Problems of Post-Communism* 47 (4).

Henderson, S. (2003). *Building Democracy in Contemporary Russia: Western Support for Grassroots Organizations*, Ithaca: Cornell University Press.

Howell, J. and Pearce, J. (2001). *Civil Society and Development: a Critical Exploration*, Boulder: Lynne Rienner Publishers.

Lendvai, N. (2005) Remaking European Governance: Transition, Accession and Integration, in J. Newman (ed.), *Remaking Governance: Peoples, Politics and the Public Sphere*, Bristol: Policy Press.

McMahon, P. (2001). Building Civil Society in East Central Europe: The Effect of American Non-governmental Organizations on Women's Groups, *Democratisation* 8 (2) 45–68.

Newman, J. (2005). Participative Governance and the Remaking of the Public Sphere, in J Newman (ed.), *Remaking Governance: Peoples, Politics and the Public Sphere*, Bristol: Policy Press.

US Congress (1992). *Freedom for Russia and Emerging Eurasia Democracies and Open Markets (FREEDOM) Support Act.*

US Department of State (2000). FY 2001 Congressional Budget Justification for Foreign Operations, Washington, DC.

USAID (21 July 1995). Core Report of the New Partnerships Initiative (internal draft), Washington, DC: USAID.

—— (November 1998). Democracy and Governance: A Conceptual Framework: Centre for Democracy and Governance, Bureau for Global Programs, Field Support, and Research.

—— (29 March 1999). U.S. Assistance Strategy for Ukraine 1999–2002.

—— (October 1999). Lessons in Implementation: The NGO Story. Building Civil Society in Central and Eastern Europe and the New Independent States: USAID Bureau for Eastern Europe and Eurasia. Office of Democracy and Governance.

—— (December 1999). From Transition to Partnership: A Strategic Framework for USAID Programs in Europe and Eurasia: USAID Bureau for Europe and Eurasia.

—— (1999). A Decade of Change: Profiles of USAID Assistance to Europe and Eurasia, Washington, DC: USAID.

—— (June 2002). Approaches to Civic Education: Lessons Learned: Office for Democracy and Governance, Bureau for Democracy, Conflict and Humanitarian Assistance.

USAID/West NIS (3 June 1996). Ukraine: Results Review and Resource Request (R4).

Van Rooy, A. (ed.) (1998). *Civil Society and the Aid Industry: The Politics and Promise*, London: Earthscan Publications.

Wedel, J. (2001). *Collision and Collusion: The Strange Case of Western Aid to Eastern Europe*, New York: St Martin's Press.

4 Civic organisations and local governance

Learning from the experience of community networks

John Diamond

Introduction

This chapter explores the relationships between UK central government funded initiatives which have as part of their remit the involvement of civic organisations and local government agencies in regeneration projects.

These relationships illustrate the emerging trend in the UK to construct a new model of local governance at the city or neighbourhood level. As the chapter demonstrates this is not without difficulty. In part this process of redrawing the boundaries between the role of the local state and civic organisations can be seen as enhancing the status and visibility of the voluntary and community sector in UK local political processes and institutions. However, it can also be experienced as a process of legitimising local state actions by incorporating key community interest groups and stakeholders into arenas and places shaped by local state institutions.

The primary source of data referred to in this chapter derives from an evaluation (undertaken by the author) of these relationships in the context of one South London authority. The evaluation included over 30 interviews with key staff and community activists, attendance at a number of meetings of the network and public agencies and a number of workshops with community representatives and front line staff involved in the local partnership. What emerges is that civic organisations place a higher premium on establishing relationships based upon trust, which are in turn informed by a developed sense of place and the needs of the local community, whereas local government actors place a much higher emphasis on meeting the requirements of central government funded initiatives, and tend to adopt an ahistorical sense of place compared with voluntary sector professionals. The resulting professional and organisational (and personal) tensions suggest that local state agencies place less emphasis on the processes of civic renewal and the capacity building of civic organisations when they appear to conflict with meeting externally set criteria. In that sense the notion of a 'new' form of local governance is experienced as the 'old' centralising and controlling tendencies of local state agencies. As a consequence we can observe how these differences of perspective get played out in the arena of highly 'localised' politics.

Context: 'new' local governance

The creation of Community Empowerment Networks (CEN) in England are a significant part of the Labour Government's Neighbourhood Renewal Strategy (NRS), and were announced at the same time as the NRS alongside the establishment of Local Strategic Partnerships (LSPs), which were, initially, focused upon the most deprived areas of England. The remit and membership of the LSPs have been more clearly defined than those of the CENs. The Local Partnerships were set up to bring together the core public service agencies in a locality in order to provide a forum within which, in the short term, the *local* neighbourhood renewal strategy could be discussed and monitored. It is here that we can observe the formation of institutions, which are congruent with the notion of a 'new' local governance.

Since 1997 the Blair Government have developed two major regeneration programmes. The New Deal for Communities (NDC) and the National Strategy for Neighbourhood Renewal (NRS) are, in some ways, a continuation of earlier initiatives (HMSO 1998; SEU 2001). They share many of the same characteristics as other contemporary UK regeneration programmes. They are area-based initiatives (ABI); adding additional layers of monitoring and delivery to existing systems and aiming to engage in facilitating a partnership between the public, private and civic organisations.

The significance of these initiatives derives from their focus on inter-agency working and the need to develop a clear succession (or exit) strategy which is dependent upon the capacity of existing local state agencies and local communities to ensure that change is maintained. In the UK the analysis which underscores these new programmes is partly based upon an evaluation of earlier schemes and upon the experience of Labour during the Thatcher years. It is argued that it is necessary to create the conditions for effective collaboration between welfare agencies and to develop a local or neighbourhood response (Burgess *et al.* 2001; Filkin *et al.* 2000; Newman 2001). In addition there is an assumption that changes in service delivery and more effective managerial systems will effect the reforms necessary.

Under the NRS, Local Strategic Partnerships (LSPs) are being set up to improve the co-ordination of public and welfare agencies (including the police) in localities (Russell 2001). These partnership boards (which are defined by central government) are not subject to local democratic accountability. As Bonny (2004) argues, this absence should not be underestimated, as strengthening representative democracy is necessary to counterbalance the influence of 'fuzzy partnerships and diffuse managed participation initiatives'.

The lack of clarity surrounding the creation of LSPs neatly highlights the contradiction at the heart of Labour's 'new' local governance project. Whilst local government reforms in the UK since 1997 have been primarily directed at modernising the institutions and processes of the local state, the reform agenda for increasing representative democracy has been less evident. For Labour new forms of governance are necessary to reform the management and delivery of public and welfare services. The LSP model contains many of the elements which we can reflect upon in terms of seeking to understand the conceptual framework which is in play. Whilst it is self-evident that all institutions contain places where political choices are made, the LSP approach seeks to create a space where choices are made within a 'neutral' or 'apolitical' context. Indeed, as has been argued elsewhere (Diamond and Liddle 2005; Newman 2005) these new institutions contain competing and contradictory elements. At the LSP table sit not only political actors (local councillors), representatives of public agencies outside local authority control (health and the police) and community and voluntary sector representatives but also statutory services, who are subject to local authority control. LSPs may be a place where local services can be discussed but it is doubtful if they represent an 'open' or 'accountable' space for decision making. In a sense Labour's model of local governance enables local elites to meet and discuss specific issues at the request of the centre. Decisions are, as this chapter suggests, taken elsewhere and as a local institution the LSP remains outside recognised forms of accountability. This lack of formal authority at the local level results in the LSP occupying a role without power but with the potential to influence decisions. In that sense it seems to fit with Labour's attempt, at the local level, to create pluralist sites of discussion without restructuring local institutions. As a consequence less powerful or independent actors (civic organisations) have to make harder choices about where and how to invest their time and scarce resources. As this chapter shows these choices can result in individuals feeling *less* powerful, rather than feeling they are participants in the new forms of decision making.

Over the past 25 years both central and local government in the UK have introduced a number of initiatives which claim to promote the 'active' participation of the civic organisations in 'partnerships' or inter-agency activity. Whilst these initiatives have often been based upon notions of enhancing public participation or renewing civil society, the experience of participants in these initiatives has been mixed (Ledwith 2005).

During the late 1970s/early 1980s a number of urban-run Labour local authorities (and some Liberal-run authorities) attempted to reform the organisation and management of their authorities by 'going local'. This usually involved attempting to decentralise service delivery away from city hall to more localised or neighbourhood-based offices. The reforms were usually accompanied by claims to enhance the capacity of voluntary organisations (including residents or tenant groups) to participate in local decision making. The extent to which these localised reforms were successful can be contested, but the experience has significantly influenced the government of Tony Blair in its introduction of the NRS (Diamond 2002a).

The NRS approach reflects the priorities and assumptions of what is possible (and desirable) in neighbourhood regeneration. It involves the identification by external agencies of a specific physical area within which a number of initiatives will be located. The classification of a neighbourhood by external welfare and professional agencies is a process in which 'local' actors (tenants and/or residents) are included only after the event (Ambrose 2005).

This, in effect, sustains the notion of a dependent and passive neighbourhood, a notion which is at the core of contemporary regeneration (Byrne 2001; Powell 1999). Thus, there is a dichotomy between the language used by regeneration professionals in which they seek the involvement of local people on the one hand and their exclusion from the initial phase of the process on the other. The neighbourhood is assumed to be incapable of engaging with the regeneration agenda and, in fact, is disempowered from the start. The agencies created to manage and to implement the regeneration initiative are, themselves, often drawn from the outside. In the UK it is certainly the case that a growing army of 'wandering' regeneration specialists has been created; they often work on temporary contracts for the lifetime of a project. They may be seconded from local welfare agencies, so many have some knowledge of the area, but they rarely live within the area subject to the regeneration process (Diamond 2001).

Local involvement is usually restricted to those who are active in local residents groups who find themselves co-opted into the initiative. Thus, for some individuals (and possibly their families) the 'benefits' of involvement may be associated with an enhanced status, an opportunity to influence particular (but discrete) aspects of the initiative, an opportunity (perhaps) to secure a job (albeit temporary) and a 'place at the table' to meet with the senior managers and professionals. This process of incorporation is not new and has been a feature of UK regeneration strategies since the mid-1960s. In effect, what is happening is that the capacity of the local community to intervene is restricted to those who 'sign up' to the initiative (Clarke 2004).

The UK has a large number of diverse civic organisations with over 500,000 paid staff and some three million volunteers in the sector (VSNTO 2003). But the diversity of the sector and the imbalance between national voluntary agencies and local community groups illustrates not only real power imbalances between civic organisations but more profound imbalances of power and access at the local or neighbourhood level.

The 'capacity' of local civic organisations to engage with local state-sponsored processes or central government programmes in the locality varies significantly. Given that civic organisations are often funded directly or indirectly via local government, then its potential to adopt an oppositional role may be restricted. 'Independent' civic organisations require some level of financial independence, but also the capacity to *act* independently and to seek to be 'representative' of their local constituent base.

Thus, we can observe currently in the UK, central government initiatives to enhance the status and role of civic organisations by focusing upon the following priority areas:

• Recruitment and retention of paid staff
• Leadership and management skills
• Networks, collaboration and information provision
• Access and investment in skills

(VSTNO 2003)

These areas which have been identified are ones which enhance the 'professionalisation' of the paid staff and seek to develop their managerial skills and techniques. They may be necessary but they are not sufficient to ensure the political autonomy of civic organisations nor do they enhance the skills of the professional staff to voice oppositional views to current initiatives.

As a strategy of containing discontent and alternative perspectives it can be very effective. While the balance of power within any regeneration initiative is significantly weighted in favour of the status quo, the long-term success of any initiative is partly dependent upon the capacity of local people to sustain their neighbourhood networks and street-based (or community) organisations after the professionals have left. It is, also, dependent upon a sustained investment in jobs and training (Atkinson 1998; Banks *et al.* 2001; Jowitt and Chapman 2001; Lowndes and Wilson 2001; Mayo and Taylor 2001; Purdue *et al.* 2000).

As these careful assessments of regeneration initiatives reveal, their long-term success is dependent upon transforming the local labour market to provide new employment opportunities, improving the knowledge and skills of local people to enter the labour market and reducing barriers to participation in the local labour market by understanding how factors such as race and gender shape what jobs are available. These structural factors present are indirectly addressed by regeneration initiatives and experience suggests that by not directly addressing them (or by using positive action initiatives or contract compliance strategies) areas remain locked into cycles of decline and exclusion. The presence of active and partly professionalised civic organisations provides an alternative 'space' to argue for a different perspective and one which, at times, questions existing initiatives.

There is, therefore, a basic mismatch between the needs of local groups and the policies which are assumed by the regeneration initiatives. This flaw in contemporary regeneration initiatives should not surprise commentators. It stems from an analysis which argues that 'communities' lack the skills and knowledge to engage sufficiently with the local state and that alternative community-based perspectives cannot be guaranteed to 'fit' with the needs of the external agencies. In this sense, the implicit model of 'the community' is a 'deficit' model.

The task, therefore, for the local state is to 'repair' the local neighbourhood sufficiently to make it safe for inward investment and development. The local state restructures localities so as to ensure its own competitive advantage over other cities and places (Cockburn 1977; Peck and Ward 2002). These developments are often ascribed to the processes of globalisation. Whilst it is possible to argue that such processes are played out in different ways in different places we can observe the impact of neo-liberalism in the UK. In particular, the marketisation of the public sector, the stress on local partnerships to take up roles previously undertaken by the state and in the stress on flexibility, flatter hierarchies and organisational capacity to respond (Clarke 2004). The NRS initiative is illustrative of these processes. At the neighbourhood level one can see in the formation of CENs an approach which mirrors these general trends. At the same time, however, such initiatives raise community expectations and pressure local initiatives to address specific and neighbourhood concerns. The space is, therefore, open to local lobbying and a struggle ensues in the identification of short-term priorities and the allocation of resources (Mayo 1997; Taylor 1995).

Community Empowerment Networks may provide an important initiative from which we can both observe and learn the extent to which autonomy is exercised. More interestingly we can explore the extent to which the value of neighbourhood-based community work is legitimised by other state-sponsored actors in this process.

Local governance and community development: capacity and legitimacy

As Banks *et al.* (2003), Hastings (2003), Henderson and Thomas (2002) and Schuftan (1996) have suggested there are a number of separate processes in play here:

- The role of community development in enhancing the confidence and skill of local community interests to articulate their voice and to identify their priorities.
- The 'political' nature of community development in seeking to occupy a different space from that which is controlled by local state agencies and local politicians.
- The skill and values associated with the community development process which are now being appropriated by local state agencies to promote local regeneration initiatives.
- The ways in which community development lays claim to a language and set of values which explicitly questions the status quo and legitimises contest and conflict.
- The implications for civic organisations of a 'professionalised' workforce which may seek less conflictual approaches.
- The traditions of community development work which have been refined and developed outside the UK and which have an explicitly radical and transforming agenda.

It is in this context that we can see the ways in which increasing the capacity of local people to engage with the regeneration initiative can lead to conflict and challenge. The need to manage such potential conflict has become a real issue for many regeneration initiatives (Diamond 2002b), and as such may provide a more interesting focus for our understanding of local governance.

The key regeneration managers will experience a tension between their relationships with local agencies, local residents and those who manage and/or fund the initiative, while local political elites will seek to exercise direct or indirect influence on regeneration initiatives.

At an initiative level there will be inter- and intra-organisational tension. The needs of the economic development teams, for instance, are likely to take priority over the needs and aspirations of the community or resident groups. In part this tension is sustained by the setting of performance indicators, against which staff are judged. Further, there may be a competing sense of time and place which is ever present in such initiatives. For those who are involved in tenant and resident liaison, the immediate needs of local groups will influence their given priorities. As they seek to renegotiate these they will have to look for 'space' within which to operate, while remaining managerially accountable to senior staff (who often have neither time nor space to engage in such reflection).

The community groups present will, themselves, reflect some of these tensions. There are, of course, important questions about the accountability and representativeness of local community leaders (Purdue *et al.* 2000). Some groups will have regeneration 'sponsors' who do receive support and resources. This, inevitably, increases their dependence but it can also increase their distance from other community groups or activists.

It is necessary, therefore, to be sensitive to the notion that the engagement of local groups in itself is a 'good thing'. Civic organisations are themselves likely sites of conflict and the exercise of unequal power, which have the effect of marginalising some individuals and groups. Paid professional staff as well as neighbourhood 'leaders' can act as significant gate keepers excluding those who offer a different perspective from the dominant or normalised view present within the sector (Purdue *et al.* 2000; Harrison *et al.* 1995).

The varied networks and partnerships associated with such initiatives increase the potential to separate local activists from their neighbourhoods, and they also can lead to ambiguity in decision making and accountability. Local community or regeneration boards may be places of formal decision making, but it is important to recognise the significance of informal decision making, and to locate its sources.

These networks or places of informal decision making can be as powerful as the roles and positions occupied by local state agencies and professionals (Parkes *et al.* 2004; Smith *et al.* 2004). Whilst the sector often values informality over formality in terms of how meetings are managed, there is a need to ensure mechanisms of accountability and governance which are pluralist and open. So despite the claims made that LSPs are a necessary element of a model of local governance, the evidence suggests that we need a more holistic map to understand the significance of local formal and informal networks.

There are models of capacity building/empowerment which suggest that it is possible to question and to challenge local state processes (Arnstein 1969; Burns 1991; Banks and Shenton 2001). These need to be contrasted with alternative approaches which take us through the complexities of decision making and the sites of power present in a locality and explore ways in which these processes can be 'opened up' to a wider audience (Bryne 2001; Mayo 1997; North 2001). These latter models of capacity building provide us with rich descriptive accounts of particular places at particular times and they offer us a 'snapshot' of what is happening. They also provide a critical reflection upon the nature of the power relationship which exists within a partnership or between a formal partnership and local community groups.

'Partnerships' are not, of course, fixed. I am not suggesting that we can read off or anticipate a particular outcome on the assumption that change is not possible (Huxham and Vangan 2000). But, without exploring the nature of power within local partnerships and between partnerships and local groups we will either miss significant changes or we will expect either too much (or too little) from regeneration projects (Diamond 2004; Mayo and Taylor 2001). The horizontal relationships formed by local partnerships, and community-based initiatives need to be contrasted with the vertical relationships with power holders ever present within a locality. The focus for those seeking to understand the power relationships present is to recognise that an understanding of positioning (according to class, race and gender and so on) may reveal likely outcomes at the points where conflict takes place – the points of intersectionality.

It is at these points of intersectionality that we can see the complexity of the relationships between the CEN, the local state actors and centrally driven initiatives being rehearsed and played out. It is here that conflict, misunderstanding and the different senses of place and time come together, which has the potential to unite the capacity of the voluntary sector to feel 'heard' and 'valued'.

Competing narratives of time and place: a case study of a Community Empowerment Network

The experience of the Community Empowerment Network (CEN) in South London and its capacity to provide an independent and critical voice in the work of the Local Strategic Partnership (LSP) can be observed by reference to:

- The relationship between those members of the CEN who sat on the LSP and the extent to which they were 'accountable' to the CEN.
- The relationship between the CEN and its voluntary sector sponsor.
- The relationship between the key activists CEN and officers of the LSP.
- The ways in which trust, methods to develop collaboration and understanding were played out, negotiated and agreed.

These emerging themes can be clustered together under the primary theme of this chapter, which is the existence of 'competing narratives' of the CEN and its historical and geographical context. It became evident that as individuals told their 'story' of their experience of the CEN (and the LSP) there were quite different narratives of place and time. Whilst the details of the same events were recalled in similar ways, the interpretations and explanations offered were often significantly different.

To some extent these different accounts were shaped by the length of time individuals had been active (either in the CEN or in their local neighbourhood or local groups) and/or where they lived. For some members of the CEN the NRS provided an opportunity to secure funds or new initiatives for the neighbourhoods which they perceived had been neglected in the past. The sense of geography and the powerful emotions associated with place and neighbourhood were key elements in framing their understanding of what the roles of the CEN and the LSP were about. Arguably, those who felt that their localities had been ignored in the past saw the NRS as an opportunity to gain access to new projects and so felt that it was 'about time' that their neighbourhoods saw some gain after years of neglect. On one level this could be seen as a positive redistribution of resources for previously neglected areas. Another interpretation might be that it illustrated not only the weakness of successive regeneration initiatives but that it presented a structural/organisational dilemma for the CEN. The CEN sought to present a 'holistic' approach to regeneration policies for the area and yet key members were arguing for a redistribution or reallocation of resources in favour of their 'space'.

As well as these spatial differences the factor of 'time' was also significant. A significant number of those interviewed who were active in the CEN had long histories of involvement with civic organisations in the local authority area. Their perception of the significance (or not) of the LSP and the CEN itself was shaped by this memory. Their narratives of meaning differed sharply from those who were employed by the LSP or who were based in the Government Office for London (GOL) as part of the NRS team.

The community activists had a sense of history, experience and a recall of success and failure which was in sharp contrast with those who were located in the LSP or GOL. Whilst local activists were steeped in the history and politics of the area, the professionals stood detached (at least in a formal sense) from this history. The former could locate the NRS along a continuum of urban regeneration experiments and could point to what they considered were evident weaknesses in the process. They perceived the formation of both the LSP and the CEN as a means to counter the negative effects of professional agencies and the local politics of the area. The CEN represented a counterweight to their negative experiences of inefficient local government and poor decision making by career politicians and poor local government staff.

The regeneration professionals distanced themselves (in the interviews) from this history and saw the LSP and the CEN as representing a new start. Their starting point and frame of reference was the NRS, their criteria for success was the extent to which the LSP in this particular authority met the objectives set and the extent to which a new approach to managing the regeneration process emerged. What is interesting to note is that whilst they articulated this view, they also marginalised or dismissed some members of the CEN by reference to their 'living in the past', or by stressing the 'newness' of the NRS.

In a significant way they sought to decontextualise the present from the past. Arguably, their claim for legitimacy and significance required them to do so. But, by presenting an ahistorical account of the NRS and by seeking to depoliticise its significance, especially at a local level, they were asserting their values over those who sat on the CEN.

These competing frameworks of understanding also saw expression in the language used. Even though there were differences in the narratives adopted by members of the CEN, they framed their observations by references to individuals, to specific places (local neighbourhoods and even collections of streets), to particular social and economic problems associated with the locality, to named groups whom they felt were 'excluded' and then to the work of the CEN or the LSP. Their accounts were *personal* and informed by reference to their direct experience or knowledge. Their 'picture' of the locality and their assessment of its needs were coloured by images of places, issues and events.

In contrast, the LSP and regional Government Office interviewees offered a much more generalised account of what was needed. In one sense this should not be surprising. However, they expressed the priorities of the LSP in terms of managing a process which was itself expressed in terms of setting objectives, allocating resources and improving service delivery. The language, itself, of managerialism can be interpreted by community-based actors as disempowering at best or at worst as dismissing their concerns and knowledge as being not relevant or too partisan or too 'emotional'. It appears from this that there is a competition between participants for definition of what constitutes appropriate knowledge.

The different accounts given by members of the CEN executive revealed some real differences in understanding the role of the CEN and the role of those who were elected by the CEN to sit on the LSP. Specifically, the unresolved issue was the extent to which CEN representatives on the LSP saw themselves as being accountable to the CEN or not, and whether or not they should act as a unified group on the LSP. This was an issue which was raised by most of those interviewed for the evaluations.

The ways in which the CEN sought to discuss (and to resolve) these accountability issues involved the use of 'away days' for the CEN executive (drawing upon outside facilitators of which the author was one), briefing meetings prior to the LSP, allocating members of the paid staff to liaise with representatives and an exploration of the issues at the CEN executive. This experience is not unusual in the voluntary and community sectors. Indeed, the uneven experience of the UK regeneration initiatives suggests that some local representatives on partnership boards will be co-opted into the processes and become distanced from their local base of support and others will adopt an oppositional role (and may, after a period, leave) (Purdue 2005).

The context of the LSP/CEN model is slightly different. The potential power and significance of the LSP approach goes beyond a local regeneration or housing initiative in which partnership boards have become the norm. The issue is not whether there should be a 'line' which all representatives sign up to, but rather the process and systems of accountability which are in place. So whilst the discussion of how to make local representatives accountable to the CEN executive may have seemed to some to be of significance, the wider set of issues was how are they accountable to their 'constituency' and how did the evident differences within the CEN shape the attitude of key members of the LSP?

It is the view of this writer that the differences were significant in how key members of the LSP (and the officers of the LSP) understood the power relations within the CEN and how they sought to use these differences as part of a wider strategy to maintain their differences in power and status.

During the course of the evaluation it became clear that the ambiguity in the relationship between the CEN and the agency could not be sustained. The main reason for this was that there was anecdotal and empirical evidence that the local agency was seeking to contain the activity of the CEN. Despite the fact that both the agency and key activists in the CEN could see the value of separation and independence over the long term, there was a clear pressure to limit and constrain the work of the CEN.

The CEN does have the potential to occupy a significant role, at the local level, of contributing to and influencing policy on behalf of civic organisations and civil society. It is able to draw together well over 200 activists and workers from its quarterly meetings. It has developed a role in providing and disseminating information about the work of the LSP and the CEN across the authority. It may be able to sustain this work as a separate and independent agency. But, this in turn leads to an important and significant examination of the way styles of leadership are developed, models and practice of decision making and the extent to which there is a shared understanding of these concepts and practices.

It is in the process of decision making, use of language and the 'style' of the meeting that the power imbalance between the CEN and some members of the LSP can be best observed. Whilst, in the UK, the emphasis on 'capacity building' with civic organisations has been focused on enhancing their capacity to sit on partnership boards, there has been relatively little work done to enhance the capacity of professional agencies to work with local groups.

There is some evidence that in small groups, or in meetings with officers of the LSP, the CEN and its paid staff have made progress in working together. Relationships with officers have improved and officers from the LSP attend CEN meetings. But, these meetings (between LSP officers and CEN staff and activists) are, by their nature, small in number and private. It is in the public arena and for the public context of their relationships that most observers are likely to conclude that imbalance in power is present, or to conclude that one particular explanation of policy (the dominant LSP view) is the more legitimate.

Conclusion

The competing narratives present within the CEN reflected to some extent the roles and experiences of those interviewed. The paid staff had a particular view and interpretation of their role, in part shaped by their understanding of the NRS and the role of the LSP. Throughout the evaluation it was apparent that this 'view' was not shared by the LSP officers or by some members of the CEN executive. Members of the CEN were, to some extent, influenced by their location, some were paid community workers, other were activists and some had a wide experience of regeneration activity. As has been noted all of those interviewed from the CEN described their experiences and understanding of the LSP in a language which drew upon a highly personalised and informed description of their sense of place and time. For many of the CEN interviewees the NRS was just another initiative. In contrast, those who were based in the LSP or the regional Government Office drew upon a discourse which emphasised the policy context of the initiative and located it within a time frame which stressed the significance of the NRS.

There remains a series of unanswered issues which the CEN/LSP approach raises. They are relevant for a broader discussion of understanding how civic or local capacity can be enhanced. There are four primary issues:

- The extent to which the CEN model is capable of developing an independent critique of the NRS.
- The congruence (or otherwise) between a strategy to enhance local capacity building and the NRS.
- The experience of those groups which choose not to participate in the CEN/NRS model.
- The extent to which local actors in the regeneration process can 'unlearn their scripts'.

CENs have presented the voice of the community within the LSPs, and therefore a necessary part of the NRS. Yet, the scope for an independent voice or an alternative perspective is limited. In part it is limited by the individuals involved at a local level and by their capacity to imagine a set of alternative perspectives in relation to the NRS and the LSP. They will, in part, be constrained by the continuation of funding as well as securing legitimacy for their work. They will also be limited by the future development of the LSP.

However, CEN are essentially dependent upon the success of the LSPs and by their perceived legitimacy to local political groups and to their constituent public agencies. By being forced to rely on the success of the LSP experiment the CENs may find themselves too dependent and may choose to adopt positions which guarantee their presence at the LSP table. To develop an independent strategy CENs will need to secure funding and to establish themselves as a legitimate voice at the local level. Whilst relative independence may be a preferred strategy for some activists, it does not, of itself, secure a sustainable future.

The UK Government (Home Office 2003) have engaged in a consultation exercise on future policy options relating to 'capacity building'. It is the view of this writer that there remains a lack of congruence between capacity building initiatives, as framed at present, and the NRS. First, the NRS is defined by reference to externally set guidelines and frameworks and primary responsibility rests with the local authority and the LSP; the local community is, in a sense, a passive partner in this process. Second, the CEN model and capacity building initiatives associated with it seek to 'represent' their views through their collaboration as an active partner within the LSP.

The issue of the 'legitimacy' of civic organisations remains. The extent to which local groups 'opt out' of the NRS is dependent either on an active choice (recognising the risks associated with this decision) or on their 'invisibility' to the LSP and NRS. Put simply, the NRS defines, to a significant extent, who is 'in' and who is 'out' of the process. Healthy (politically and financially) independent civic organisations are necessary in any event. As civic organisations are increasingly drawn into the provision of services their ability to stand back and give support to those groups which are not given legitimacy remains doubtful.

Finally, there is a separate but related issue of how participants make sense of these policy initiatives. A recurring theme of the CEN evaluation experience was the way in which individuals 'understood their script' and how threatened they appear to be if asked to step outside their understanding.

This process was evident with all participants and not just welfare professionals employed by the local state. A crucial role for those engaged in local evaluations is to invite the participants to consider alternative interpretations or to develop a different vocabulary to explain their experience. 'Unlearning our script' should, perhaps, be seen as a means of not only developing alternative perspectives but also of different interpretations of what has happened and what is possible. In this way the 'capacity' of a number of key actors to imagine new ways of working may be enhanced.

References

Ambrose, P. (2005) 'Urban Regeneration: Who Defines the Indicators' in D. Taylor and S. Balloch (eds) *The Politics of Evaluation: Participation and Policy Implementation*, Bristol: The Policy Press.

Arnstein, S. (1969) 'A Ladder of Citizen Participation' in *Journal of the American Institute of Planners* 35: 216–224.

Atkinson, P. (1998) 'Countering Urban Social Exclusion: The Role of Community Participation and Partnership' in R. Griffiths (ed.) *Social Exclusion in Cities* Occasional Paper 8, University of the West of England.

Banks, S. and Shenton, F. (2001) 'Regenerating Neighbourhoods: A Critical Look at the Role of Community Capacity Building' in *Local Economy* 16(4): 286–298.

Banks, S., Butcher, H., Handerson, P. and Robertson, S. (eds) (2003) *Managing Community Practice*, Bristol: The Policy Press.

Bonny, N. (2004) 'Local Democracy Renewed' in *The Political Quarterly* 75(1): 43–51.

Burgess, P., Hall, S., Mawson, J. and Pearce, G. (2001) *Devolved Approaches to Local Governance*, York: York Publishing Service.

Burns, D. (1991) 'Ladders of Participation' in *Going Local* 18.

Byrne, D. (2001) *Social Exclusion*, Buckingham: Open University Press.

Clarke, J. (2004) 'Dissolving the Public Realm? The Logic and Limits of Neo-liberalism' in *Journal of Social Policy* 33(1): 27–48.

Cockburn, C. (1977) *The Local State: Management of Cities and People*, London: Pluto Press.

Diamond, J. (2001) 'Managing Change or Coping with Conflict' in *Local Economy* 16(4): 272–285.

Diamond, J. (2002a) 'Decentralisation: New Forms of Public Participation or New Forms of Managerialism' in P. McLaverty (ed.) *Public Participation and Innovations in Community Governance*, Aldershot: Ashgate.

Diamond, J. (2002b) 'Strategies to Resolve Conflict in Partnerships' in *International Journal of Public Sector Management* 15(2): 296–306.

Diamond, J. (2004) 'Capacity Building – For What?' in *Community Development Journal* 39(2): 177–187.

Diamond, J. and Liddle, J. (2005) *Management of Regeneration*, London: Routledge.

Filkin, G., Stoker, G., Wilkinson, G. and Williams, J. (2000) *Towards A New Localism*, IPPR/NLGN.

Harrison, L., Hoggett, P. and Jeffers, S. (1995) 'Race, Ethnicity and Community Development' in *Community Development Journal* 30(2): 144–157.

Hastings, A. (2003) 'Strategic, Multilevel Neighbourhood Regeneration: an Outward-looking Approach at Last?' in R. Imrie and M. Raco, *Urban Renaissance*, Bristol: The Policy Press.

Henderson, P. and Thomas, D. (2002) *Skills in Neighbourhood Work*, London: Routledge.

HMSO (1998) Bringing Britain Together: A National Strategy for Neighbourhood Renewal, Report by the Social Exclusion Unit, Cm4045.

Home Office (2003) Building Civic Renewal: A Consultation Paper, London.

Huxham, C. and Vangan, S. (2000) 'What Makes Partnership Work?' in S. Osborne (ed.) *Public – Private Partnerships*, London: Routledge.

Imrie, R. and Raco, M. (2003) *Urban Renaissance*, Bristol: The Policy Press.

Jowitt, A. and Chapman, J. (2001) 'Community Leaders and Community Regeneration: a Pilot Project for Neighbourhood Renewal'. Paper presented to the 5th Learning and Skills Research Conference, University of Cambridge, 6–7 December.

Ledwith, M. (2005) *Community Development: A Critical Approach*, Bristol: The Policy Press.

Lowndes, V. and Wilson, D. (2001) 'Social Capital and Local Governance: Exploring the Institutional Design Variable' in *Political Studies* 49(4): 629–647.

Mayo, M. (1997) 'Partnerships for Regeneration and Community Development' in *Critical Social Policy* 52: 3–26.

Mayo, M. and Taylor, M. (2001) 'Partnerships and Power in Community Regeneration' in S. Balloch and M. Taylor (eds) *Partnership Working*, Bristol: The Policy Press.

Newman, J. (2001) *Modernising Governance*, London: Sage.

Newman, J. (ed.) (2005) *Remaking Governance*, Bristol: The Policy Press.

North, P. (2001) 'Conflict Within Regeneration Partnerships – Help or Hindrance'. Paper presented to the 2nd Regeneration Management Workshop, University of Durham, 7 November.

Parkes, T., Taylor, M. and Wilkinson, M. (2004) 'From Protest to Participation' in M. Todd and G. Taylor (eds) *Democracy and Participation*, London: The Merlin Press.

Peck, J. and Ward, K. (eds) (2002) *City of Revolution: Restructuring Manchester*, Manchester: Manchester University Press.

Powell, M. (ed.) (1999) *New Labour, New Welfare*, Bristol: The Policy Press.

Purdue, D. (2005) 'Community Leadership Cycles and the Consolidation of Neighbourhood Coalitions in the New Local Governance' in *Public Management Review* 7(2): 247–266.

Purdue, D., Razzaque, K., Hambleton, R. and Strewart, M. with Huxham, C. and Vangan, S. (2000) *Community Leadership in Area Regeneration*, Bristol: The Policy Press.

Russell, H. (2001) *Local Strategic Partnerships*, Bristol: Policy Press and JRF.

Schuftan, C. (1996) 'The Community Development Dilemma: What is Really Empowering' in *Community Development Journal* 31(3): 260–264.

Smith, G., Stoker, G. and Maloney, W. (2004) 'Building Social Capital in City Politics: Scope and Limitations at the Inter-organisational Level' in *Political Studies* 52(3): 508–530.

Social Exclusion Unit (2001) *A New Commitment to Neighbourhood Renewal*, London: Cabinet Office.

Taylor, M. (1995) *Unleashing the Potential*, York: Joseph Rowntree Foundation.

Taylor, D. and Balloch, S. (eds) (2005) *The Politics of Evaluation: Participation and Policy Implementation*, Bristol: The Policy Press.

Part II

Civic societies and social movements from local to global

Arenas for mobilization and action

5 Social movement scenes

Infrastructures of opposition in civil society

Sebastian Haunss and Darcy K. Leach[1]

In their efforts to create change in the larger society, social movements enter into relationships of coalition, competition or conflict with other political actors, becoming embedded in a wider set of social and political networks that structures activists' opportunities and choices. Theories of civil society and theories of social movements can both be relevant starting points for investigating these relationships. In this article we discuss a particular kind of network, overlooked in both of these literatures, that often constitutes an important part of a movement's sphere of action.

Civil society authors have focused on weak and strong ties between individuals, networks of trust and the creation of social capital (Cohen 1999; Cohen and Arato 1992; Putnam 2000; Skocpol and Fiorina 1999). Social movement scholars have investigated the impact of personal ties on recruitment (della Porta 1992; Diani 1995; McAdam 1986; Ohlemacher 1996; Snow *et al.* 1980), organizational membership (McAdam 1982; Morris 1984) and interorganizational networks (Diani and Bison 2004). They have also looked at the roles such ties play in the formation and transformation of collective identities (Cohen 1985; Haunss 2004; Melucci 1988, 1995, 1996) and the development of certain cultural forms (Eyerman and Jamison 1998; Fantasia 1988). For the most part, however, movements' environments have been conceptualized as "political opportunity structures", incorporating such components as the society's formal political structure, the relative openness of conventional channels of interest representation, and the availability and position of potential elite allies (Kitschelt 1986; Kriesi 1995; Tarrow 1994).

There is a similar gap in both of these literatures. On the social movement side, there has been little investigation into social structures that help constitute movement cultures and identities, as opposed to simply structuring their strategic and tactical choices or directly affecting their capacity to mobilize. On the civil society side, while most have argued that civic participation fosters feelings of generalized reciprocity and trust which in turn help sustain democracy (Putnam 2000; Skocpol 1999), some have noted that more radical social movement groups may be an exception to this rule. That is, they often cultivate attitudes which *undermine* representative democracy, either because they reject/neglect democratic values or because they see the representative form as not democratic enough. As Fung notes, "those associations that are most capable of offering political resistance may be unlikely to foster a range of civic virtues such as tolerance, generalized reciprocity and trust, and respect for the rule of law" (Fung 2003: 522–523). In the movement discussed below, for example, the social network we refer to as a movement scene fosters a high degree of trust *among its members*, but not a generalized trust in existing social institutions or a feeling of reciprocity with citizens outside the scene. More work needs to be done to differentiate the cultural attributes that are cultivated in different kinds of movement structures and to investigate their influence on various forms of democracy – including those the movements may be trying to bring about.

One of the reasons for these shortcomings is that research in both of these areas – and on civil society – has focused too exclusively on formal organizations as its unit of analysis. Movements and civil society are both fluid structures that change over time, have blurred borders, and can take on a range of organizational forms. When operationalizing network connections in a particular social movement or civil society actor, scholars often fall back on reductionist approaches and concentrate on the more readily quantifiable links and interactions. Putnam has been criticized for overemphasizing the role of organizations in his analysis of the changing structure of civil society (Cohen 1999). In the study of social movements, resource mobilization and political process models have been similarly challenged for having too narrow a focus on formal organizations and institutional relationships. While organizations certainly play an important role in most social movements, a movement cannot be reduced to its constituent organizations.

We argue that a closer examination of social movement scenes would be beneficial for two reasons: first, because scenes constitute an important non-organizational component of civil society that shapes the kind of contribution social movements make to democracy; and second, a scene is often an influential social structure in the environment of a social movement that is more stable than interpersonal networks, but that is still generally not embedded in formal organizations. We begin by defining the concept of a scene and illustrating it in the context of the German autonomous movement. Then we discuss four ways in which scenes can affect the character and development of a movement, and close with a discussion of what might be gained by incorporating scenes into our conception of civil society as well as our analysis of the structural environments within which social movements develop and grow.

Scenes

What are scenes and how do they differ from other similar social structures? In the only systematic study that has been done on scenes (Hitzler *et al.* 2001), three salient characteristics emerge that are shared by those groups they consider to be scenes.

First, scenes are social networks made up of like-minded individuals who are involved in face-to-face interaction focused around a particular topic. To be part of a scene, it is not enough just to share the scene's signs and symbols. One must also share its convictions and be actively and directly engaged with other members. This engagement, however, is generally only a part-time activity and does not structure the totality of a person's everyday life.

Second, scenes are self-constituted dynamic entities whose internal and external boundaries are constantly in flux. The transition between core members and those less integrally involved is fluid, as is the transition between members and non-members. Neither the boundaries of a scene nor its membership criteria can be determined from the outside, because a scene is ultimately constituted through a process of self-identification and mutual recognition. This process also marks social territory, lending distinction to scene members by establishing membership criteria and a common identity that distances them from other social groups.

Lastly, the geographic aspect of scenes is expressed in the fact that they form around recognized scene locations – meeting places like bars, clubs, parks, street corners and parts of town – where being part of a scene can be physically experienced and the signifiers of membership can be enacted. Knowing where such places are located is often itself a badge of membership. Since scenes are not just collections of random individuals, but networks of both individuals and groups, one can often become part of a scene simply by being connected to a group or circle of friends that is itself part of that scene.

Incorporating these points and based on our own research, we offer a general definition of a scene as *a network of people who identify as part of a group and share a certain belief system or set of convictions, that is also necessarily centred around a certain location or set of locations where that group is known to congregate.*

It is important to note here that a scene always has two dimensions: it is at once both a social structure and a geographical location. This geographic and social duality – its simultaneous designation as both a network of people and the infrastructure that sustains it – is the most distinguishing feature of a scene. As a social group, a scene has its own culture. In addition to shared convictions, those who are part of a scene often share distinct dress codes, aesthetic tastes, social norms, linguistic patterns, signs and symbols, and sets of knowledge that differ from those of the larger society. Where a social movement and a scene are tightly connected we speak of "*movement scenes*". But not all scenes are related to a movement; many are purely life-style oriented. Until now, it is only this subcultural aspect of the scene as an alternative life-style that has garnered scholarly attention.

As the discussion thus far suggests, scenes are less rigid and more intentionally constructed than milieus, more directly interactional and less culture-oriented than subcultures, and less demanding and all-encompassing than countercultures. In fact, *movement* scenes are social spaces where subcultures, countercultures and social movements meet and influence each other. In contrast to milieus, scenes are less determined by cultural and economic capital, even though they are usually not independent from this. They are actively enacted and reproduced by their participants – scene membership is more a product of conscious decision than of social position. On the other hand, being part of a scene, in contrast to a subculture, is also more than just an expressive act or a question of style. Even though expressive forms play a central role, scenes can not be reduced to "sign-communities" (Hebdige 1979). They are more an attempt at *building* social structure than they are an expression of it.

To move now from the abstract definition of a scene to a more concrete setting, in the following section we describe the scene surrounding the German autonomous movement. We contend that the features of this particular movement scene can be found in the environment of other movements as well, and therefore can serve to flesh out the general concept. Our description of the movement and its venues and discourses is based on a deconstructive textual analysis of articles published in movement newspapers between 1988 and 2001 (540 issues) and extensive fieldwork conducted by the authors for separate projects, including a year of participant observation in an autonomous anti-nuclear group (2000–2001), several years of participation in an autonomous cultural centre and in the Berlin and Hamburg scenes more generally, and in-depth interviews with 32 movement participants in six Autonomen-style groups from various German cities.

The autonomous movement scene in Germany

The German autonomous movement developed out of remnant strands of the post-'68 New Left. Activists from Frankfurt's "Spontis" who rejected the parliamentary path of leading figures like Joschka Fischer and Daniel Cohn Bendit, along with radicals in the anti-nuclear movement whose political agenda went beyond ecological issues to include a system-level critique, were the first to call themselves "Autonome". Influenced by writings of the Italian "autonomia operaia" they developed their oppositional politics around a militant anti-authoritarian subjectivism and opposition to the dogmatism of both the old and new left. In contrast to the Italian conception of autonomy as a form of working-class organization, autonomy in the German case more closely resembles the civic concept of individual autonomy and self-determination. The frame of reference for the Autonomen is not the working class or "the people" but a "politics of the first person". As such their vision of social change tends to be centred around local projects and a belief that oppressed groups must mobilize around their own interests in solidarity with other such groups, rather than mobilizing *on behalf* of, or claiming to speak for anyone but themselves.

As a movement, the Autonomen first became visible in the mid- to late 1970s as the militant wing of the anti-nuclear movement. In 1980, with the rise of squatters' movements across Europe, the Autonomen became part of a growing "alternative" scene in Berlin, at one point involving up to 100,000 people, that was characterized by a local infrastructure of bars, retail collectives, info-shops, concert venues, squats, living projects and alternative media groups. These locales played a central role in the self-conception and self-construction of the

Autonomen, and many have since become a part of the autonomous/radical leftist scene. In the 1980s a potent Autonomen identity emerged containing the following core elements: a radical oppositional subjectivism and emphasis on self-determination, the devaluation of paid work, Punk and "hardcore" music, a distinctive clothing style, communal forms of living and a commitment to the ideal of participatory, non-hierarchical organization.

In the last 25 years the Autonomen have been concerned with a number of issues ranging from community organizing and squatting to anti-nuclear struggles, anti-fascism, anti-racism and solidarity with international anti-capitalist and social justice struggles. Most of these issues have been recurrent themes in the movement without ever being its sole focus. Though it is virtually impossible to formulate one overarching principle of autonomous politics, it is safe to say that the Autonomen have never been a single-issue movement. Wherever they have been active, however, the central values underlying their engagement have been autonomy, self-determination and a general rejection of formal authority.

Throughout its history the autonomous movement has always been embedded in local scenes. These radical leftist/autonomous scenes, which still exist in many German cities, consist of dense webs of alternative locales and institutions run either by the activists themselves or by people sympathetic to the movement. These projects, whether they are for-profit commercial establishments or non-profit voluntary associations, generally reflect the movement's preference for non-hierarchical, collectivist-democratic structures of "self-administration" and are relatively autonomous from the dominant institutions of the larger society. Together they form a set of locations where movement activists can have regular meetings, attend panel discussions on political topics, go to a party, find a cheap meal, see a political film or just talk politics over a drink.

Scene venues are usually geographically concentrated in one neighbourhood (or, in larger cities, in a small number of neighbourhoods). This concentration has important consequences. First, it positively affects the movement's ability to react quickly to political challenges. An action can be mobilized in as little as a few hours by distributing flyers and posters through the network of bars and shops that are sympathetic to the movement. These postings also make it easy for people who are curious about the movement to find out about movement activities. Second, the concentration and diversity of the infrastructure promotes an overlapping of informal social networks, cultivating a community based on close social ties and a shared culture. Activists and sympathizers not only meet at political events but also at parties, concerts or in bars where, interspersed with small talk and gossip, information about political campaigns and first-hand accounts of protest actions are exchanged. Verbal communication thus becomes an important part of the movement's information infrastructure, with all of the advantages and disadvantages that entails. On the one hand, word of mouth communication is an efficient way of quickly transmitting certain kinds of information. On the other, one has to frequent the right bars, parties or events regularly or at least maintain close contact with those who do in order to stay abreast of the movement's activities.

Like all movements that exist for longer periods of time, the Autonomen are constantly faced with problems of commitment and continuity. As mobilization cannot be maintained at the same high level over time, other ways must be found to bind activists to the movement. One strategy for accomplishing this goal is formal organization; the maintenance of cultural spaces in close proximity to the movement can be another. Inasmuch as the Autonomen reject formal organization they have had to rely on the latter strategy.

In the autonomous movement the scene is the social structure in which subcultural attitudes and preferences are negotiated, maintained and transformed. The following brief analysis of autonomous movement discourses illustrates the importance of this structure for the movement, revealing that the Autonomen have used the scene to align their attitudes and preferences with their political values, norms and convictions; that is, there has been a close connection between scene and movement or, in more abstract terms, between their collective action frames and their everyday practices. This integration of everyday practices, subcultural preferences, and collective action frames generates what we call *commitment frames* – collectively shared concepts of political activism as an expression *of* a subcultural identity that is also necessarily expressed *in* one's everyday life-style choices. Because of their integrative character, commitment frames form strong anchor points for processes of collective identity in social movements (Haunss 2004: 243ff.).

As became evident in our analysis of key movement discourses from the last 20 years, the scene has been a central reference point in processes of collective identity in the autonomous movement. In contrast to their public image as "black bloc" street-fighters, the Autonomen are a very self-reflective, discursive movement in which almost every issue of their political agenda has been repeatedly subjected to critical internal scrutiny and debate. Debates over three perennial issues have generated by far the highest number of contributions in the movement's publications:

- organizational structure and process;
- the meaning of militancy and its proper form; and
- gender relations.

In the discourse on each of these issues, commitment frames were forged that connected scene and movement and formed the central building blocks of the autonomous movement's collective identity.

The debates about organizational structure and process revolved mainly around the question of whether the Autonomen should adopt a more formal organizational model. Autonomous movement organizations are usually organized around an informal plenum where in principle everyone has the right to speak and a right of veto in decision-making. There have been some attempts to modify this structure, but they have ultimately failed, due to a feature of autonomous politics mentioned above – the commitment to a "politics of the first person". According to this principle, authentic individual experience is the necessary starting point for political engagement. If no one can speak legitimately about anyone's suffering but their own, then any structure in which representatives decide on others' behalf without a specific mandate is necessarily illegitimate.

While organizationally, this radical principle of self-representation dictates a preference for directly democratic structures, interpersonally, it is expressed in the saying, "the way is the goal" – that accomplishing movement goals such as equality and emancipation requires that egalitarian and non-oppressive forms of interaction be learned/practised in the everyday process of struggle. The separation between political and private life is rejected, and there is an expectation that one lead a life-style consistent with one's political beliefs. While political activities are organized in the movement, the scene becomes the place where autonomous principles organize a broader range of life-style practices. A formal organizational model would have undermined this close link between life-style and politics. Such an approach was repeatedly proposed and consistently rejected, even though radical life-style norms often alienated potential recruits and made it more difficult to join the movement.

The second set of debates, about militancy and legitimate forms of political action, focused on two interrelated questions: (1) which forms of violence were acceptable and (2) whether or not the movement should take on the form of a militant avant-garde organization. Without going into too much detail, what is interesting for our current purposes is that in these debates a conflict between two collective action frames emerges, in which movement and scene are positioned very differently in relation to one another. We can label these frames the *movement militancy frame* and the *revolution frame*.

From the perspective of the *revolution frame*, militancy is understood and justified as a necessary component of revolutionary change. In this frame, only militant actions are valued and expected to lead to fundamental social change. An avant-garde function of militant organizations is more or less openly stated, and local movement activity is interpreted as part of a wider framework of worldwide revolutionary movements. In this frame, immigrant youth gangs and "international revolutionary movements" are more common referents than the scene or other domestic movements. The life-style model embraced in this frame – that of the clandestine revolutionary fighter – stands in stark contrast to the image they associate with the "petit bourgeois revolt" of the movement mainstream and the scene. Yet in the absence of any contemporary German guerilla movement, the scene – despite its devaluation – is still important as the space in which the habitus of the revolutionary fighter is cultivated.

In contrast to the revolution frame, the scene is the central point of reference for proponents of the *movement militancy frame*, the stronger of the two currents in the movement. In this frame militancy is not inflated as revolutionary action but propagated as a useful collective action strategy in situations where non-militant means of action are regarded as being too limited. Here a distinction is made between political violence directed against property (which is condoned) and violence against persons (which is not). In this perspective the decision for or against militant forms of action is largely a tactical one that needs to be discussed with those involved. From this perspective the scene is the space where discussions about militant forms of actions take place, and most of the texts published around this issue are addressed to the scene as much as to the movement.

Since the revolution frame called for clandestine organizational forms in which no easy integration of the activists' daily practices and their political programme was possible, only the movement militancy frame was capable of binding these two areas, and thus of serving as a commitment frame. The last set of debates – those around gender relations – have been a constant feature of the autonomous movement from the beginning. These debates have revolved around four main points:

- the necessity of separate women's organizations;
- issues of sexual violence;
- sexuality and desire; and
- more general debates about patriarchy.

In keeping with the autonomous principle of a politics of the first person, these issues were only discussed in a very personal and concrete manner. Movement debates about sexism and gender have almost never been carried beyond the boundaries of the autonomous/radical leftist scene and have therefore had no impact on public perceptions of the Autonomen. This contrasts sharply with the internal importance of these struggles, especially as evidenced by recurrent conflicts around sexual violence and harassment. These conflicts have revolved mainly around the questions of who should have the right to define sexual violence and what the sanctions for offenders should be.

With respect to the question of how to deal with offenders, the penalty usually proposed for men accused of rape was expulsion from the scene. That this was regarded as the severest possible sanction (compared, for example, to humiliating them, stripping them of responsibilities, or even beating them up) is a telling indicator of the importance of the scene to activists. Among those involved in these debates, there was an assumption that the scene was integral to the activists' political and personal lives, so much so that expulsion from the scene would be tantamount to expulsion from political engagement itself. Given that movement engagement usually lasts no more than a few years, expulsion from the scene might seem to outsiders to be a relatively weak sanction. The fact that activists saw it as the most severe possible punishment, points to the remarkable strength of a countercultural movement identity that is anchored in the scene.

Commitment frames that emerged in each of these debates integrated collective action frames with the activists' everyday practices, and thus played a central role in the construction and maintenance of an autonomous collective identity. A movement scene facilitates this process: when a movement's goals are compatible with the cultural orientation of a nearby scene, the movement can tap into the scene's networks and connect them to the political project of the movement. In the case of the Autonomen this integration was very successful, so that movement and scene have become almost indistinguishable. The transition between the two has become fluid, with entrance to and exit from the movement largely mediated through the scene.

It is important to note that the three debates we have highlighted here are not unique preoccupations of the autonomous movement. In fact, inasmuch as they emphasize the issue of finding an appropriate relationship/connection/boundary between political ideals and personal behavioural choices, the debates among the Autonomen about militancy, organizational structure and gender all reflect central axes of concern for any movement wing or faction intent on accomplishing deep structural and cultural change without reproducing within the movement itself the very forms of oppression it is trying to eliminate in the larger society.

The function of the scene for social movements

Building on the roles a movement scene has played for the Autonomen, we can generate a few tentative hypotheses about the relationship between movements and scenes in general. Our separate and combined analyses of the autonomous movement (Leach 2005; Haunss 2004) suggest that scenes may have at least four important functions for social movements.

Movement scenes can be a mobilization pool for social movements and a site for the development of oppositional consciousness

Because they offer a life-style and at the same time, as part-time communities, require only a relatively low level of commitment, scenes attract a much larger group of participants than the movement does. Just as membership in the countercultural core of a scene requires that one submit to a more thoroughgoing life-style transformation, engagement in the movement requires a higher level of commitment than the scene and often the willingness to engage in high risk activities. In the autonomous movement – as in for example the women's and gay rights movements – certain parts of the scene's infrastructure have developed out of and in support of movement activities. Their subcultural attractiveness stems in part from this political history, which provides scene venues with an additional flair of authenticity and edginess. Subcultural activities like concerts and parties in turn have brought a large number of people into contact with the movement who would otherwise not have had anything to do with the Autonomen.

This overlapping of scene, movement and sub- and counterculture blurs the distinctions between them. In a relatively large transitional zone it becomes quite difficult to distinguish whether people actually belong to the movement or are just culturally involved in the scene. Someone who is active in the movement can safely be presumed to be connected to the scene in some way, but s/he may or may not be a member of the sub- or counterculture. Scenes offer a "soft" way of joining a movement, with subcultural identification as the first step. The decision to make a larger political commitment can be left open for a relatively long period of time.

Movement scenes can be sites of experimentation with alternative forms of self-governance

For a movement like the Autonomen whose ultimate aim is to create a "power-free society", the scene is an invaluable space in which to experiment with alternative ways of structuring daily life. Students of social movements have long noted the importance of institutional space for a movement. The political process model, for example, has noted the key role played by Black churches in the US civil rights movement (McAdam 1982; Morris 1984), or by the Catholic church in the Polish Solidarity movement.

What we are talking about, however, goes beyond that role. A scene is not just a place to be, it is a particular *kind* of space that allows a movement to "be" in a particular way. For the relationship between scene and movement to function smoothly, the scene must be structured in a way that reflects the principles and central values of the movement. In the cases highlighted by political process theorists, movements made use of existing institutions that were outside the main halls of political power but nonetheless fairly integrated into the logic of the system. As established bureaucratic structures with a degree of political leverage and credibility, these institutions could provide a relatively safe space for movement groups to meet and most importantly, social capital in the form of a cohesive network of people with an effective system of communication.

However, the very characteristics that made these institutions useful umbrellas for other movements would make them problematic as scene locations for autonomous movements. In order to experiment with *alternative* structures of self-governance and decision-making, a movement needs a space that is free of external control, or at least some agreement must be reached allowing the movement maximum autonomy from the institution whose space they are using. Indeed, for an autonomous movement, the utility of a space depends very much on how that space is structured, not just whether the institution is sympathetic and willing to help. To the degree possible, the scene should consist of "free" space that is not already hierarchically organized or subject to pre-existing rules that run counter to the principles of the movement.

Movement scenes play a central role in processes of collective identity

As shown above, by providing a place where life-styles and collective action frames can be linked, scenes help to generate commitment frames, which are central building blocks in processes of collective identity. One such commitment frame of the autonomous movement is the anti-patriarchy frame connecting a feminist political analysis with the call to abolish patriarchal structures in the activists' private lives. The general injunction to realize the revolutionary goals of the movement in the everyday practices of the movement and in personal interaction is another such commitment. When a social movement manages to interject its political identity into the life-styles and practices of one or more scenes, this can create an atmosphere whereby that identity is constantly regenerated, stabilizing and rejuvenating the movement from one wave of protest to the next.

The Autonomen have constantly maintained a very close link between movement and scene. In this way they have profited from the youth-culture attractiveness of the scene and maintained a relatively constant level of mobilization, despite the so-called "crisis of the autonomous movement" that has been repeatedly proclaimed by movement activists since the late 1980s. The movement discourses of the 1990s regularly and explicitly problematized the relationship between movement and scene as too intimate and exclusive, but nevertheless, a constant exchange of personnel, ideas and styles between movement and scene has de facto broadened the reach of the autonomous collective identity beyond the limits of the movement itself.

Movement scenes can serve as movement abeyance structures

Scenes offer not only an easy way into the movement; they also offer an easy way out. Taylor and Whittier have described this possibility for activists to "hibernate" in the scene during times of low mobilization, characterizing the structures of a scene as "social movement abeyance structures" (Taylor 1989; Taylor and Whittier 1992). As they point out, these structures provide highly committed radical activists the chance to leave the question of further activism open for a time, for example if the movement as a whole starts to take a more reformist turn. Beyond being temporary abeyance structures, scenes also make it possible to retreat permanently from movement activities without having to sever all ties to it. In the scene, former activists can stay more or less sympathetic to the movement without actively engaging in movement activities. As they do not break completely with the movement, they may still be available for later mobilization under certain circumstances.

In addition to serving as a shelter for activists in times of low mobilization, scenes function as abeyance structures in another sense as well, by serving as culture-carriers for movement traditions, norms and history. Scene locations such as movement archives, book stores and movie-houses can do this in a very concrete and explicit way, acting as the institutional memory of the movement. But to the degree that scene organizations are also organized according to the principles of the movement and operate according to movement norms, they also preserve those norms and traditions in their praxis, keeping them alive and modelling them for future generations of activists. Bars, communes, book stores, housing projects or print shops, for example, that are run as collectives, can continue to work out the kinks in this structure and pass on the lessons they learn, though in times when militant activism ceases to police the boundaries, such groups also show a tendency to re-adapt to the dominant culture over time.

Generally speaking, with the exception of the first, which probably applies equally to all movements, these four functions seem especially important for a certain broad category of movement that includes what have been called "left-libertarian" (della Porta and Rucht 1995), "expressive" (Rucht 1990), and "non-violent direct action" (Epstein 1991) movements. Movements like these, that operate with a predominantly value-rational orientation rather than an instrumental one, that reject traditional forms of organization, and aim to transform fundamentally the logic and institutional structure of society, may find it especially critical to have space in which to put their politics into practice.

Movements, scenes and civil society

Thus far in the discussion, we have introduced the concept of a scene and distinguished it from other social structures such as community, subculture, counterculture and milieu; illustrated the role of scenes in the construction of movement identities, through an analysis of internal debates within the German autonomous movement; and outlined four functions that scenes linked to social movements can have for the movement. In this concluding section, we will outline some of the implications of our investigation for the study of social movements and for investigations into the nature of civil society and the relationship between associations and democracy.

First, with respect to research on social movements, our case suggests that where scenes arise around social movements, they can have a strong impact on movement trajectories and longevity, and that therefore, the relationship between scenes and social movements merits further investigation. The recent cultural turn in social movement research notwithstanding, there has been a tendency in theories of social movements to overemphasize formal organizations on the one hand and institutional political opportunity structures on the other. As geographically embedded social networks, scenes are a structured part of the environment of some movements that do *not* comprise formal organizations, but may nevertheless have an important impact on their behaviour. Especially for the kind of movements mentioned above, the presence of a scene and its relationship to the movement is an aspect of the political opportunity structure – alongside such factors as the openness of political institutions, the stability of political alignments, the availability of influential allies and divisions within the elite (see also Purdue *et al.* 1997; Tarrow 1994: 87ff.) – that can critically affect a movement's trajectory.

There is much to learn about why scenes come into being around some movements and not others, why the relationship between movement and scene takes different forms from one movement to the next, and the consequences of each form for the movement. With respect to the latter question, we have argued that scenes can function in at least four different ways to support movement progress, by serving: (1) as a mobilization pool; (2) as a social space in which movements can experiment with new organizational structures, deliberative styles and modes of interaction; (3) as a "free space" for political debate and the exchange of information, in which new ideologies and collective identities are constructed and reproduced; and (4) as a set of "abeyance structures" that can be the institutional memory of the movement, preserving and transmitting movement culture, ideals and practices from one generation of activists to the next. We have seen in the German autonomous movement that there has been a strong symbiotic relationship between scene and movement, which has for the most part proved beneficial to the movement. But this relationship can work out differently from one movement to the next. Scenes can hinder as well as facilitate progress toward movement goals. The influence scenes have on movements very much depends on the kind of relationship that develops between them, and that relationship is not always a complementary one. More work needs to be done to flesh out the various kinds of relationships that exist, the conditions that give rise to them and their consequences for the movement.

A second area of scholarship in which the concept of scenes may prove useful is in the study of civil society. There are two points here. First, we argue that for certain kinds of investigations, it would be meaningful and productive to conceptualize scenes as a distinct sector of civil society. As in social movement research, the tendency in research on civil society, especially on the question of associations and democracy, has been to foreground participation in formal organizations at the expense of other forms of association. But at least in the German social movement sector, and we suspect elsewhere as well, social movement activists are seldom loyal to any one movement or social movement organization. Individual activists frequently move from one group to another, often participating in several different issue-based movements within a period of months or even weeks. Their participation in the *scene*, however, is much more constant. And while some collective decision-making goes on in social movement groups, it is in these informally structured locales and networks – in their politically oriented *Wohngemeinschaften* (living groups), movie theatres and scene bars – where the more intensive political debates, strategy discussions and even action planning goes on. In short, it is primarily in the scene that they have the sustained interaction to learn the skills and attitudes of democratic engagement. For that reason, it seems to make little sense to think of "associations" only in formal organizational terms. At least in the context of these kinds of movements, the scene may be the more meaningful and relevant form of association on which to focus when investigating the relationship between associations and democracy.

While *including* scenes in our conception of civil society, it is also important to distinguish between movement scenes and the more traditional kinds of voluntary associations, such as fraternal organizations, parent–teacher associations and bowling leagues, that are the usual referents for studies on associations and democracy. Just as traditional voluntary associations are said to produce broader engagement in the political processes of a democratic state (Putnam 2000), the alternative structures and networks of movement scenes also generate substantial political action. The form of that engagement, however, as well as its impact on democracy, is likely to be substantially different.

The central argument in relation to associations and democracy has been that by teaching citizenship skills and fostering civic virtues such as trust, respect for the rule of law and a sense of generalized reciprocity, voluntary organizations encourage political participation, which is generally conceived of in conventional terms to include such activities as voting or writing to one's political representatives (Putnam 2000; Skocpol and Fiorina 1999). This kind of participation helps stabilize democracy in that it supports the legitimacy of existing political institutions and serves to prevent any obvious move toward a less democratic form of governance. But scholars have qualified this claim by arguing (1) that the contributions made by social movement organizations may differ substantially and in conflicting ways from those made by traditional voluntary associations; (2) that the degree to which associations are themselves democratically organized affects how well they can cultivate democratic civic virtues and participation; and (3) that associations with the same organizational structure may still make very different contributions to democracy, depending on the political context in which they operate (Fung 2003). To the degree that scenes are closely aligned with social movements, are made up of democratically structured groups and networks, and constitute an important part of a movement's political context, these findings all suggest that movement scenes may make a distinctive contribution to democracy.

Our second point with respect to scenes and civil society is that the *relationship* between scenes and social movements may be an important variable in assessing the democratic contributions of both kinds of association. We can theoretically consider not only the direct effects of both movement organizations and movement scenes on democracy, but also how various relationships *between* scenes and movements may mediate the contributions of each. For example, movements embedded in scenes may make a different kind of contribution than movements that do not give rise to scenes, and movements that are closely connected with a scene may make different contributions than those with a more antagonistic relationship.

There are certain tensions inherent in the relationship between movement and scene. Most significantly, scenes tend to be more experience-oriented while movements reach out and are more project-oriented. Scenes can, therefore, become lightning rods for ambivalence about competing instrumental and expressive logics within the movement. In the autonomous movement these different logics have repeatedly led to conflict, particularly around the question of whether the movement should focus its mobilization efforts only within the scene or reach out more to groups outside of it. That such an outreach strategy has never been able to gain hegemony in the autonomous movement is due mainly to the intimate connection between scene and movement. In contrast, the women's movement in Germany was also embedded in a similar structure of women's centres, bars, bookshops and a growing social support structure. But in the case of the women's movement, a growing distance between the movement and its scene developed throughout the 1980s. Professionalization on the one hand and "spiritualization" on the other led to a growing differentiation of the scene and a growing alienation between the women supporting scene institutions and the women active in the movement. The resulting differentiation of activist life styles has led to the development of parallel, redundant and largely disconnected activist structures and a shift within the movement's scene to a strategy of what Rucht (1990) calls "subcultural retreat".

In the German gay movement as well, a growing alienation between movement and scene took place throughout the 1980s which led to a more or less rigid separation between the two, and finally to the dissolution of the movement into a traditional lobbying organization. In this case the separation of lifeworld and politics – scene and movement – had the effect of gradually stripping the movement of its ability to mobilize significant numbers of activists (Haunss 2004: 256ff.).

These examples suggest that different kinds of relationships between movement and scene yield different kinds of outcomes with respect to political engagement. Where there was a close connection between scenes and movements, as in the German autonomous movement, scenes allowed the movement to construct commitment frames that stabilized collective movement identities and, as such, helped to sustain the movement and foster their particular style of civic engagement. In the women's and gay rights movements in Germany, where the relationship between scene and movement became estranged or antagonistic, respectively, subcultural retreat and traditional lobbying – two other forms of civic engagement – were the outcomes.

In closing, we have argued that scenes are an important non-organizational element in the environment of some social movements. Their most distinguishing feature is that they are simultaneously a network of people with a shared set of beliefs, tastes and convictions and a network of places where those who identify with the scene congregate and feel welcome. Our investigation of the autonomous movement and other movements in the German social movement sector suggests that where there is a close connection between scene and movement, scenes can help movements sustain mobilization, develop alternative forms of organization and self-governance, construct collective identities and reproduce their culture over time. Where the relationship between movement and scene becomes antagonistic, scenes can also divide or marginalize the movement, push it toward subcultural retreat or conventional forms of interest representation and otherwise impede its ability to mobilize. Because of this variety of effects scenes can have on movements, we believe that the relationship between scene and movement may also be an important intervening variable, mediating the movement's response to the political opportunity structure, and, as a distinct non-organizational sector of civil society, mediating the movement's impact on the quality of democracy.

Note

1 Authors listed alphabetically for convenience.

References

Cohen, Jean L. (1985). "Strategy or Identity: New Theoretical Paradigms and Contemporary Social Movements". *Social Research* 52 (4): 663–716.

—— (1999). "Trust, Voluntary Association and Workable Democracy: The Contemporary American Discourse of Civil Society". pp. 208–248 in *Democracy and Trust*, edited by Mark E. Warren. Cambridge: Cambridge University Press.

Cohen, J. and A. Arato (1992). *Civil Society and Political Theory.* Cambridge, MA: MIT Press.

della Porta, Donatella (1992). "Introduction: On Individual Motivations in Underground Political Organizations". *International Social Movements Research* 4: 3–28.

della Porta, Donatella and Dieter Rucht (1995). "Left-Libertarian Movements in Context: A Comparison of Italy and West Germany, 1965–1990". pp. 229–272 in *The Politics of Social Protest*, edited by J. Craig Jenkins and Bert Klandermans. Minneapolis, MN: University of Minnesota Press.

Diani, Mario (1995). *Green Networks: A Structural Analysis of the Italian Environmental Movement.* Edinburgh: Edinburgh University Press.

Diani, Mario and Ivano Bison (2004). "Organizations, Coalitions, and Movements". *Theory and Society* 33: 281–309.

Epstein, Barbara (1991). *Political Protest and Cultural Revolution: Nonviolent Direct Action in the 1970s and 1980s.* Berkeley, CA: University of California Press.

Eyerman, Ron and Andrew Jamison (1998). *Music and Social Movements: Mobilizing Traditions in the Twentieth Century.* Cambridge: Cambridge University Press.

Fantasia, Rick (1988). *Cultures of Solidarity: Consciousness, Action, and Contemporary American Workers.* Berkeley, CA: University of California Press.

Fung, Archon (2003). "Associations and Democracy: Between Theories, Hopes, and Realities". *Annual Review of Sociology* 29: 515–539.

Haunss, Sebastian (2004). *Identität in Bewegung. Prozesse kollektiver Identität bei den Autonomen und in der Schwulenbewegung.* Wiesbaden: VS Verlag für Sozialwissenschaften.

Hebdige, Dick (1979). *Subculture: The Meaning of Style.* London: Routledge.

Hitzler, Ronald, Thomas Bucher and Arne Niederbacher (2001). *Leben in Szenen. Formen jugendlicher Vergemeinschaftung heute.* Opladen: Leske + Budrich.

Kitschelt, Herbert (1986). "Political Opportunity Structures and Political Protest: Anti-nuclear Movements in Four Democracies". *British Journal of Political Science* 16(1): 57–85.

Kriesi, Hanspeter (1995). "The Political Opportunity Structure of New Social Movements: Its Impact on Their Mobilization". pp. 167–198 in *The Politics of Social Protest*, edited by J. Craig Jenkins and Bert Klandermans. Minneapolis, MN: University of Minnesota Press.

Leach, Darcy K. (2005). "The Way is the Goal: Ideology and the Practice of Collectivist Democracy in German New Social Movements", Department of Sociology, University of Michigan.

McAdam, Doug (1982). *Political Process and the Development of Black Insurgency 1930–1970.* Chicago: University of Chicago Press.

—— (1986). "Recruitment to High-Risk Activism: The Case of Freedom Summer". *American Journal of Sociology* 92: 64–90.

Melucci, Alberto (1988). "Getting Involved: Identity and Mobilization in Social Movements". pp. 329–348 in *International Social Movements Research*, edited by Bert Klandermans, Hanspeter Kriesi and Sidney Tarrow. Greenwich, CT: JAI Press.

—— (1995). "The Process of Collective Identity". pp. 41–64 in *Social Movements and Culture*, edited by Hank Johnston and Bert Klandermans. London: UCL.

—— (1996). *Challenging Codes: Collective Action in the Information Age*. Cambridge: Cambridge University Press.

Morris, Adlon D. (1984). *The Origins of the Civil Rights Movement: Black Communities Organizing for Change*. New York: Free Press.

Ohlemacher, Thomas (1996). "Bridging People and Protest: Social Relays of Protest Groups against Low-flying Military Jets in West Germany". *Social Problems* 43: 197–218.

Purdue, D., Dürrschmidt, J., Jowers, P. and O'Doherty, R. (1997). "DIY Culture and Extended Milieux: LETS, Veggie Boxes and Festivals". *Sociological Review* 45(4): 645–667.

Putnam, Robert D. (2000). *Bowling Alone: The Collapse and Revival of American Community*. New York: Simon & Schuster.

Rucht, Dieter (1990). "The Strategies and Action Repertoires of New Movements". pp. 156–175 in *Challenging the Political Order*, edited by R.J. Dalton and M. Kuechler. Cambridge: Polity Press.

Skocpol, Theda (1999). "Advocates without Members: the Recent Transformation of American Civic Life". pp. 461–510 in *Civic Engagement in American Democracy*, edited by Theda Skocpol and Morris P. Fiorina. Washington, DC: Brookings Institute Press.

Skocpol, Theda, and Morris P. Fiorina (eds) (1999). *Civic Engagement in American Democracy*. Washington, DC: Brookings Institute Press.

Snow, David A., Jr., Louis A. Zurcher and Sheldon Ekland-Olson (1980). "Social Networks and Social Movements: A Microstructural Approach to Differential Recruitment". *American Sociological Review* 45(5): 787–801.

Tarrow, Sidney (1994). *Power in Movement: Social Movements, Collective Action and Politics*. New York: Cambridge University Press.

Taylor, Verta (1989). "Social Movement Continuity: The Women's Movement in Abeyance". *American Sociological Review* 54(5): 761–775.

Taylor, Verta and Nancy Whittier (1992). "Collective Identity in Social Movement Communities: Lesbian Feminist Mobilization". pp. 104–129 in *Frontiers in Social Movement Theory*, edited by A.D. Morris and C.M. Mueller. New Haven, CT: Yale University.

6 Between horizontal bridging and vertical governance

Pro-beneficiary movements in New Labour Britain

Manlio Cinalli

Asylum and unemployment in Britain: an introduction

This chapter focuses on the mobilisation of two national movements in Britain, and in particular, on the web of ties forged by 'altruist' organisations that act 'on behalf' of the poor and weak. Research on mobilisation on behalf of the poor and weak has so far relied on relatively few empirical accounts that are informed by original comparative data (Giugni and Passy, 2001), and has received limited attention by scholars of social movements, where the tendency is to focus on collective action when the beneficiary of the political goal does not differ from the constituency group that mobilises. I start with the investigation of the main pro-beneficiary actors in two key fields of exclusion, namely, asylum and unemployment, and then analyse

- their horizontal networks amongst themselves and with civil society organisations in the public domain, and
- their vertical networks with policy-makers and institutional actors in the policy domain.

Sub-sets of research questions can be formulated along these two main dimensions of investigation. As regards the first dimension consisting of horizontal networks: What is the precise nature of horizontal ties in each of the two fields and how are they sustained in each case? Are the networks of a similar size? Are these ties based on identity, regular exchange of information or short-lived issue coalition? Or are they merely limited to loose contacts based on simple cohabitation within the same issue-field? As regards the second dimension consisting of vertical ties: What is the precise nature of these vertical ties in each of the two fields and how are they sustained in each field? In this case, it is also crucial to focus on the correlation between patterns of networks at the horizontal level and at the vertical level. Is the strength and nature of horizontal networks in the public domain related to particular patterns of vertical ties with institutional actors in each policy domain?

Asylum and unemployment are indeed two key fields of exclusion in contemporary Britain. Long-term and unskilled unemployed people have faced the continuous erosion of their welfare entitlements, declining level of daily social conditions, and falling expectations to be reinserted into the labour market (Van den Berg and Van Ours, 1994). Asylum seekers have been the object of a raft of restrictive measures underscoring New Labour's negative agenda of deterring new arrivals, rather than a positive will to provide full entitlements and protection for those who flee persecution. The introduction of restrictive measures has also been matched by increasing politicisation of these issues, with politicians regularly throwing facts and figures at each other about employed and unemployed, arrivals and deportations. In addition, asylum seekers and unemployed people have faced resentment in public discourse with disputes taking place with regard to 'bogus asylum seekers' and 'welfare scroungers'. Collective action across these two issue-fields has thus been characterised by a limited direct participation of asylum seekers and unemployed people themselves (Cinalli, 2004). Although they have engaged in direct protests against government throughout the 1980s and the first half of the 1990s, unemployed people have not voiced their claims beyond the local level during the last decade, mobilising only occasionally and as result of specific industrial disputes. This weakness also prevented British unemployed people from playing any active role during widespread marches of unemployed people across Europe. Asylum seekers, too, have rarely mobilised visibly in the public domain. With the exception of a few symbolic protests (e.g. *Guardian*, 31 May 2003), they have usually contained their (invisible) action within grassroots and community groups at the local level. In sum, given their relatively small size, marginal political position and ownership of very few resources for autonomous mobilisation, asylum seekers and unemployed people have had to rely on the support of organisations willing to act on their behalf.

The next section presents the theoretical foundations on which this chapter is based, while at the same time systematically specifying the criteria of my comparative analysis. I emphasise the distinct function of horizontal and vertical networks, in keeping with the concepts of social capital and governance which play a central role in this book. Horizontal networks can be considered as 'resources', that is, channels for 'bonding' capital within movements and 'bridging' capital between these movements and larger civil society. Vertical networks consist of exchanges across the public and policy domains, thus connecting movements to the state. In particular, the shape of these 'links' emphasises the changing combinations of opportunities and constraints that exist between institutions and civil society, within different forms of governance. The following two sections debate the main findings, analysing in detail horizontal networks and vertical networks between pro-beneficiary movements, civil society organisations, political parties and core state policy-makers. In particular, I emphasise the contrasting patterns of horizontal and vertical ties that have developed in the two selected issue-fields. Finally, the last section focuses on factors impacting upon the decision which actors take when shaping their horizontal and vertical exchanges. A central explanatory role is given to the 'constraining opportunities' that New Labour has brought for pro-beneficiary movements in the two fields of asylum and unemployment. I also discuss the relevance of different levels of political action, ranging from the national to the local and grassroots.

Finally, I should emphasise that a more holistic approach, which takes overall network patterns as an independent variable to explain actors' mobilisation and their attributes, is out of the scope of this chapter. Network analysis can be used to investigate both independent and dependent variables when focusing on social movements and collective action. In the first case, the overall network structure is the *explanans* and actors' attributes follow as the *explananda*. An alternative approach takes network patterns as the dependent variable, focusing on the explanation of decisions which individual actors take when building their relationships. This is the approach that I follow in this chapter.

Altruist mobilisation in multi-organisational fields: focusing on networks

While scholarly interest in relational characteristics of collective action and social movements is at least three decades old (Curtis and Zurcher, 1973) and it can indeed be traced well back into Simmel's works of classic sociology, it is only in more recent times that social scientists have fully engaged with a research approach which evaluates forms of collective action starting from the appraisal of their structural properties. Scholars of social capital have for example emphasised the importance of resources embedded in social networks, which can be accessed by individuals wishing to increase likelihood of success in a purposive action (Lin, 2001). At the meso-level, scholars have argued that networks of obligations and recognition are the basis on which members of a clear-cut (and privileged) group maintain and reinforce their social capital as a collective asset (Bourdieu, 1986); that social networks not only sustain individuals within social structures but provide resources (that is, social capital) to the structures themselves (Coleman, 1990); and that participation, associations and exchanges are indicators of well-being in societies, since they promote collective norms and trust (Putnam, 1995).

In sum, networks enhance the outcomes of collective action. Through these networks a wide range of embedded resources can be accessed, thus facilitating the flow of information about choices otherwise not available, influencing the agents who play a critical role in decision-making, as well as reinforcing identity, recognition, public acknowledgement and support. At the same time, network analysis has found extensive applications in specific research questions of social movement analysis and contentious politics, such as inter-organisational networks and overlapping memberships (Diani, 1995), processes of mobilisation and counter-mobilisation (Franzosi, 1997), protest across traditional cleavages in deeply divided societies (Cinalli, 2003), the influence of individuals' relational contexts on their decision to mobilise (Passy, 2001) and the impact of whole communities' network structures on the development of their collective action (Gould, 1995). Many of these investigations have made use of networks to analyse the social and political context within which actors operate, thus offering a different viewpoint from theories of social capital (which rather consider networks as an internal resource to mobilise for sustaining collective action). This type of analytical development can thus fit in ongoing studies of emerging forms of governance, referring to the involvement of multiple actors 'from below' in processes of decision-making alongside policy elites and institutions, in a dynamic renegotiation of boundaries between civil society and the state.

It follows that the analysis of networks is at the core of current debates on social capital and governance. Networks allow for 'bonding' within social movements, that is, it enables their individual groups and organisations to unite in common projects that go well beyond the achievement of individual goals. Outwardly, networks provide these same movements with resources for 'bridging' their distance from potential allies in civil society, in a process of further access to social capital and wider acknowledgement of their objectives. Lastly, the development of 'links' across different levels of political power and territory enable movements to seize opportunities so as to influence decision-making, thus shaping *de facto* new patterns of governance.

It is thus crucial to provide a more explicit definition of the central tenets of network analysis that guide the specific investigation of this chapter. First, actors are interdependent rather than independent units, and the relations amongst them are the most meaningful focus of analysis. Second, many relevant characteristics of these actors are correlated to their network features. Last, relational ties between these actors provide channels for the flow of both material and non-material resources, as well as opportunities for accessing higher levels of policy-making. Put simply, I operationalise the two issue-fields of asylum and unemployment in terms of networks amongst units, that is, a set of nodes which differ according to the control of and access to embedded resources in their positions. Actors can thus be viewed as a focus from which lines radiate horizontally and vertically to other nodes (that is, actors with which it is in contact). In particular, I refer to some of the central characteristics of a network and its actors. My networks are sets of co-operative ties connecting a set of actors (or nodes), that is, they depict actors connected *by relations of close co-operation*. I refer to a relation between any two actors as an 'edge'. If there is an edge joining two actors these actors are adjacent. A 'path' is a chain of edges that connect two actors. The number of actors adjacent to an actor expresses its 'degree' or 'point-centrality', that is, a measure of centrality within the network. The most important structural characteristic of a network, which I consider in general terms, is density. A network is relatively dense if a large number of actors are linked to each other. Last, my analysis focuses especially on network portions, that is, segments or compartments of networks with a high density.

As regards the method, my research is mostly based on analysis of 60 in-depth semi-structured interviews conducted with core policy-makers, political party representatives, civil society organisations, pro-beneficiary groups and movements. The interview schedule for each category of actors is strictly comparative. It is specifically designed to analyse where they locate themselves in relation to other actors in the field. These interviews include not only qualitative in-depth questions (examining, for example, the framing of their political claims) but also sets of standardised questions, which aim to investigate action repertoires, mobilisation and communication strategies, institutions on which demands are made, as well as relationships of disagreement and co-operation with other actors in the field. In particular, the analysis of inter-organisational networks has been based on the elaboration of lists of actors engaged in the two issue-fields. In this chapter, I focus systematically on exchanges between actors that have been interviewed (listed, with abbreviations, in Appendix). Other available relational data between interviewed and non-interviewed actors are here used only as narrative evidence. At the same time, a wide range of secondary sources, such as existing literature, organisations' publications, press articles and official documents from political and institutional authorities, has been used to deepen the analysis of actors and key contextual dimensions.

Horizontal networks: 'bonds' and 'bridges' in the issue-fields

Bonding in the pro-asylum field

Having divided the two issue-fields into comparable network portions, it is possible to focus first of all on the analysis of the inter-organisational ties which pro-asylum and pro-unemployed actors decided to build amongst themselves. Figure 6.1 shows the map of edges between 16 pro-asylum organisations, where each edge indicates the existence of a relationship of close co-operation between a pair of these actors. The first evident characteristic of this portion of networks among pro-asylum organisations was its high density, owing to the fact that many actors interact with each other. The majority of these organisations have forged ties of co-operation with more than half of the actors in the network, and some of them (namely, the Joint Committee for the Welfare of Immigrants, Refugee Council, Amnesty International and Oxfam) stand out for their remarkable point-centrality.

At the same time, all the organisations with lowest point-centrality (namely, the Children's Society, Jesuit Refugee Centre, Campaign for Closing Camps-field and the Commission for Racial Equality) interact directly with two or more organisations with the highest point-centrality, and hence, they are no more than one single edge away from any other organisation within the network. The issue-field is thus characterised by extensive 'bonding'. This development of rich and meaningful ties promotes not only a fast and efficient flow of information amongst the different nodes, but also the strengthening of solidarity among the organisations and a wider sense of belongingness in the overall network.

In sum, pro-asylum organisations can access, exchange and develop a wide range of material and non-material resources through their extensive web of inter-organisational exchanges. These ties seem to be particularly useful for increasing the flow of information across the nodes, for facilitating allocation of responsibilities and flexibility of action, and hence, for achieving their goals.

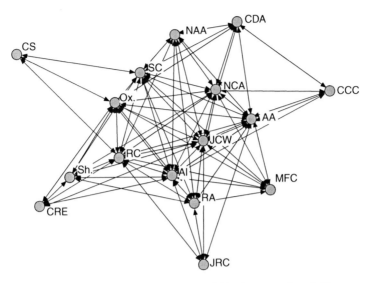

Figure 6.1 Inter-organisational networks within the pro-asylum field.

Many organisations have decided to engage actively in the Asylum Rights Campaign, which functions as an information-sharing umbrella that informs the campaigning work of its members. At the same time, it is important to emphasise the relevance of networks at the level of single organisations. For example, the Joint Committee for the Welfare of Immigrants (JCWI) has debated for years on its internal structure, emphasising the convenience of a network, rather than a membership organisation. In the words of one of its leaders:

> Networks are much more flexible and much more responsive. There's a possibility of dividing the work up much more quickly so we've got people who are in a position to respond quickly ... The whole asylum agenda has been based on the possibility of establishing, particularly as far as reception issues are concerned, basically a co-ordinated strategy which will strap important NGOs in the process right from the very beginning.

Inter-organisational exchanges have strengthened solidarity and belief of sharing similar purposes for action, encouraging the formation and reproduction of bonds downward at the local and grassroots level, reaching the level of individual activists. For example, Oxfam has actively worked to promote and sustain a common agenda within the wider pro-asylum voluntary sector, fostering not only a dense network of inter-organisational connections at the national and sub-national level but also extensive overlapping memberships, with many supporters active in more than one organisation at the same time. In the words of one of its leaders:

An Oxfam supporter isn't just an Oxfam supporter. I know myself that I'm a member of Oxfam, a supporter of Oxfam, I support Amnesty, Christian Aid, a variety of different groups but I'm the same person. And I really think that our supporters love it, and I would use that verb, they love it when we work with other people with a common agenda. And they hate it when we're standing up individually.

Through its connections, the Refugee Council (RC) has successfully guided other organisations to rediscover and strengthen their own concern for asylum. This successful transformation of 'bridges' in potential 'bonds' is clear when considering the solidarity and sense of common belongingness that have been mobilised at crucial times. For example, a wide number of pro-asylum organisations have stood together to boycott the implementation of the Government's food voucher scheme. Not only did this campaign prove that pro-asylum organisations could successfully unite in their efforts for political change, but it has especially demonstrated that the instrumental function of networks is only a part, albeit the most evident part, of their meaning, since overwhelming symbolic resources can at times be mobilised through these same networks. The resolute participation of the Refugee Council to the campaign of protest – notwithstanding its role of assistant agency under the same Act which had introduced the vouchers – provides important evidence for this type of argument.

Bonding in the pro-unemployment field

Moving to the analysis of (portions of) ties amongst pro-beneficiary actors in the issue field of unemployment, it is evident that pro-unemployed organisations have decided to shape their reciprocal ties according to a completely different pattern. Figure 6.2 shows the map of edges between organisations working on behalf of unemployed people, where each edge represents the existence of a relationship of close co-operation between a pair of these actors. This time, the first evident characteristic of this network was its very low density, with a large number of actors disconnected from each other or only related through long paths. Only a few organisations were characterised by a somewhat significant point-centrality, namely, the Joseph Rowntree Foundation, the Centre for Economic and Social Inclusion, and the Work Foundation. By interacting with one of these latter organisations, many actors could communicate with each other even if only through long paths which shape the network in the model of a star. A significant number of pro-unemployed organisations, however, had not built extensive relationships of co-operation. In sum, actors working on behalf of unemployed people appeared to be unwilling to forge strong bonds of cohesive co-operation, while aiming to keep some basic degree of information flow within the network.

The low number of exchanges provided only limited space for collective action across levels, encouraging pro-unemployed organisations to specialise in a few specific techniques which were used exclusively at the national level.

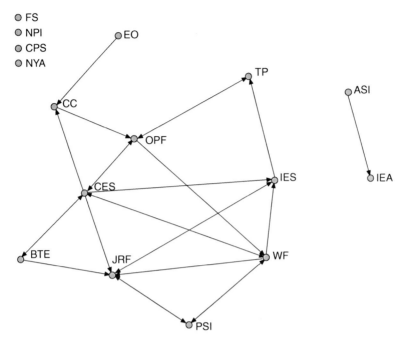

Figure 6.2 Inter-organisational networks within the pro-unemployed field.

Indeed, the unemployment voluntary sector is occupied by two main kinds of actors:

• national organisations which consider the promotion, production and dissemination of research and knowledge to be the major means to intervene on unemployment policy (for example, the Institute of Economic Affairs and the Joseph Rowntree Foundation), and

• national organisations which, albeit also engaged in research, had decided to play a direct role in the formulation, implementation and development of government policies (for example, the Centre for Economic and Social Inclusion and the Institute for Employment Studies).

Low density and the lack of clique-shaped relationships in any part of the network were thus matched by a lack of significant connections with groups of beneficiaries at the local and grassroots levels. In fact, the National Unemployed Centres Combine (CC) stood out as the only important organisation which actually involved unemployed people in its own organisational activities, working for the bottom-up promotion of their interest rather than for the elaboration of top-down solutions to tackle unemployment. CC was also engaged in campaigning and direct action, linking together various local 'unemployed workers centres' across Britain.

Bridging to wider civil society

I will turn my attention from the bonds internal to the pro-beneficiary movements, to assess the extent to which pro-asylum and pro-unemployed actors have decided to bridge the gap with their potential allies in broader civil society, and to explore whether these bridging exchanges complement the network patterns hitherto examined. In this case, it is crucial to analyse relationships of co-operation between pro-beneficiary organisations actors on the one hand, and trade unions, political parties, churches, professional and other independent organisations from civil society on the other hand. Figures 6.3 and 6.4 compare network patterns between pro-beneficiary actors and civil society allies across the two issue-fields.

My attention is here exclusively focused on bridges across two different sets of actors, with no attention paid to reciprocal ties forged amongst actors within the same set. These data, again, confirm that pro-asylum and pro-unemployed organisations differed greatly in terms of their respective decisions to build horizontal ties. Actors working on behalf of unemployed people have scarcely managed to make any bridging connections with broader civil society. Although a large majority of actors have built at least one tie of co-operation with trade unions, churches and/or political parties, no node is characterised by high point-centrality and a few organisations are disconnected from the overall network. Figure 6.4 shows that CC has decided to build an important web of relationships with civil society allies, and hence, occupies a relatively important position

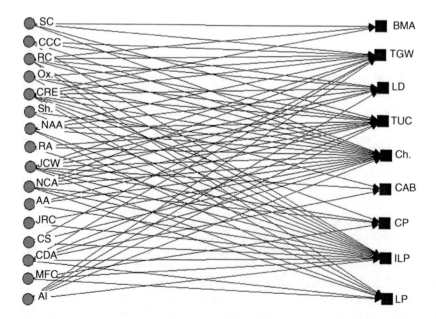

Figure 6.3 Horizontal networks in the asylum issue-field: pro-beneficiary vs. civil society.

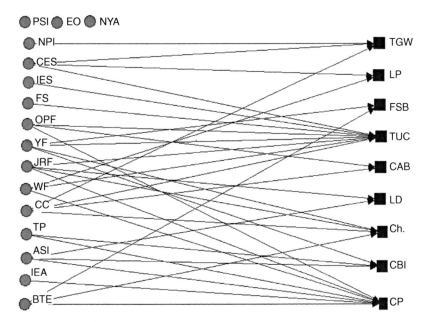

Figure 6.4 Horizontal networks in the unemployment issue-field: pro-beneficiary vs. civil society.

within the overall pro-unemployed people's movement in spite of its scarce exchanges with other pro-beneficiary organisations. However, it is crucial to emphasise that this organisation progressively reduced the scope and intensity of its action since the mid-1990s, facing some major obstacles in promoting the direct involvement of unemployed people. In particular, its network of local centres gradually shrunk due to tightening funding constraints, a halt in street protest and new political conditions, which have forced groups to demobilise and strengthen their links with the unions, as well as adapting to government strategies. Having dealt with the restrictive legislation of three successive Conservative governments, these centres generally decided to support New Labour policies after 1997. CC thus worked to strengthen its ties with trade unions, churches and other civil society organisations in order to connect to policy-makers.

On the other hand, pro-asylum organisations developed a denser network structure, characterised by extensive bridges with civil society allies. In particular, it is worth noticing that the high point-centrality of JCWI and RC within the pro-beneficiary network is matched by similar high values when considering this larger portion of network. JCWI and RC emerged as the main organisations which pulled resources horizontally across the pro-beneficiary movement and civil society. At the same time, it is crucial to emphasise that the Council for Racial Equality occupied a strategic position of exchange with civil society allies, and hence, should be considered to be an important organisation within the overall movement in spite of its limited linkages with other pro-beneficiary actors. In sum it is clear that pro-asylum organisations have decided not only to bond among themselves, but to forge at the same time a burgeoning web of horizontal exchanges which built bridging connections to all the main organisations of civil society. These 'external' horizontal networks have further facilitated the flow of information and definition of common beliefs. I have already mentioned the widespread campaign to 'scrap the vouchers'. This was the most visible episode of protest on behalf of asylum seekers, which brought together a wide range of organisations. A key union, namely, the Transport and General Workers' Union, led this campaign together with RC and Oxfam, while national and local churches have played an important role alongside professional associations (e.g. the British Medical Association), local authorities and other civic organisations commonly not engaged in the asylum issue-field (e.g. Barnardos and the Body Shop).

However, it is worth analysing further evidence about bridges between pro-beneficiary groups and civil society. First, Asylum Aid worked in partnership with the Central London Advice Service (CLAS) and with the Refugee Education and Training Advisory Service (RETAS) in the Rope project. While RETAS gave guidance on employment and access to education, CLAS provided further advice on accessing the National Asylum Support Service. Second, Amnesty International set up an ad hoc inter-organisational forum for debating and exchanging information on asylum seekers. This 'working group' connected Amnesty with the Refugee Legal Centre, the Immigration Law Practitioners Association, the United Nations High Commissioner for Refugees, the Jesuit Refugee Service, the Medical Foundation for the Care of Victims of Torture, Friends House, Oxfam, RC and JCWI. Amnesty also co-operates with Liberty and the Law Society, while relying at the same time on more extensive connections through Reach Out, which linked Amnesty with the Lawyers' Committee for Human Rights, Oxfam, Save the Children and the UNHCR's protection unit. Last, the Refugee Council and Refugee Action were active alongside other refugee voluntary organisations within a national multi-agency partnership. In particular, Refugee Action has developed its relationships especially at the regional level throughout the North of England, building linkages with the North West Development Agency, regional Community Health Council, regional volunteer bureaux, North West Consortium, accommodation providers, Princes Trust and Learning Direct, as well as hundreds of ties with different organisations at the local level such as refugee support groups, refugee community organisations and education suppliers.

Hence, this extensive web also spread through co-operation with a wide range of actors at the grassroots level, such as community and faith groups, education service and student groups, refugee community organisations and local voluntary groups, as well as asylum support networks that include the beneficiaries themselves. The pro-asylum organisational field was clearly characterised by dense exchanges which have filled in the gap between main national organisations and local grassroots groups. For example, Asylum Aid is in close contact with many refugee groups in areas where asylum seekers have been dispersed, working closely with these groups in order to produce a concerted and unified front of refugee organisations. The JCWI relied on a network of more than 2000 groups and individuals throughout Britain, working in direct contact with local groups, committees and families. Trade unions and other formal organisations could not affiliate to the National Coalition for Anti-Deportation Campaign (NCADC), which only built selected links of co-operation with other national voluntary actors to guarantee that the control of its own activities remains firmly in the hands of people facing deportation. In the words of a NCADC member:

> It does constrain us in that the trade union organisations can't really affili-
> ate, can't make donations, which is a bit of a handicap but we can't see a
> way round it because we are quite adamant that those fighting deportations
> will stay in control ... They ultimately are our employers. They can make
> the decisions.

This practice facilitated the broadening of ties at the local level, where NCADC forged an extensive web of exchanges through co-operation with grass-roots refugee groups, local committees of the socialist workers party, churches and trade unions branches.

Oxfam co-operated with faith-based groups such as Islamic Relief, informal organisations and committees, as well as with local branches of trade unions. In particular, the voucher campaign enabled Oxfam to develop extensive connections with organisations working directly on asylum. In the words of one of its members:

> I went to a brilliant group in Newham, the east end of London, Newham
> Refugee Forum, who were using Oxfam cards in the east end. They had
> never had any contact with Oxfam, barely knew who Oxfam were, but
> wanted to be part of this campaign ... The Northern Refugee Centre, again
> a group with no real links with Oxfam, got in touch and started distributing
> thousands of cards in Sheffield ... And all the cards came back ... from
> every part of the country, all political persuasions.

RC provides a further example of a key national organisation which was working alongside local refugee community organisations and a large number of grassroots groups for the reintegration of asylum seekers and refugees. In the words of a RC member:

> Refugees are part of our community and therefore as such the fundamental
> thing for me is to stop them being marginalised, stop them being seen as a
> separate thing ... It's to try and make sure that we can influence as much of
> that as possible.

My analysis has so far demonstrated that pro-beneficiary actors can take very different decisions when shaping their horizontal inter-organisational networks amongst themselves and with other organisations from civil society. The data indicate that extensive networks provide a distinctive advantage in the mobilisation of both material and non-material resources. In the asylum issue-field, the high number of ties among pro-beneficiary actors, as well as with civil society allies, was matched by

- the substantial and constant flow of information throughout the overall network, which led to the setting up of a national information-sharing umbrella, namely, the Asylum Rights Campaign (ARC),
- the decision to differentiate and harmonise their widespread interventions in a multitude of specific actions, bringing about the mushrooming of numerous ad hoc issue coalitions across the national and the local level, and
- the gradual development of a cohesive feeling of solidarity and belongingness within the network, which, in the case of the voucher campaign, also proved capable of prevailing on individual actors' pursuit of their own specific interests.

In the unemployment issue-field, ties of co-operation amongst pro-beneficiary actors were so loose that it was difficult to distinguish a well-defined cluster of organisations effectively co-operating with each other. Organisations working on behalf of unemployed people appeared to be interested in sustaining the minimum number of horizontal ties (with each other and with civil society allies) required to guarantee some basic information flow. They did not share any sense of solidarity, nor did they unite in pervasive common action or form ad hoc coalitions.

Vertical networks: 'links' with policy-makers compared across both issue-fields

Turning to the engagement in governance through vertical links with institutions and policy-makers reveals a contrast to the patterns of bonding and bridging capital built up inside civil society. Figures 6.5 and 6.6 compare links between pro-beneficiary organisations and core policy actors in each issue-field.

Whereas the pro-asylum movement had strong connections within civil society and the pro-unemployed people's movement was relatively much weaker, the roles were reversed when it came to links into governance, where the pro-asylum movement was quite weak and the pro-unemployed people's movement had much stronger connections. From the point of view of vertical governance connections, pro-unemployed actors no longer stand out as socially and politically marginalised organisations. While building a loose web of horizontal exchanges, they successfully forged an extensive web of links with influential policy-makers. The Centre for Economic and Social Inclusion (CESI) worked closely with policy-makers from 1997, when its strategy changed as a result of the election of the New Labour government. CESI no longer targeted the wider public or grassroots groups of unemployed (a normal practice through-

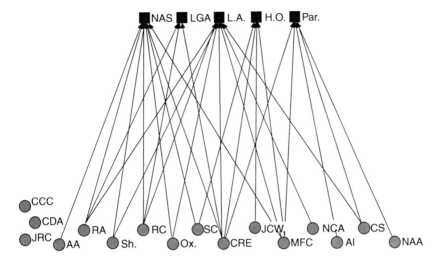

Figure 6.5 Vertical networks in the asylum issue-field: pro-beneficiary vs. core policy actors.

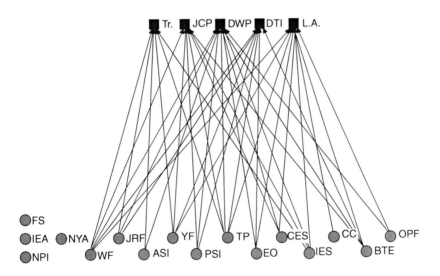

Figure 6.6 Vertical networks in the unemployment issue-field: pro-beneficiary vs. core policy actors.

out the previous Conservative governments), but instead played a crucial role beside government bodies in the design and formulation of different measures aimed to increase the employability of unemployed people (e.g. the transitional programme STEP-UP, the New Deal for young people, and the New Deal for long-term unemployed). Similarly, the Institute for Employment Studies (IES) worked in close contact with the Department of Work and Pension and Jobcentre-Plus, dealing with unemployment and labour market issues with the objective of changing policy from within. In the words of one of its members:

> We have always worked with policy makers and government, with them and for them. We have very good links with them ... We find it more fruitful to use the inside track, than the outside track.

In particular, IES was extensively involved in the elaboration of the New Deal programme for job seekers. It gave evidence to select committees and circulated most of its work throughout government departments, while placing many reports in the House of Commons library and briefing ministers and politicians.

The Joseph Rowntree Foundation (JRF) organised and co-hosted seminars with the Department of Work and Pension, bringing together policy-makers and researchers to discuss unemployment. JRF also launched many reports at day conferences, which were attended by ministers and keynote policy-makers. Tomorrow's People (TP) relied on a solid web of ties with government bodies and core policy actors. Indeed, far-reaching exchanges across the policy field were considered to be the best resource with which to help people who were excluded from the labour market to get out of long-term unemployment, welfare dependence and homelessness and into jobs and self-sufficiency. In the words of a TP member:

> Speaking to policy makers directly is much more effective ... The public does not have sufficient technical interest in the issues of concern and it is more effective therefore to deal with policy makers.

Lastly, the National Council for One Parent Families (OPF) focused most of its efforts on strengthening direct contacts with policy-makers and civil servants so as to participate in the development of policy. In particular, OPF worked closely with the Employment Service on the New Deal for Lone Parents and was responsible for training advisers. It also co-operated with the Treasury and Inland Revenue in the development of the tax credit system, and by briefing MPs for ad hoc debates, OPF had some influence on social security legislation and the 1998 Welfare Reform and Pension Bill.

I have already argued that in the asylum issue-field pro-beneficiary actors decided to privilege the building of horizontal ties, both inwardly amongst themselves and outwardly with civil society allies. Yet, the data in Figure 6.5 suggest that pro-asylum organisations, albeit opposing government policies, did not overlook the potentialities of forging direct links with policy elites and institutions so as to play some role in processes of decision-making. Mentioning only a few examples, the Commission for Racial Equality built an extensive web of vertical ties, owing to the special acknowledgement of its functions under the terms of the 1976 Race Relations Act and the 2000 Race Relations (Amendment) Act. In particular, this organisation worked actively with public bodies to promote laws, policies and practices which take full account of the Race Relations Acts and the protection they give against discrimination. Save the Children played a key role in the Young Unaccompanied Asylum Seekers stakeholders group, while participating at the same time in other stakeholder groups where the groundwork for legislation was being made and policy effected. Last, the Refugee Council (RC) was one of the assisting agencies set up in the aftermath of the 1999 Immigration and Asylum Act. It was part of a multi-agency partnership with other refugee voluntary organisations that aimed to plug asylum seekers into the National Asylum Support Service, providing them with support and independent advice on a wide range of questions. The RC also worked with local authorities to provide a service of home-hostels.

In sum, my findings can be summarised as follows. In the asylum issue-field, vertical links enabled pro-beneficiary actors to strengthen their intervention on behalf of asylum seekers, entering processes of governance through direct contact with institutions. Yet, pro-asylum organisations engaged more in accumulating bonding and bridging social capital through far-reaching exchanges among themselves and with civil society allies than concerning themselves with governance. These horizontal networks facilitated the flow of information and material resources, allowing for a balanced allocation of tasks and responsibilities. They were also valuable in sustaining symbolic and expressive actions. At times of mobilisation, pro-asylum actors with direct links in the policy field preferred to support other pro-beneficiary organisations, in spite of their interest in showing allegiance to institutions and policy-makers. Within an issue-field so 'horizontally-stretched', pro-asylum organisations have proved to be capable of merging their efforts within a unified front, drawing at the same time on the support of grassroots groups of beneficiaries and civil society allies.

By contrast, in the unemployment issue-field there was little bonding and bridging capital, with only a few loose horizontal exchanges. Pro-unemployed organisations did not share any sense of solidarity, nor have they ever united in pervasive common action, or formed large ad hoc coalitions. Rather, the entire issue-field is 'vertically-stretched', with extensive links into governance across the public and policy domains. Actors aim to access different social positions so as to strengthen their role in processes of governance. Policy-makers are interested in the support which pro-unemployed organisations can provide in terms of welfare services, production of knowledge, sharing of expertise and public legitimisation. In exchange, pro-unemployed organisations obtain a privileged access to higher political positions and financial resources, thus reinforcing their organisational strength and public acknowledgement. This leads to increasing competition amongst pro-unemployed actors to reach the top level of the policy domain, while fostering distance of beneficiaries (unemployed people themselves) at the grassroots level.

Explaining networks: political constraints in New Labour Britain

My analysis of horizontal ties (bonds and bridges) and vertical links in the two issue-fields of asylum and unemployment in Britain has focused on two distinct patterns of networks forged by pro-beneficiary actors. I can now take them as my dependent variable and analyse which factors impact upon pro-beneficiary organisations when they build their preferred combination of networks. In particular, I draw on theories of 'political opportunity structure' (Tarrow, 1998). This approach is indeed well-known in studies of social movements' scholarship. It shares many common features with the broadly influential 'neo-institutionalist' perspective (Hall and Taylor, 1996), but it is characterised at the same time by a stronger attention for collective action within the public domain. Hence, it can be particularly valuable to explain the different decisions that pro-asylum and pro-unemployed movements take in their own issue-field with regard to their actions and exchanges. While different authors have provided different definitions and operationalisations of the concept of political opportunity structure, my attention here is focused on some key dimensions which are particularly relevant for my cross-issue comparative study, namely,

- legal arrangements,
- configurations of alliances at the level of party system, and
- the prevailing strategies of ruling elites.

Starting with the analysis of legal arrangements, asylum seekers and unemployed people have both faced the implementation of restrictive measures. Since its first mandate, the New Labour government has promoted significant reforms to the labour market in order to move more people from welfare to work. These include the working families' tax credit, changes to the system of national contribution, a national minimum wage and the New Deal, which started as a specific policy directed at young people, but was soon extended to older people, single parents and disabled people. In particular, a new principle of 'conditionality' can be seen at the core of New Labour's welfare to work agenda. Within the New Deal programme, failure to take up one of the four work/training options has often amounted to punitive benefit cuts and suspensions (CESI, 2002). As regards asylum, there have been substantial reforms underscoring the government's negative agenda of deterring new arrivals. Three main pieces of legislation have come into force, namely, the Immigration and Asylum Act 1999, the Nationality, Immigration and Asylum Act 2002 and the Asylum and Immigration Act 2004, which have extended penalties on carriers, introduced (and then changed) the voucher scheme as an important instrument of welfare support, extended policies preventing arrivals at British ports and made provision for a new system of compulsory dispersal to reduce asylum seekers' presence in London and the South-East of England. In particular, the 2004 and 2002 Acts followed on the footsteps of the 1999 Act, extending the application of some appeals and establishing the withdrawal of welfare support for in-country applicants.

Nevertheless, these two groups face diverse (combinations of) types of exclusion. In particular, they access different bundles of legal and political rights, which sanction that unemployed people have at least full juridical inclusion through their entitlement as British nationals. A comprehensive examination of the constitutional and social nature of citizenship in Britain can thus offer some valuable insights on the relationships between different dimensions of exclusion (White, 1999). My argument suggests that the holding of British citizenship (with its entitlements and duties) may have a relevant impact upon exchanges in the two issue-fields, clearly accounting for different network patterns between pro-beneficiary movements and groups of beneficiaries at the grassroots level. Unlike unemployed people, asylum seekers face high barriers to obtaining acknowledgement of their most basic rights, including official residence entitlements, and are consequently dependent upon pro-beneficiary organisations for all their daily needs. It follows that pro-asylum organisations need to work actively with local asylum support networks and grassroots groups of beneficiaries, thus filling in the gap between beneficiary and pro-beneficiary space. In a certain sense, the very meaning and practice of altruism change across the two issue-fields. Different legal and constitutional arrangements impact upon the very substantive content of 'mobilising on behalf of' in each case, thus influencing the decisions which built different patterns of co-operation.

My investigation, however, extends beyond the analysis of exchanges between pro-beneficiaries and beneficiaries, entailing the consideration of two further dimensions, namely, the alliances of political parties, and the specific strategies of policy actors. My data indicate that political parties are somewhat minor protagonists in the unemployment policy field, whereas they are central actors for decision-making on asylum. While pro-asylum organisations decided to build an extensive web of bridges with allies in civil society, their exchanges with political parties were characterised by low density as a result of the extensive inclusion of political parties in the policy field. In the unemployment policy domain the opposite occurred, where the marginal presence of parties stabilised the loose horizontal exchanges within the unemployment public domain.

Lastly, it is necessary to focus on the strategies of policy-makers and institutions. I have already emphasised that three successive New Labour governments have brought about the introduction of many restrictive provisions in both issue-fields. However, these provisions seem to fit only partially with the standard interpretation of a dichotomous split between opportunities and constraints. New Labour seems to be capable of providing and co-ordinating a mix of 'constraining opportunities' so as to predict and control collective action across different issue-fields. In the unemployment issue-field, the responsiveness of institutions and policy-makers strategies of co-option have constrained the use of direct action and widespread intervention in the public domain (to be sustained through dense horizontal networks), but at the same time have provided opportunities for small specialist organisations that target relevant policy-makers. The demise of an unemployed people's protest movement in the public domain coincided with New Labour taking on responsibility for government. Yet, New Labour strategically 'opened up' institutional channels of access so as to encourage pro-unemployed people's organisations to strengthen their forms of direct involvement in processes of governance. This has attracted a wider range of voluntary organisations willing to seize this new mix of constraints and opportunities, and whose involvement has led to further marginalisation of grassroots groups of unemployed people.

In the asylum issue-field, the New Labour government has preferred a classic strategy of prevailing constraints so as to reinforce the restrictive social, political and legal context for pro-beneficiary movements. Pro-asylum organisations thus strengthened their horizontal networks, in order to tie in other campaign organisations and transform the beneficiary-specific claims into visible political demands in opposition to state policy-makers.

Ultimately, my study suggests focusing on and comparing different issue and political fields to assess more precisely the intermediate space between explanatory factors on the one hand and collective action on the other hand. It is in the specific relational configurations of these fields that social movements forge reciprocal bonds, establish bridges with civil society allies and attempt to play an active role in wider processes of governance through links with policy-makers. A political opportunity structure approach is valuable in explaining the different decisions which actors take when shaping their exchanges. Yet, I emphasise that opportunities are not cut off from, but rather mixed with, constraints. New Labour seems indeed to have gone a long way in packaging sophisticated mixes of opportunities and constraints so as to predict and control collective action. In addition, these mixes should not be treated as if they could be uniformly applied across all issue and political fields, impacting equally upon all kinds of challenging groups in a given political context. My final findings show the striking differences between the politics of asylum and unemployment in New Labour Britain. While the issue-field of asylum resembles a classical state–challenger dichotomy in which pro-beneficiary actors aim to develop their horizontal ties through both instrumental and expressive actions in order to strengthen their position against government, the issue-field of unemployment stands out as a pacified multi-organisational field in which there is complete governance synchrony between state, civil society and pro-beneficiary actors.

Appendix: list of interviewed actors and their abbreviations in figures

Asylum issue-field

AA	Asylum Aid
AI	Amnesty International
BMA	British Medical Association
CAB	National Association of Citizens Advice Bureaux
CCC	Campaign to Close Campsfield
Ch.	Churches' Commission for Racial Justice
CDA	Committee to Defend Asylum Seekers
CP	Conservative Party
CRE	Commission for Racial Equality
CS	Children's Society
HO	Home Office
ILP	Immigration Law Practitioners' Association
JCW	Joint Council for the Welfare of Immigrants
JRC	Jesuit Refugee Centre
LD	Liberal Democrats
LA	Local Authority
LGA	Local Government Association
LP	Labour Party
MFC	Medical Foundation for the Care of Victims of Torture
NAA	National Assembly Against Racism
NAS	National Asylum Support Service
NCA	National Coalition of Anti-Deportation Campaigns
Ox.	Oxfam
Par.	Parliament
RA	Refugee Action
RC	Refugee Council
SC	Save the Children
Sh.	Shelter
TGW	Transport and General Workers Union
TUC	Trade Unions Congress

Unemployment issue-field

ASI	Adam Smith Institute
BTE	Black Training and Enterprise Group
CAB	National Association of Citizens Advice Bureaux
CBI	Confederation British Industry
CC	Network of Unemployed Centres Combine
CES	Centre for Economic and Social Inclusion
Ch.	Church of England
CP	Conservative Party
CPS	Centre for Policy Studies
DTI	Department for Trade and Industry
DWP	Department for Work and Pension
EO	Employment Opportunities
FS	Fabian Society
FSB	Federation of Small Businesses
IEA	Institute of Economic Affairs
IES	Institute of Employment Studies
JCP	Jobcentre Plus
JRF	Joseph Rowntree Foundation
LA	Local Authority
LD	Liberal Democrats
LP	Labour Party
NPI	New Policy Institute
NYA	National Youth Agency
OPF	National Council for One Parent Families
PSI	Policy Studies Institute
TGW	Transport and General Workers Union
TP	Tomorrow's People
Tr.	Treasury
TUC	Trade Unions Congress
WF	Work Foundation

References

Bourdieu, P. (1986) 'The Forms of Capital', in Richardson, J.C. (ed.), *Handbook of Theory and Research for the Sociology of Education*, Westport, CT: Greenwood Press, pp. 241–258.

CESI (2002) 'New Deal Sanctions', *Training and Employment Network Weekly Briefing*, No. 194, London: Cesi, available at www.cesi.org.uk/_newsite2002/newdeal/weekly-briefing/brief194.htm.

Cinalli, M. (2003) 'Socio-Politically Polarized Contexts, Urban Mobilization and the Environmental Movement: A Comparative Study of Two Campaigns of Protest in Northern Ireland', *International Journal of Urban and Regional Research*, 27 (1): 158–177.

Cinalli, M. (2004) 'Horizontal Networks vs. Vertical Networks in Multi-Organisational Alliances: A Comparative Study of the Unemployment and Asylum Issue-Fields in Britain', EurPolCom working paper 8 (4), University of Leeds.

Coleman, J. (1990) *Foundations of Social Theory*, Cambridge, MA: Harvard University Press.

Curtis, R. and Zurcher, L. (1973) 'Stable Resources of Protest Movements: The Multi-Organizational Field', *Social Forces*, 52: 53–61.

Diani, M. (1995) *Green Networks: A Structural Analysis of the Italian Environmental Movement*, Edinburgh: Edinburgh University Press.

Franzosi, R. (1997) 'Mobilization and Counter-Mobilization Processes: From the Red Years (1919–20) to the Black Years (1921–22). A New Methodological Approach to the Study of Narrative Data', *Theory and Society* (Special Issue), 26: 275–304.

Giugni, M. and Passy, F. (2001) (eds) *Political Altruism? Solidarity Movements in International Perspective*, Lanham, MD: Rowman & Littlefield Publishers.

Gould, R. (1995) *Insurgent Identities: Class, Community and Protest in Paris from 1848 to the Commune*, Chicago: University of Chicago Press.

Guardian (2003) *Kurdish Poet Finds his Voice*, 31 May 2003.

Hall, P. and Taylor, R. (1996) 'Political Science and the Three New Institutionalisms', *Political Studies*, 44 (5): 936–957.

Lin, N. (2001) *Social Capital: A Theory of Social Structure and Action*, Cambridge: Cambridge University Press.

Passy, F. (2001) 'Socializing, Connecting, and the Structural/Agency Gap: A Specification of the Impact of Networks on Participation in Social Movements', *Mobilization*, 6: 173–192.

Putnam, R. (1995) 'Bowling Alone: American's Declining Social Capital', *Journal of Democracy*, 6 (1): 65–78.

Tarrow, S. (1998) *Power in Movement*, Second Edition, Cambridge: Cambridge University Press.

Van den Berg, G. and van Ours, J. (1994) 'Unemployment Dynamics and Duration Dependence in France, The Netherlands and the United Kingdom', *Economic Journal*, 104: 432–443.

White, P. (1999) 'Ethnicity, Racialization and Citizenship as Divisive Elements in Europe', in Hudson, R. and Williams, A.M. (eds), *Divided Europe: Society and Territory*, London: Sage.

7 Networks of protest on global issues in Greece 2002–2003

Moses A. Boudourides and Iosif A. Botetzagias

Introduction

This chapter explores the impact of political differences on networks at a national level in the case of Greece, mobilization on global social movements and global issues. Mario Diani (1992, 2003) has clearly and extensively argued on the value of treating social movements as networks if the aim is to identify the distinctive characteristics of such contentious forms of collective action which differentiate them from other social processes and social actors (like non-conflictual movements, political organizations and coalitions). For Diani, social movements are defined as networks 'of informal interactions between a plurality of individuals, groups or associations, engaged in a political or cultural conflict, on the basis of a shared collective identity' (Diani 1992, p. 13). In fact, this is the starting point of what we intend to discuss here concerning contentious protest in Greece centered on global issues during the two years, 2002–2003. Actually, that contemporary social movements around global issues constitute and represent a paradigm 'par excellence' of a networked form of mobilization is an idea to which many would have no difficulty in subscribing. For instance, Arturo Escobar claims that the most apt metaphor to describe the anti-globalization movement is that of networks. Furthermore, drawing upon the collateral concept of a 'meshwork' advanced by Manuel de Landa (1997), Escobar suggests that 'anti-globalization struggles are best seen as horizontal, self-organizing mesh-works of heterogeneous sites/struggles brought together by diverse interfaces and catalysts, particularly NGOs and pioneering social movements' (Escobar 2000, p. 12).

Our aim here is to study the network structure of these conflictual social dynamics in order to understand two important aspects of contemporary social movements: (i) how the organizational actors, the collective protagonists, of these protests develop their strategies of complex interweaving through which they are constructing their contentious political agendas and their engagement in social conflict; and (ii) how the relational niche of such social movement networks resonates with and is conditioned by the 'cognitive mechanisms' (Tarrow 2002) or the 'master frames' (Snow and Benford 1992) of the contentious collective action.

Stated more concretely, our aim is to analyze newspaper data on contemporary social protest in Greece in order to be able to answer the following two sets of questions:

- How do organizations constitute the observed protest networks? What patterns of ties do they form? Besides their primary strategy to confront a common enemy, how are these organizations positioned inside the emerging network of collective action with respect to each other?
- The observed protest events might be decomposed in certain recurrent episodes (or cycles) of events each focused on a distinctive group of protest issues. We may see these issues as amalgams of collective ideas, opinions, claims and frames which are embedded in a dynamic social movement network. How are the protest networks structured in relation to the prevailing contemporary protest issues? Do these issues mobilize the same or different actors in the issue-specific protest networks? So, from a relational point of view, how are the dominant protest issues related to each other?

It is immediately clear that the perspectives of our analysis touch the very details of how actors weave the complex web of their interdependent relationships into a social network. In other words, we would like to center our investigation of social movement networks on the concept capturing all the complexity of a network, i.e. that of a 'tie,' which constitutes the most basic unit of social network analysis (White 1992). Furthermore, a social tie is not unitary, but possesses a composite character of multiple dimensions. It is the multiplexity (of a tie) which indicates how interdependent and interlocked the various dimensions of a tie are. Furthermore, social network analysts know very well that these dimensions need not be homogeneous in any sense. In a social network, ties might reflect cooperation as well as competition, friendship as well as hostility, 'conflict as well as solidarity' (Lorrain and White 1971, p. 78).

Thus, our primary consideration is to investigate what the implications are (at the network level) of existing polarities (at the level of connected dyads) among various types of ties. Do such local tensions reshuffle the network so that coherence might be lost and new diversity might emerge?

We would like to answer these questions drawing upon a number of methodological approaches developed in theories of social networks. A first approach to the analysis of network heterogeneity that one could follow proceeds with an investigation of exactly the opposite direction. Under what conditions and mechanisms does homogenization persist? Is convergence towards an attractive network pattern guaranteed? One answer is given by theories of 'homophily,' through which one could study the tendency of individuals to interact with others sharing similar attributes (Kandel 1978; McPherson *et al.* 2001). However, if homogenization is the expected outcome of homophily, then in social networks the same result of structural cohesion could be attained at least locally by processes of social influence without any assumption of homophilic interactions (Friedkin 1984). Furthermore, often an alternative explanation of homophily makes more sense: 'homophily is largely a byproduct of its antipole' (Macy *et al.* 2004, p. 164). Thus, in many cases, a 'repulsion hypothesis' as an unintended consequence of xenophobia may cause the same effects with homophilic attractivity (Rosenbaum 1986).

Beyond theories of homophily, there is a second sociological strand trying to explain network heterogeneity and polarization processes. This is related to an old problem in social network analysis, which concerns the stability of social networks with signed links – some of the relationships are positive and some are negative. In other words, this is the setting of the so-called 'balance theory' Heider (1946). Heider suggested that certain patterns of attitudes are more stable than others and he called them 'balanced' – depending on how individuals are connected to each other and with what sign of relationships (Heider 1946). For instance, triads with two negative relationships are as well balanced as triads with positive product of signs for all their relationships. In fact, if the latter happens, the whole network (or 'graph') is said to be balanced. Defined in this way, balanced networks are shown to possess a very important property of 'differentiated clusterability': actors are partitioned in a finite number of blocks such that inside all blocks relationships are positive while among all blocks relationships are negative (Davis 1967).

Could we observe such a property of clusterability over protest networks we are studying here? Of course, our case is more complicated than the above setting of balance theory: multiplexity or multiple relationships are now present. However, social network analysis techniques of clustering or decomposition into blocks have already been applied in the study of social movements (Bearman and Everett 1993; Diani 2002; Forno 2003). In our case, the fact is that one is able to single out at least two 'opposite' relationships connecting protest organizations, which are the collective actors in protest networks.

- On the one hand, there is a relationship of 'co-participation' (we will say just 'participation' when communality is obvious) when two or more organizations participate in a certain protest event.
- On the other hand, there is a relationship of 'anti-participation' when two organizations (or, in general, more dyads of organizations) decide to participate at two different protest events taking place at the same time in different locations of the same city (or area) instead of mobilizing themselves in a common protest event.

Underlying this differentiation between the two types of participation is the hypothesis that a protest event – as any organizational or 'policy event' (see Laumann and Knoke 1987) – can be uniquely identified by the time and space of its occurrence: it happens on a certain date, for a certain duration and in certain geographical locations (possibly multiple). In this sense, co-participation and anti-participation might be considered as opposite relationships in the network composed of organizations participating in multiple protest events: say, co-participation is positively signed and anti-participation is negative. However, these two relationships are not mutually exclusionary: it is possible that two organizations co-participate in certain protest events and anti-participate in some others. But what one could easily guess in such situations is that co-participation should be negatively correlated with anti-participation: the more two organizations participate in common protest events, the less (it is reasonable to expect that) they would decide to disassociate themselves by deliberately and systematically showing up in different co-occurring protest events. Indeed, this is what we find in our analysis of protest networks in Greece compiled from newspaper data for the period 2002–2003.

One might hypothesize that the length of the time period over which protest events are monitored should be important for the intensity of the negative correlation between co- and anti-participation. Focusing on rather short periods of, say, a couple of months should give robust enough patterns of co- and anti-participation among organizations taking part in the protest events of such periods. If such fragmented or even segregated patterns are sustained, either a trans-organizational solidarity is built over time, an antagonism or competition develops between protest organizations motivated by the same cause and usually confronting the same enemy. However, it is also possible that the membership inside these patterns formed by relationships of co- and anti-participation might be variable. An organization which at some period co-participates with certain others might later change strategy and enter a coalition with these previously antagonistic organizations.

Therefore, from a dynamic network perspective of social movements, what is interesting to analyze is the evolution over time of all these patterns of co- and anti-participation from the point of view of not only stability (organizational robustness) but also instability (organizational dissolution) as well as the mobility (organizational volatility) of coalitions and individual protest organizations. In practice, the proper techniques and methodologies of social network analysis, which facilitate the study of fragmentation of networks in distinctive patterns of positions and roles, are those of structural equivalence and blockmodeling (White et al. 1976). Therefore, the above patterns of co- and anti-participating organizations can be studied as blocks of structurally equivalent actors (organizations) in the protest network, which is structured by two relationships (co- and anti-participation). However, instead of treating the two opposite relationships simultaneously, we have chosen to follow a blockmodeling procedure (Breiger et al. 1975) based solely on the co-participation relationship and then using the anti-participation relationship in order to interpret the attractivity of organizations inside blocks (high co-participation and low anti-participation) and the repulsiveness of organizations belonging in different blocks (low co-participation and high anti-participation). As a matter of fact, the usual clustering techniques of blockmodeling (e.g. through Pearson product–moment correlations) need to aggregate different sociomatrices (each corresponding to a different relationship) into a joint sociomatrix and they do this algebraically. However, a methodological confusion might arise when two relationships are opposite in sign but their addition does not annul nor obliterate them! For instance, two organizations might have equal number of co- and anti-participations but summing them up one would end with a tie weight equal to zero. Then, the problem would be that zero tie weight might be confused with no tie at all, i.e. the case of no connection with any type of participation, which of course is not the case here.

Finally, let us remark that in addition to the above interpretation of the composition of blocks through a combined effect of co-participatory attractivity and anti-participatory repulsion, one could validate the resulting blockmodels using attributes of actors in order to describe their positions inside blocks. Since the actors are various political or protest organizations and other civil society associations, their characteristics of political affiliation or socio-economic orientation might suffice to clear up the organizational composition of the emerging blocks. However, note that such a validation through exogenous (to the network) actor attributes brings back into action the basic assumptions of homophily, but this time by skipping any social influence model and following the routes of network clustering through blockmodeling.

Apart from the social network theory implications stemming from the analysis of our data, another important dimension we are interested in exploring is the temporal development of the (generic) 'anti'- or 'alter'-movement of the late 1990s. It is by now common knowledge not only that each cycle of protest largely depends on previously established networks of acquaintance and interaction but also creates a useful 'bank' of 'warm-feeling' individuals, waiting to be re-mobilized in the future, over similar issues. These issues, albeit an integral part of our ongoing research, will not be addressed in this chapter, where we are following the structural-dynamical network perspective: rather, we are interested in a larger picture of the actual organizations involved.

The period under investigation is one compromising many stimuli for the (generic) 'anti'-movement. In less than three years we witnessed the establishment of the World Social Forum, the 9/11 attack, the Afghanistan and the Iraq wars and, in the Greek context, an EU summit: certainly, a great deal of issues for the movement to act upon. Furthermore, especially in the case of the war, the general public exhibited an enhanced interest and opposition, making it especially conducive for the movement to materialize on this widespread discontent.

These stimuli presented new mobilizing opportunities for the Greek left libertarian movement. In addition, though, they opened up a new arena for the ongoing competition between the two major Greek left political parties, the Greek Communist Party (*KKE*) and *SYN* (Coalition of the Left, the Social Movements and the Ecology). Ever since the last Greek military junta of 1967–1974, these two larger Greek left parties have been embroiled in bitter conflict. The former, nicknamed 'KKE-*exterior*,' upheld Communist orthodoxy, looking to Soviet Union for guidance. The latter, nicknamed 'KKE-*interior*,' in the early 1980s, was associated with the European left. The two parties had only rarely cooperated while the latest coalition split (in the early 1990s) had not yet healed. KKE (interior) renamed itself SYN and has struggled to safeguard its parliamentary presence (failing to do so in the 1993 elections, just after the last split) while KKE (exterior) went on to establish itself as the major Greek left party: it has established its own trade union organizations, organized its own protests and marches (e.g. on the traditional 1 May march, the KKE-affiliate organizations demonstrate on their own) while it has repeatedly turned down all calls for (even tactical) collaboration with SYN. In other words, and in rather typical Marxist–Leninist fashion, KKE has (tried to) seal off and discredit its 'revisionist opponents.' This age-old delimitation reasserted itself with the emergence of the novel alter-globalization movement: KKE did not participate in the Greek Social Forum (where SYN plays a prominent role) while in the anti-globalization and anti-war demonstrations (at the Thessaloniki 2003 EU summit and the 2003 and 2004 Iraq war marches, respectively) the KKE protested on its own, hand-in-hand with the union and/or social movement organizations it controlled.

This chapter, then, focuses on analyzing (through network blockmodel decompositions) the Greek movements' development as it was conditioned by instances of important stimuli. In other words: how and when did the first movement organizations emerge? Were they established ad hoc or had they sprung out from pre-existing groups/schemes (and if so, from which)? Were they politically autonomous or have they aligned themselves with existing political families? How have they developed? Have some ceased to exist (or merged into larger ones) once the specific stimulus was removed or have they chosen to broaden their scope, taking action on new issues? What about the creation and/or the appearance rate of new social movement organizations (SMOs)? Can we identify larger coalitions of SMOs (of a limited number) or do the movements demonstrate centrifugal tendencies? If the former is the case, what separates and what unites these larger SMO-families and how do they position themselves vis-à-vis the (pre-) existing civil society actors (especially political parties and NGOs)?

Data and methods

We have been analyzing protest events happening in Greece during the two years 2002–2003 as far as these protests were referring to international issues around the effects of globalization and expressing an opposition to certain wars occurring in the same period. Our source of information about these protest events has been the Greek daily newspaper *Eleftherotypia* (meaning 'Free Press'). From the online editions and archives of this newspaper, we have collected 596 articles referring to protests of interest that have occurred in Greece and all over the world in this period.[1] Our concern was to code information about distinctive protests throughout the collected newspaper articles. As we have already mentioned, a protest event is identified by the time and space of its occurrence: it occurs on a certain date, lasts a certain duration and takes place in certain geographical locations (possibly multiple). In other words, we associated a specific time and a specific geographical area with each distinctive protest event. Concerning the 'timing' of the protest event, we primarily use the date it starts: two protest events, starting at the same date but at different hours were considered different events, even when they were happening at the same location, as far as they were mobilizing different constituencies of organizations and they were focused on different issues and frames. Concerning the 'geographical area' of the protest event, we use the location or place where the protest was taking place for most time or otherwise where the most important episode of the event had happened. Usually, this geographical area was a square, a street or a neighborhood in a city or village or other geographical location. Protest events occurring simultaneously in the same wider area but converging temporarily with others at the same places (where they could terminate or just meet for a short period and then separate again) were taken as different. Furthermore, let us add that it was possible from a single newspaper article to collect information about more than one distinct protest event and that information about a single protest event might have been collected through more than one newspaper article. In this way, by aggregating information on the same protest events coming from multiple articles, we were able to identify 725 distinct protest events among which 329 occurred in Greece while 406 occurred abroad. The evolution over time of all the events (inside and outside Greece) is shown in Figure 7.1. As one could immediately observe, the bulk of the protest events took place in the first semester of 2003; the time evolution of protests in that period is shown in Figure 7.2 in the Appendix.

For each protest we coded two dominant issues or foci of the mobilization (which constitute the frame of the collective action). Table 7.1 shows the coded issues, the majority of which is distributed over three main groups of issues: anti-war, summit-related and anti-globalization. Furthermore, we coded the organizations (both initiating-organizing and participating) in each protest event.

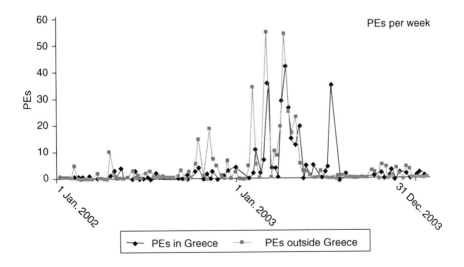

Figure 7.1 Time evolution of protest events (PEs).

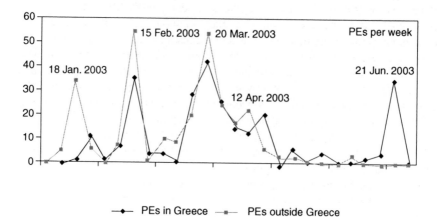

— PEs in Greece ....■.... PEs outside Greece

Figure 7.2 Protest events (PEs) during January–July 2003.

Table 7.1 Issues of protest events (PEs)

Issues	PEs in Greece	Total no. of PEs
Anti-war	211	554
Against war in Iraq	205	539
Against occupation in Iraq	2	5
Peace	2	4
Against war in Afghanistan	1	3
Other	1	3
Summit-related	88	114
EU Summit	87	94
WTO Summit	1	6
G8 Summit	0	4
World Summit on Sustainable Development	0	3
World Economic Forum	0	2
Other	0	5
Anti-globalization	24	60
Resisting globalization	21	48
Bush's Visit	0	5
Other	3	7
Middle East conflict	8	22
Against war in Palestine	2	5
Solidarity to Israel	0	1
Solidarity to Palestinians	6	16
Miscellaneous	20	27
Against racism	5	5
Labor Rights	5	5
Global Environment	0	4
Anniversary of Polytechnion Uprising	3	3
Environment	2	2
Educational policies	1	2
Protest against Italy	2	2
Other	2	4

The structure of protest networks over time

Observing the time evolution of the protest events (Figure 7.1), we can discern the following periodization of the main protest waves in 2002–2003:

Period 1: *January–September 2002:* Anti-globalization and peace protests peaked around the Second World Social Forum at Porto Alegre, 31 January to 5 February 2002, the pro-Palestinian demonstrations of 13–14 April 2002 and the EU Summit at Seville, 21–23 June 2002.

Period 2: *October–December 2002:* Anti-globalization and peace protests intensified during the October 2002 anti-war protests and the European Social Forum in Florence, 7–10 November 2002.

Period 3: *January 2003:* Anti-globalization mobilizations at the informal meeting of the EU Ministers of Employment and Social Policy at Nafplio, 24 January 2003, and peace protests due to the Iraq crisis peaked around the demonstrations of 18 January 2003.

Period 4: *February 2003:* Anti-war mobilizations due to the Iraq crisis peaked around the demonstrations of 15 February 2003 and at the end of February 2003.

Period 5: *March–April 2003:* Anti-war mobilizations due to the Iraq crisis peaked around the demonstrations of 20 March 2003 (official start of the war) and 12 April 2003.

Period 6: *May–June 2003:* Anti-war and anti-globalization protests culminating at the EU Summit in Greece on 21 June 2003.

Period 7: *July–October 2003:* Anti-globalization protests intensified during the WTO Summit at Cancun around 13 September 2003.

Period 8: *November–December 2003:* Anti-globalization and anti-American demonstrations on the occasion of Bush's visits around the world.

In each of these periods, we constructed three networks, each based on the duality between organizations and one of the three main issues of protest events (i.e. anti-war, anti-globalization and summit-related). This means that, in each period, we were considering those organizations appearing in the protest events which were characterized by a certain issue (among the above three broader categories of issues). These organizations were taken to be related to each other with respect two types of relationships:

- In the relationship of *co-participation*, two organizations, say, i and j, are considered connected if they both participate in at least one protest event, P – in this case we say that organizations i and j co-participate. The number of distinct protest events P, in all of which these two organizations co-participate, defines the weight of the link of co-participation between organizations i and j.

- In the relationship of *anti-participation*, two organizations, say, i and j, are considered connected if there exists a pair of two distinct protest events taking place at the same time in different locations of the same area, say, P_k and P_m, such that organization i participates in P_k, where organization j abstains, and organization j participates in P_m, where organization i abstains (or the other way around, by permuting i with j) – in this case we say that organizations i and j anti-participate. The number of pairs of such protest events (P_k, P_m), in all of which these two organizations anti-participate, defines the weight of the link of anti-participation between organizations i and j.

Therefore, by the duality of organizations and issues (Breiger 1974), our data produce 24 networks (eight periods times three issues), each of which possesses double relationships (co- and anti-participation). Notice that these networks correspond to valued undirected graphs (without self-loops); in other words, the corresponding adjacency matrices are symmetric, without any diagonal entries and with non-diagonal entries taking positive integer values (the weights).

These networks have been analyzed with CONCOR (Breiger *et al.* 1975), a frequently employed algorithm for detecting structural equivalence of actors in a network. In this analysis, we have been using solely the networks of co-participation and we have managed to derive all the produced blocks of co-participating organizations together with the corresponding density matrices. Notice that in our density matrices we have included two densities: the density of and among blocks of co-participating organizations and the density of and among the corresponding blocks but the second time with respect to the relationship of anti-participation.

From these blockmodels of co-participation in the three main areas of mobilization issues (anti-war, anti-globalization and summit-related), it is not hard to observe that two divergent coalitions of organizations emerge:

- *Coalition A*: a group of organizations aligned with the Greek Social Forum.
- *Coalition B*: a group of organizations aligned with KKE (the Communist Party of Greece).

The constituencies of both coalitions include an invariant core of organizations (although beyond the core they were variable at a different degree during the first three periods). Both coalitions were definitely stabilized in February 2003 and thereafter they held more or less almost all their adherent organizations, which had already converged within the blocks occupied by each of the two coalitions. Coalition A (led by the Greek Social Forum) attracted a group of organizations including Initiative Genova 2001 (a Greek anti-globalization organization), SYN (the second biggest Greek left party) and various Greek Trade Unions (ADEDI, GSEE, EKA and OLME). The hard core of the constituency of coalition B (led by KKE, the Greek Communist Party) included PAME-DRASI and Action Thessaloniki 2003 (a trade union controlled by KKE) (an anti-globalization organization), EDYETh (a peace movement organization), EDOTh (a trade union) and DIKKI (a left party created by ex-members of PASOK, the Greek Socialist Party).

The blockmodels of the networks we found suggested that these two coalitions were strongly antagonistic in three senses and, thus, they could be considered to form the two antipoles of the contemporary Greek social movement.

First, the two coalitions always occupied different blocks in each network. This means that their structural characteristics (positions and roles) were quite distinctive. However, although they occupied separate blocks during all periods, after March 2003 each coalition engaged with all three of the issues of mobilization (but always kept to different blocks with respect to each other), a fact that generates some very interesting implications about the relational miscibility of frames of contentious collective action in Greece during 2002–2003, as we will see in a moment.

Second, we observe that the corresponding blocks of the two coalitions in each period and on each issue have variable densities of co-participating and anti-participating links. In the network of co-participation, the density of links connecting the blocks of coalition A with B is rather low: almost always 0. The exceptions were the anti-war network in February 2003 (0.4) and in March–April 2003 (0.386) and the summit-related network in May–June 2003 (0.67). These relatively high values of the density of links of co-participation between the two rival blocks in these exceptional cases can easily be explained. February to March 2003 was the hottest period of anti-war mobilizations and exposure to public attention increased the strategic value of joint actions. Moreover, in June 2003 Greece was hosting the EU Council Summit at Chalkidiki and the public pressure (both from national and international sources) was very high necessitating that Greek organizations should show up in common demonstrations. On the other hand, although the blocks of the two coalitions started with a rather high density of anti-participating links (0.6 in the beginning of 2002 and 0.4 in February 2003), subsequently in the hot period from February to June 2003 this density dropped almost to zero. In other words, what our data show is that an initial sensitivity towards maintaining the distinctive political identities of the organizations in these blocks has gradually declined, driven by the change of focus of the master-frame of the mobilizations.

Third, the trajectories of the two antagonistic coalitions when they were encountering the three main mobilization issues (anti-war, anti-globalization and summit-related) were very dissimilar before February 2003 but subsequently they normalized into a common pattern, which was uniformly dense in all three issue areas – in the sense that the two coalitions engaged with all three issues. This is shown in Figure 7.3, where we see that although both coalitions started from anti-globalization mobilizations (in the beginning of 2002, i.e. the period just following 9/11 and the Afghanistan war), in their next transitions the two coalitions bifurcated towards their own trajectories, with coalition A shifting to summit-related mobilizations, while coalition B passed almost immediately into anti-war mobilizations. However, the subsequent passage was common to both coalitions and it turns out to be extremely crucial since after that step both coalitions follow similar routes (but always in disjoint blocks). This turning point was February 2003, during which both coalitions were engaged in peace

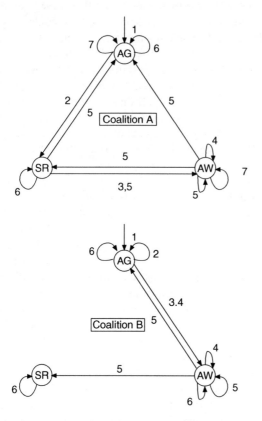

Figure 7.3 Trajectories of two rival coalitions, A (led by the Greek Social Forum)
and B (led by KKE, the Greek Communist Party).

Notes
AW, Anti-war issues; AG, Anti-globalization issues; SR, Summit-related issues.
Numbers on arrows indicate the periods when the corresponding transitions are happening (see
list in text).

mobilizations (due to the impending war in Iraq). In the subsequent months, it
appeared that the strategies of both coalitions were orchestrated and coordinated
in a common pattern of mobilization frames, which included all the three main
protest issues, with which we were concerned. Both coalitions A and B, after
February 2003, channeled their struggles into anti-war, anti-globalization and
summit-related mobilizations. But this common march lasted only until the end
of June 2003, a period after which the contentious collective dynamism of the
spring seemed to deflate into the torpor of a warm summer. (The summer of
2003 was indeed one of the warmest summers of the last decade.)

A last important point we observed was that the three main issues driving
protest events in the period from February to June 2003 were all tuned up to a

shared pattern of mobilizations, if we see them from the perspective of the social movement networks sustaining these forms of collective action. By this we mean that there were no organizations or blocks of organizations 'specialized' in mobilizations on a certain issue but that all organizations appeared in any event on any issue at that time. Undoubtedly, each issue is embedded in a different 'cognitive' frame and it is related to distinctive political and socio-historical causes and effects. However, what we observed in these circumstances was that all the issues were mobilizing and were mobilized by the same (social) network(ed) agencies. Therefore, our data show a spontaneous diffusion and inter-fusion of three social movement mobilizations (peace, anti-globalization and counter-summit), which in other periods and in other contexts might have appeared uncoupled. This situation is an example (based on relational-network arguments) of what Snow and his collaborators have named 'frame bridging' (Snow *et al.* 1986, p. 467), a concept upon which Tarrow more recently has based his notion of 'frame condensation' (Tarrow 2002, p. 22).

Conclusions

This chapter has analysed the impact of national political tensions in mobilizing on a series of more or less related global issues in a national context. The use of concepts of co- and anti-participation allows us to develop a network theory of mobilization combining some classical social network analysis techniques (like affiliation networks and blockmodeling) in a novel way.

In particular, in the context of mobilizations, we tried to focus on internal antagonistic (competitive or overt hostile) friction in the relationships of political organizations with each other. This is manifested by the reluctance of some organizations to participate in protest events when some of their rivals either organize them or just participate in them. Such inter-organizational micro-ruptures are not only responsible for a proliferation of the number of protest events – after all pluralism is a democratic virtue. More importantly, such local micro-tensions might trigger a chain of structural and dynamical reactions which in certain cases could be the cause of macro-patterns of fragmentation or even segregation.

The network paradigm is a very convenient theoretical tool to study such effects of a micro–macro linkage and social network analysis does provide a number of theoretical instruments to be employed in this respect. In particular, by so studying the emergent patterns of organizational heterogeneity and diversity in the context of contemporary mobilizations in Greece, our aim was to trace the strategies that organizations are employing when they are building their alliances in a network. These are all cases of cumulation of strategic interactions through processes of selective coupling–decoupling, interlockings and disjunctions, as well as diffusion, brokerage and condensation of frame alignments. 'Identities come from turbulence,' Harrison C. White argues (2002, p. 1).

Acknowledgment

The authors wish to thank cordially Alexandros Mantzoukas for all his assistance in the implementation of so many scripts, filters and other programmable devices employed in an effort to survive from the computational chaos of SPSS, Pajek and UCInet. Also, our sincere thanks go to Dimitris Kalamaras, Solomon Eleftheriadis, Antonis Polentas and Dimitris Kapetanakis for helping us in collecting and coding the protest events.

Note

1 Newspaper data are a common source of information in social movements research; how relatively appropriate, accessible, biased, valid, reliable, etc. they are is often discussed in the literature in comparison with other quantitative sources of information on social movement mobilization, such as official statistics, yearbooks, police or other authorities archives, etc. (Snyder and Kelly 1977; Franzosi 1987; Olzak 1989; Kriesi *et al.* 1995; Rucht *et al.* 1999; Klandermans and Staggenborg 2002).

References

Bearman, P. and Everett, K. (1993) The structure of social protest, 1961–1983. *Social Networks*, vol. 15, pp. 171–200.

Breiger, R. (1974) The duality of persons and groups. *Social Forces*, vol. 53, no. 2, pp. 181–190.

Breiger, R., Boorman, S. and Arabie, P. (1975) An algorithm for clustering relational data with applications to social network analysis and comparison with multidimensional scaling. *Journal of Mathematical Psychology*, vol. 12, pp. 328–383.

Davis, J. (1967) Clustering and structural balance in graphs. *Human Relations*, vol. 20, pp. 181–187.

de Landa, M. (1997) *A Thousand Years of Nonlinear History*. New York: Zone Books.

Diani, M. (1992) The concept of social movement. *Sociological Review*, vol. 40, pp. 1–25.

Diani, M. (2002) Britain re-creates the social movement: Contentious (and not-so-contentious) networks in Glasgow. Paper for the Conference 'Contentious Politics and the Economic Opportunity Space' in honour of Charles Tilly, University of Crete, Rethymno, 17–19 October 2002.

Diani, M. (2003) Networks and social movements: A research program. In M. Diani and D. McAdam (eds), *Social Movements and Networks: Relational Approaches to Collective Action*, pp. 299–319. Oxford: Oxford University Press.

Escobar, A. (2000) Notes on networks and anti-globalization social movements. Paper presented at the Session on 'Actors, Networks, Meanings: Environmental Social Movements and the Anthropology of Activism,' 2000 AAA Annual Meeting, San Francisco, 15–19 November 2000.

Forno, F. (2003) Protest in Italy during the 1990s. Paper presented at the ECPR Joint Sessions Workshop 'New Social Movements and Protest in Southern Europe,' Edinburgh, 28 March to 2 April 2003.

Franzosi, R. (1987) The press as a source of socio-historical data: Issues in the methodology of data collection from newspapers. *Historical Methods*, vol. 20, pp. 5–16.

Friedkin, N. (1984) Structural cohesion and equivalence explanations of social homogeneity. *Sociological Methods and Research*, vol. 12, no. 3, pp. 235–261.

Heider, F. (1946) Attitudes and cognitive organization. *Journal of Psychology*, vol. 21, pp. 107–112.

Kandel, D. (1978) Homophily, selection, and socialization in adolescent friendships. *American Journal of Sociology*, vol. 84, pp. 427–436.

Klandermans, B. and Staggenborg, S. (eds) (2002) *Methods of Social Movement Research*. Minneapolis, MN: University of Minnesota Press.

Kriesi, H., Koopmans, R., Duyvendak, J. and Giugni, M. (eds) (1995) *New Social Movements in Western Europe: A Comparative Analysis*. Minneapolis, MN: University of Minnesota Press.

Laumann, E. and Knoke, D. (1987) *The Organizational State: Social Choice in National Policy Domains*. Madison, WI: The University of Wisconsin Press.

Lorrain, F. and White, H. (1971) Structural equivalence of individuals in social networks. *Journal of Mathematical Sociology*, vol. 1, pp. 49–80.

McPherson, M., Smith-Lovin, L. and Cook, J. (2001) Birds of a feather: Homophily in social networks. *Annual Review of Sociology*, vol. 27, pp. 415–444.

Macy, M., Kitts, J. and Flache, A. (2004) Polarization in dynamic networks: A Hopfield model of emergent structure. In R. Breiger, K. Carley and P. Pattison (eds), *Dynamic Social Network Modeling and Analysis: Workshop Summary and Papers*, pp. 162–173. Washington, DC: The National Academy Press.

Olzak, S. (1989) Analysis of events in the study of collective action. *Annual Review of Sociology*, vol. 15, pp. 119–141.

Rosenbaum, M. (1986) The repulsion hypothesis: On the non-development of relationships. *Journal of Personality and Social Psychology*, vol. 51, pp. 1156–1166.

Rucht, D., Koopmans, R. and Neidhardt, F. (eds) (1999) *Acts of Dissent: New Developments in the Study of Protest*. Lanham: Rowman and Littlefield Publishers, Inc.

Snow, D. and Benford, R. (1992) Master frames and cycles of protest. In A. Morris and C. McClurg Mueller (eds), *Frontiers in Social Movement Theory*, pp. 133–155. New Haven, CN: Yale University Press.

Snow, D.A., Burke Rochford, E., Jr., Worden, S. and Benford, R. (1986) Frame alignment processes, micromobilization, and movement participation. *American Sociological Review*, vol. 51, no. 4, pp. 464–481.

Snyder, D. and Kelly, W. (1977) Conflict intensity, media sensitivity and the validity of newspaper data. *American Sociological Review*, vol. 42, pp. 105–123.

Tarrow, S. (2002) The new transnational contention: Organizations, coalitions, mechanisms. Paper presented at the Panel on 'Social Movements and Transnational Social Movements,' APSA Annual Meeting, Chicago, 31 August to 1 September 2002.

White, H. (1992) *Identity and Control: A Structural Theory of Social Action*. Princeton, NJ: Princeton University Press.

White, H. (2002) Strategies and identities by mobilization context. Working Paper. Center on Organizational Innovation, Columbia University.

White, H., Boorman, S. and Breiger, R. (1976) Social structure from multiple networks. I. Blockmodels of roles and positions. *American Journal of Sociology*, vol. 81, pp. 730–779.

8 Protest and protesters in advanced industrial democracies

The case of the 15 February global anti-war demonstrations[1]

Joris Verhulst and Stefaan Walgrave

Introduction

Social and political protest is a means by which groups or segments of a given society try to influence public discourse and political decision-making on a variety of issues. In recent years, it has evolved from an 'unconventional' to a 'normalized' form of political action in the Western world. More and more social and political organizations dealing with diverging issues seem to turn to protest as a legitimate and obvious way to display their grievances, and as a common stage in ongoing campaigns (Barnes and Kaase, 1979; Norris, 2002; Norris *et al.*, 2004). And thus, more and more people take part in these protests. Assuming that participation optimists are right when they say that protest activism does not substitute for, but rather supplements, traditional political participation (like voting) (Norris, 2002), this trend surely benefits a country's democratic quality, and it is a very strong indicator of the strength of national civil society.

Yet, in the last few decades political decision-making has progressively been shifting from the national to the global level, and political claims-making is steadily catching up. Increasingly, movements worldwide join their forces in the staging of transnational protest events and ongoing campaigns, aimed at national and international authorities and corporations. Movement scholars did not let this level shift go by unnoticed, and transnationalism steadily became a key field in the study of social movements (see among many others: della Porta *et al.*, 1999; Smith *et al.*, 1997; Smith and Johnston, 2002; Tarrow, 1998). All kinds of social movement-like phenomena are presently studied under the transnational movements' label, yet the most of interest to us here are the transnational social movement *networks* to which Tarrow (2002), della Porta *et al.* (1999) and Duyvendak and Koopmans (1995) refer. These are primarily rooted in and confined to their national political contexts, but coordinate their actions to bring about transnational collective action. Their transnational character lies in '*the links among non-state actors – most notably, in this context, mobilization by contentious social movements that crosses borders*' (Tarrow, 2002: 4). For some scholars, the originality of the present day transnational contention is exactly that it can bypass national political opportunities. Gathering resources, membership and even mobilization can be truly transnational activities, these authors claim (Smith *et al.*, 1997). Yet, all movements have '*both a domestic and an international political environment*' (Oberschall, 1996: 94), and '*nation states are still the principal actors in international relations, and the national political context continues to constitute a crucial filter which conditions the impact of international change on domestic politics*' (della Porta and Kriesi, 1999: 4), and '*national political opportunity structures affect the variable likelihood of transnationalism*' (McCarthy, 1997: 256).

It is exactly this dichotomy that defines the object of study of this article. Transnational contention is defined as: 'the coordinated struggle of actors and organizations from more than one society against a state, international economic actors, or international institutions' (Tarrow, 2002: 7). So to what extent is transnational protest to be considered as truly transnational contention? To what extent do national contexts play a role when it comes to protest goals and targets, and to the kinds of people that are attracted to engage in protest? In tackling these questions, our case will be one of the most recent and most notable examples of such a transnational protest event: the 15 February 2003 (in short: F15) protests against war in Iraq. On that day, millions of people worldwide took to the streets to voice their discontent and to try to prevent the invasion of Iraq in a day of global mass demonstrations. Taken altogether, these were the largest and most momentous transnational anti-war protests in human history (Epstein 2003: 109), all occurring on one single day. In the US the F15 demonstrations were the largest since those against the Vietnam War. In Europe they outshone the 1991 anti-Gulf war protests by far. In some countries, like Spain and Italy, they even dwarfed the 1980s protest against NATO nuclear armament in Europe, which had long been considered an unprecedented wave of political protest (Rochon, 1988). Politicians, commentators, scholars and even movement members and leaders worldwide were startled by the amount and immensity of the F15 demonstrations.

Furthermore, throughout the globe, these protests were all very much alike concerning protest trigger, issue, target and action repertoire, and, obviously, protest timing. Slogans like 'Not in My Name' and 'No War on Iraq' could be heard and read in the streets of cities in all continents. According to many, a 'new superpower' had stood up: since 15 February there were 'two superpowers on the planet: the United States and World Public Opinion' (Cortright, 2004: xi). The fact that the timing, trigger, issue, goal and action repertoires of the 15 February protests seem to have been identical throughout the world makes it an exceptional and unique example of a truly transnational protest event, and many characteristics of the protests and of their organization might lead us to find this to be true indeed. Conversely, there are several important obvious differences between countries (for example the extreme differences in mobilization levels between, for example, Italy and Belgium), which prove that national circumstances do still matter in some way. Furthermore, the different waves of worldwide, or at least European-wide, peace protest in the past have been strongly determined by the specific national political contexts (Ruzza and Bozzini, 2003);

the peace movement has always been a reactive movement and more sensitive to national opportunities than many of its new social movement colleagues.

Data and methods

To grasp F15 in its full essence, we need information on the actual F15 protest participants in different countries. We obtained that information from the F15 protesters themselves, by the use of protest surveys. Interviewing participants at protest demonstrations is not a common research technique. Favre and colleagues even speak of 'a strange gap' in the sociology of mobilizations (Favre *et al.*, 1997). To the best of our knowledge, few studies have used this approach. Most elaborate is the work of the French research team including Favre *et al.*, who developed a method designed to offer all participants an equal opportunity of being interviewed, and which was later refined by van Aelst and Walgrave (1999). In December 2002, a group of social movement scholars in eight nations (Belgium, the Netherlands, Germany, Switzerland, Spain, Italy, the UK and the US)[2] began forging a network in order to survey the expected anti-war demonstrations to be staged in the next few months. They agreed on a common questionnaire and a field work method. In all eight countries, except for Italy, the actual survey process to establish a random sample of demonstration participants was twofold. First, fieldwork supervisors counted the rows of participants, selecting every nth row, to ensure that the same number of rows was skipped throughout. Then a dozen interviewers selected every nth person in that row and distributed questionnaires to these individuals during the actual protest march. The selected participants were asked to complete the questionnaire at home and to mail it back. However, the Italian team followed another sampling track and interviewed participants on trains on their way to the demonstration in Rome. In a later study, we will carefully compare the outcome of the Italian field method with the results of the other country's approach.

This International Peace Protest Survey (IPPS) carried out on 15 February covers a random sample of demonstrators engaged in 11 different demonstrations in eight countries involving 6,753 respondents in total. The overall response rate for the postal survey (Italy with its 100 per cent not included) was more than 53 per cent, with no country's response rate lower than 37 per cent, which is satisfactory for an anonymous survey without reminders.

15 February: timing, set-up and organization

The US plans to invade Iraq had been obvious since early 2002, when President Bush gave his famed speech on the 'Axis of Evil', a 'thread of threat' constituted by the countries of North Korea, Iran and Iraq. From that time on, debates in the US Congress and UN Security Council led to the respective authorization of an attack of Iraq in October 2002 by the US Congress and the approval of UN Resolution 1441 in November 2002. In this resolution Iraq was forced to cooperate fully with UN weapons inspectors, but it did not contain the legitimization of an eventual use of force. UN weapons inspectors were installed in Iraq, but did not get enough cooperation from the Iraq government. In late January, the leaders of eight European countries issued a joint statement in all major European newspapers to promote the invasion of Iraq. By then, the first armed skirmishes had already taken place and had resulted in the first deaths of Iraqi civilians. Near the end of January, it became very clear that war was imminent.

The common slogans, identical date and action repertoires of the F15 worldwide protests did not just appear out of thin air. They were the fruit of months of intensive contacts and preparations. Starting as a European initiative, the call for major demonstrations of 15 February 2003 was launched at the Florence European Social Forum (ESF) in November of the year before. One month later, the transatlantic bridge was forged at a subsequent ESF preparatory meeting, where the newly founded American peace group, United for Peace and Justice, was present, which would become the driving force behind the F15 protest on American soil, and was also to be an avid player in international coordination. After this second meeting, intense contacts between the different national (umbrella) organizations through a few consecutive European and World Social Forums, as well as by means of intensively used e-mail circuits, kept the idea of F15 very much alive. As already mentioned, by the end of January, war seemed inevitable, and it became clear that the demonstration date that was set several months earlier would be ideal. According to the Belgian leader of the peace group 'Vrede' ('Peace'),[3] the final true go-ahead for the set-up of mass demonstrations was actually triggered on 5 February, when the US Secretary of State presented the US evidence of the Iraqi arsenal of weapons of mass destruction; evidence the authenticity of which was contested. So, although the mobilizations were carefully planned and coordinated, it was the presentation of dubious evidence that really triggered them. To conclude: initiated because of the fear for war, and triggered by the effective prospect of war, all protests were planned on the same day, 15 February. Although many smaller protest gatherings took many other forms, the standard action form was that of peaceful protest marches,[4] which took place simultaneously in all large cities throughout the West.

National contexts

Worldwide or global protest evidently means protest throughout different places in the world. Different protest loci also imply, amongst other things, different protest cultures, opportunities and cycles; different issue-relevance and different targets, all of which could have their impact on who would take to the streets. In this section, we will focus on two aspects that had an immediate relevance for differences between different countries in the F15 protests and protesters: the official national government positions towards the possibility of war, and national protest cultures. We have elaborated on the different positions of government and opposition before (Verhulst and Walgrave, 2007); we present a brief résumé of these findings here.

Looking at the different national governments' stances on war, we could more or less place our countries on a spectrum from an official pro-war position to an official anti-war stance, with the US being the most anxious to take up arms and Germany being the most reluctant to do so. In the US, the governing party (Republicans) supported war, as did part of the opposition (Democrats). For the most avid follower of the US in its war race, the UK, governing party Labour (the only centre-left government with pro-war attitudes) was divided on the issue, as was the opposition (split between the pro-war Conservative party and the anti-war Liberal Democrats). In all three war-supporting countries, Spain, Italy and the Netherlands, which are ranked according to their degree of active involvement, government was unanimously in favour of war but received full resistance from all opposition parties. The Netherlands, however, was an exceptional case, since the national ruling coalition had split up and a general election was held, but at the time of the protests it was still unable to form a new Cabinet and the old Government continued to rule. In the three remaining countries, government as well as opposition unanimously opposed the possibility of war, though tacitly in Switzerland, moderately pronounced in Belgium and with international voice in Germany.

A second important country variable is constituted by the variation in protest culture and political climate in the countries surveyed. This is a very complex matter that goes far beyond the scope of this chapter, but European Social Survey and World Value Study[5] evidence can give us some clue of the national protest climate in the eight countries under study. Not the general lifelong indication (that also includes once-in-a-lifetime protesters, 1960s student protesters and 1980s anti-missile protest participants), but the differences in actual protest levels in the one-year period before F15 are of interest to us here. There is a lot of variation on this country variable too; the least active protesters in 2001 were the Dutch (3 per cent) and the British (4 per cent) populations; most active were the Spanish citizens: 16 per cent of them had taken part in a lawful demonstration in the past year. The Germans and Italians (both 11 per cent) were more than averagely active; the Swiss and Belgian somewhat less. When we interpret these numbers in protest terms, they could be regarded as indicators of a phase in a national protest cycle. In Germany, Italy and most of all Spain, protest was 'up'; in Belgium and Germany it was more or less stable (or average); in the Netherlands and the UK, protest seemed to have reached rock bottom in the period under study. Did these differences in national contexts have their effects on who took to the different streets in our eight countries? That is the question that we will tackle in the rest of this chapter.

Inside the F15 protests: dissent or dissenting protesters

Socio-demographics of the F15 protesters

The 15 February protesters were predominantly relatively young to middle-aged men and women with higher education, employed as office workers in the more 'soft' professional sectors. They were, on the whole, the classic example of new social movement (NSM) protesters (Norris, 2002; Norris *et al.*, 2004; Van Aelst and Walgrave, 2001). But between countries, we find some striking differences: only in Belgium did the men outnumber the women, in all other countries the opposite was true, with an exceptional 63 per cent of women in the US. In addition, the American protesters were hyper-educated and relatively older (more than half of them was over 45), and mostly professional workers. At the other end we find the Swiss and Spanish protesters: the Swiss were the youngest and least educated because of a large amount of youngsters and students; the Spanish were also somewhat younger, less educated, and disproportionably many of them were manual workers. Apart from the relatively low educational level of the Dutch protesters, they, as did the Italian, Belgian, German and British protesters, had commensurable socio-demographic profiles that link up with the expected NSM profile. Three countries really stand out: the American protesters with an extreme new social movement profile, the younger and (thus) less educated Swiss demonstrators and the Spanish protesters seem to least fit the NSM profile. Obviously, these socio-demographic variations have specific origins like, for example, specific mobilizing structures. Looking at these differences, we could presume that the American protesters were predominantly mobilized through new social movement organizations, the Spanish relatively more through labour unions, and the Swiss through youngsters' organizations. But first, let us have a look at some more data of the F15 protesters (Table 8.1).

Knowing who demonstrated on F15, the question now is: what was it that drove people onto the streets on 15 February? Who or what were the protests targeted on, what were the protest goals; how did the participants feel about politics in general and about the possibility of war in particular?

Issue-related attitudes and general political attitudes

'What are we fighting for?' was a popular slogan used by the American peace movement after the war had started on 20 March 2003. Yet it is the question 'Who are we fighting against?' that is vital for protest organizers. Very often, the issues on which protest demonstrations are organized are not straightforward, and protestors often attribute the blame for their grievances on many actors and institutions. This is the case not only for the Global Justice Movement, but also for national and transnational peace movements: in both cases the issues and grievances have become relevant because of geopolitical developments and a globalized economy.

Whereas the transnationalist thesis would suppose one joint target, things are likely to be somewhat more complicated. It is reasonable to assume that governments' positions on war in our eight nations are closely related to the different protest targets. In the three war-opposing countries, for example, there was no need for protestors to convince their own governments. So, were the demonstrations in these countries purely expressing solidarity with their counterparts in less peaceful countries? Or did these demonstrators intend to target world public

Table 8.1 Socio-demographic profiles (in %) of the F15 protesters (n = 5,710)

		War initiating countries		War supporting countries			War opposing countries			Average
		US	UK	SP	IT	NL	SW	BE	GE	
	n:	705	1,129	452	1,016	542	637	510	781	
Sex	Male	37	46	50	48	45	49	57	47	47
	Female	63	54	50	52	55	51	43	53	53
Age	0–24	11	16	27	13	19	31	23	26	21
	25–44	35	38	46	48	36	39	38	36	39
	45–64	43	39	25	36	38	26	35	31	34
	65+	11	7	2	3	7	4	5	7	6
Education	None & primary	0	2	2	2	3	9	2	1	3
	Lower second	1	7	11	7	6	23	5	10	9
	Higher second	6	15	41	15	31	26	21	25	23
	Non-univ higher	15	9	6	18	23	13	27	3	13
	University	78	67	40	58	37	30	46	61	52
Profession	Manual worker	6	8	31	9	5	4	4	7	8
	Office/professional worker	50	49	41	33	48	36	53	42	43
	Manager	6	6	0	2	4	2	3	3	3
	Not working/student	15/12	13/20	12/10	11/32	16/21	18/32	17/22	13/35	14/24
	Other	10	4	6	14	7	7	2	1	7
Work	Industrial	17	12	–	18	11	13	12	17	15
	Private services	21	11	–	14	23	25	19	14	18
	Health, education, care	42	47	–	27	43	44	37	33	38
	Government	6	5	–	16	11	12	20	9	11
	Charity	12	11	–	6	10	4	10	8	9
	Other	2	14	–	19	0	2	2	19	9

Source: International Peace Protest Survey (IPPS) 2003, coordinated by M2P, University of Antwerp.

opinion and world leaders? Although we did not include any specific question on protest targets, we do have some variables that might give us a clue (Table 8.2).

The demonstrators' satisfaction with their government's effort to prevent a war is obviously related to the stance these governments took in the war debate. For the protesters in the five countries that were actively initiating or supporting war, this satisfaction was close to zero. In Switzerland, the government position of tacit opposition to the war did not suffice for the F15 demonstrators; the more pronounced oppositional position of the German and Belgian governments, however, was very much appreciated by their national demonstrators. Logically, the more discontent exists on the way the government is dealing with the object of grievance, the more it will be regarded as a target of protest.

In general, over 60 per cent of all F15 protesters believed in the 'efficacy' of the F15 demonstration they took part in. That is, they believed that the protest would improve the chances that outbreak of war could be prevented. Only in Switzerland, the Netherlands and Italy did this figure fall to about one in two. These are interesting results: there were no huge differences in perceived efficacy between protesters who were satisfied and those who were dissatisfied with the efforts of their own government to prevent a war. This means that, although there are no clear national protest targets, protestors do conceive of their protest effort as instrumental in achieving their goals, not mere acts of solidarity with protesters elsewhere. The impact they wished to make was at a transnational level, and not necessarily via their own national government.

The same unifying slogans were chanted in all major cities in the Western world on 15 February showing the connection and solidarity between the different protests in the different countries. Slogans like 'No War in Iraq', 'No Blood for Oil' and 'Not in our Name' served as a common master frame for F15 (Koopmans, 1999). Ruzza and Bozzini (2003) systematically analysed the official discourses of the major 15 February movements in most of the countries under study here and established clear and strong similarities between the organizers' issues and goals, mainly consisting of a new form of moral and legalistic anti-Americanism. The question now is whether this organizational frame was reflected in the motivation of the protesters themselves. Did they share the same aims and did they define the Iraq War issue in the same way? The ubiquity of common slogans and logos would make us expect this to be the case, but the national differences in targets and turnouts make this claim appear less obviously true, not least because targets and goals are logically interrelated. In Table 8.3, we have put together several protest goals, and in Table 8.4 several demonstration themes.

The protest goals in Table 8.3 were propagated by many national F15 organizers on their websites in their mobilizing campaigns. We asked our respondents to rank these goals in order of importance. It is clear that, although all protesters wanted to prevent war, their preferred means to do so (or maybe their sense of reality) differed considerably. Clearly, American and, to a lesser degree, the British and Dutch protesters were most keen on a diplomatic solution of the

Table 8.2 Protest targets and usefulness of the F15 protesters (% agree) (n = 5,710)

	War initiating countries		War supporting countries			War opposing countries			Average
	US	UK	SP	IT	NL	SW	BE	GE	
n:	705	1,129	452	1,016	542	637	510	781	
Demo will raise understanding of public opinion	83	84	84	90	78	84	77	83	4
This demo raises the chance that a war can be prevented	65	65	60	52	55	49	67	63	60
Satisfied with own government's efforts to prevent war	2	0	0	1	1	38	84	68	24

Source: International Peace Protest Survey (IPPS) 2003, coordinated by M2P, University of Antwerp.

Table 8.3 Protest goals of the F15 protesters (percentage 'put as first goal') (n = 5,710)

	War initiating countries		War supporting countries			War opposing countries			Average
	US	UK	SP	IT	NL	SW	BE	GE	
n:	705	1,129	452	1,016	542	637	510	781	
The [country] government must seek a diplomatic solution to the conflict with Iraq	72	58	33	25	56	32	49	44	47
The [country] government must renounce all U.S. military plans against Iraq	17	15	31	35	20	23	21	15	22
[country] should in no circumstances give support to any acts of war in Iraq and the region	12	25	30	37	20	32	21	36	27
The [country] government must urge the Security Council to lift the embargo on Iraq	1	4	9	7	5	15	9	9	6

Source: International Peace Protest Survey (IPPS) 2003, coordinated by M2P, University of Antwerp.

Table 8.4 Anti-war attitudes of the F15 protesters (% agree) (n = 5,710)

	War initiating countries		War supporting countries			War opposing countries			Average
	US	UK	SP	IT	NL	SW	BE	GE	
n:	705	1,129	452	1,016	542	637	510	781	
A war is justified to bring down a dictatorial regime	3	7	7	4	5	4	7	2	5
A war against Iraq is justified when authorized by the UN Security Council	15	17	10	5	14	6	11	8	11
War is always wrong	42	44	88	82	67	79	79	74	67
This is a racist war	48	40	26	31	24	35	31	30	34
The USA is conducting a crusade against Islam	37	42	48	42	45	42	45	37	41
Saddam Hussein and the Iraqi regime are a threat to world peace	31	27	17	21	41	23	20	28	26
The Iraqi regime must be brought down to end the suffering of the Iraqi people	20	52	58	39	76	56	42	45	47
The USA wants to invade Iraq to secure national oil supply	85	83	83	86	79	82	91	85	85

Source: International Peace Protest Survey (IPPS) 2003, coordinated by M2P, University of Antwerp.

conflict. On the following two goals, which point out active support of and involvement in a possible war, all three countries' protesters score below average. So, in their views war seemed to be more justified in relation to the other countries, but first all diplomatic means should have run out. Somewhat the opposite was true for, again, the Spanish and Italian demonstrators. They were not as much concerned with diplomatic solutions for the conflict; they just did not want their governments to be *involved* in any acts of war. Again, this shows that the targets were in the first place national governments, and that targets and goals are closely related. The Swiss obviously wanted their government to give more voice to their non-support. The Belgian and German protesters were first and foremost concerned with a diplomatic solution to the crisis; on top of that the Germans by no means wanted their government to give any kind of support to such a war.

In Table 8.4 we present an overview of the anti-war attitudes of the F15 protesters. Some of these propositions most demonstrators seemed to agree on: in all countries, large majorities of the protesters believed that war has economic motives (getting hold of oil supplies), and practically none of them (between 2 and 7 per cent) approved of war that served to bring down a dictatorial regime. Inter-country variation is also low on the proposition that the US were conducting a crusade against Islam (on average 41 per cent of the protesters believed this was true; in Spain nearly one in two). On average 11 per cent of the protesters believed that war would be justified when authorized by the UN Security Council; with the Italian and Swiss protesters disagreeing the most strongly with this proposition. In the US and the UK, about one in six demonstrators thought this would be justified. The protesters in the different nations more or less agreed on these four propositions. They were the shared frames of the anti-war mobilization.

Yet, confronted with four other questions, respondents answered in more diverging ways. Protesters in the UK, and most of all the US, were more likely to see a possible war as being based on racist grounds than those in the other countries. On the other hand, both countries' demonstrators were less likely to agree with the idea that war is always wrong. Whereas in the other countries on average 78 per cent of the protesters agreed with this, in the US and UK this was the case for less than half. This confirms the finding of Table 8.3 that in both these countries, the F15 demonstrators took to the streets less out of pure pacifism, which could in fact point to more instrumental intended outcomes of their protest participation. The Dutch protesters also took an exceptional position on some propositions. They were the most concerned with the negative influence of the Iraqi regime on world peace (41 per cent of them believed that Iraq posed a threat for world peace) and on the Iraqi people (76 per cent agreed that they should be delivered from their regime, though not by means of war). There was far from general agreement on this latter issue among American protesters – only one in five thought that the Iraqi people would benefit from regime change.

In spite of many similarities, we also find a lot of variance in the anti-war attitudes of the protesters in the different countries. The American, British and

Dutch protesters again had attitudes that diverged from the other countries. Yet, it is not easy to account for these differences. Maybe a closer look at more general attitudes of the F15 protesters can tell us somewhat more (Table 8.5).

On the whole, the F15 protesters considered themselves to be leftists. They were all very much interested in politics, yet in the US this was the case for nearly all protesters, in the Netherlands and Belgium this was true for only about half of them. On average about four-fifths of all F15 demonstrators positioned themselves as being (far) left. In Italy, however, exactly twice the average number of people considered themselves to be far-left. The Italian protesters were also the ones with the lowest belief in the political efficacy of their action and the lowest support for the way the political system in their country operates. In sum, the Italians seemed to have the most radical political beliefs of all the F15 protesters.

Political behaviour and organizational embeddedness

As is clear from Table 8.6, F15 protesters converted their left views into left votes, with almost all of them voting for left and green parties. The Belgian demonstrators seemed to be the greenest voters of all; the American protesters cast the most moderate votes. In the UK, some of the F15 demonstrators had already reprimanded their Labour government (that most 'fits' their profile) by voting for the Liberal Democrats, who took up an anti-war stance, and the Conservatives, who did not. The Italian protesters appeared to have the most extreme political values, and translated their beliefs into voting massively for far-left parties.

Apart from voting, which is the most institutionalized form of political behaviour, the F15 protesters were also very experienced in all sorts of (collective) protest repertoires. In all countries, nearly all of them had engaged in more conventional political action in one way or another. The Italian protesters had the most radical action profiles, followed by the Spanish and Swiss. Four out of ten Italians had engaged in violent action, squatting houses and/or the occupation of public buildings. The Spanish and Swiss protesters were also more than averagely involved in non-conventional and radical action repertoires. In the other countries, radicalism occurred at a more or less uniform lower level. A similar pattern was revealed for past experience in protest participation: Spain and Switzerland displayed an average rate of newcomers to protest, whereas in Italy, where a high proportion of protesters had already taken to the streets ten or more times, newcomers were underrepresented. On the other end of the spectrum we found many first timer protestors in the Netherlands (55 per cent), the UK (50 per cent) and the US (30 per cent) and overall, these three countries had far less frequent protesters. For the Italians, this radical action profile tallies with their more radical political attitudes as described above. For the other countries, things are less clear. Organizational membership and recruitment may provide a more enlightening approach to this phenomenon.

Indeed, since F15 was indeed the outcome of ongoing efforts of substantial

Table 8.5 General political attitudes (in %) of the F15 protesters (n = 5,710)

		War initiating countries		War supporting countries			War opposing countries			Average
		US	UK	SP	IT	NL	SW	BE	GE	
	n:	705	1,129	452	1,016	542	637	510	781	
Interest in politics	A lot	**94**	78	69	86	55	70	53	83	75
Left–Right self-placement	Far left	21	14	19	**44**	17	27	14	14	22
	Left	**64**	63	61	46	**64**	58	62	63	60
	Centre	15	**22**	18	8	17	14	20	**22**	17
	(Far) Right	1	1	1	2	**3**	1	**3**	1	2
Political efficacy[a]	(higher = more)	2.8	2.7	2.6	2.2	**3.2**	3.0	3.0	2.7	2.8
System support[b]	High	18	15	34	3	42	**45**	36	31	26
	Intermediate	20	20	23	6	26	26	**27**	23	20
	Low	62	65	43	**91**	32	30	37	43	54

Source: International Peace Protest Survey (IPPS) 2003, coordinated by M2P, University of Antwerp.

Notes

a This variable was constructed by taking the mean of the answers on several survey questions, all on a five-point scale – (1) completely disagree to (5) completely agree. The questions were (*coding reversed for scale construction): 'I don't see the use of voting, parties do whatever they want anyway*', 'Most politicians make a lot of promises but do not actually do anything*', 'In politics, a lot of things happen that are undisclosed*', 'People like myself do have an influence on what the political authorities do', 'Political parties are only interested in my vote, not in my ideas and opinions*', 'When people like myself voice opinions to politicians, these are taken into account'.

b This variable was constructed with the mean of the answers on two survey questions, all on a five-point scale – (1) completely disagree to (5) completely agree. The questions were: 'I admire the way our political system is organized', 'Most of our politicians are very competent people who know what they are doing'. Subsequently, the variable was recoded as follows: 1–2.75: 'low'; 2.76–3.24: 'intermediate'; 3.25–5: 'high'.

Table 8.6 Relevant political behaviour (collective action experience) and specific organizational embeddedness of the F15 protesters ($n = 5,710$)

	War initiating countries		War supporting countries			War opposing countries			Average
	US	UK	SP	IT	NL	SW	BE	GE	
n:	705	1,129	452	1,016	542	637	510	781	
Political behaviour									
Political action[a] conventional	99	96	91	94	93	98	94	96	95
non-conventional	15	16	28	27	12	28	11	17	20
radical	6	6	13	40	6	12	9	9	15
Protest experience first time	30	49	21	9	54	26	22	23	27
2–5	49	39	53	33	36	47	54	43	44
6–10	12	6	12	22	4	14	14	15	13
10+	9	6	13	36	5	13	10	19	16
Voting behaviour Far left	0	13	27	45	34	2	6	24	18
Green	33	11	3	7	39	21	56	37	25
Social-democrats	65	40	58	44	20	73	26	36	44
Christian-democrats/ Conservatives	1	13	12	1	2	2	6	2	6
Liberal-democrats	0	24	0	3	5	2	6	2	8
Specific organizational embeddedness									
Active organization member (yes)	85	76	54	71	72	73	74	58	71
Active member of:									
Peace organization	28	4	4	7	6	6	7	5	8
Transnational Org. (NoGlobal; Anti-racist; Human rights; 3d World)	41	29	34	27	45	47	42	17	33
Interest Representation Org. (Pol. Party; Union; Neighbourhood group)	68	43	34	40	44	43	48	32	41
NSM Org. (Women; Environmental)	49	26	13	18	44	53	41	36	41

Social Org. (*Charities; Cultural and Educational; Church and Religious*)	71	59	21	35	46	53	41	36	41
Youth Org. (*Sports; Student*)	27	29	23	30	37	33	26	19	26
Informed about demonstration by:									
ads/flyers	18	39	13	16	22	17	28	32	23
posters	41	23	33	15	29	31	34	31	29
organization	26	22	12	31	20	20	31	18	23
website	25	25	6	7	16	11	13	11	13
mailing list	26	8	4	5	8	5	12	6	9
Member organizing organization (yes)	13	11	17	31	22	21	24	16	20
Attended demo with fellow members (yes)	16	12	9	21	11	10	19	12	14

Source: International Peace Protest Survey (IPPS) 2003, coordinated by M2P, University of Antwerp.

Note

a A respondent is categorized as having taken part in *conventional* action, when he/she has indicated to have engaged in *at least one* of the following activities: contacted a politician; contacted an organization or association; contacted a local or national civil servant; worn a pin or hung a flyer/poster/sticker of a political campaign; signed a people's initiative or referendum; signed a petition; taken part in a product boycott; bought a product for political, ethical or ecological reasons; made a donation; contacted or appeared in the media.

A respondent is categorized as having taken part in *non-conventional* action, when he/she has indicated to have engaged in *at least one* of the following activities: set up a petition or gathered signatures for a petition; taken part in a strike; raised funds.

A respondent is categorized as having taken part in *radical* participation, when he/she has indicated to have engaged in *at least one* of the following activities: engaged in a sit-in; engaged in the occupation of a public building/school/university; engaged in the squatting of houses/abandoned areas; engaged in violent forms of action.

groups of contemporary civil society, the question remaining is: in what way and to what degree was civil society (in this case, movements in general) represented on the streets? Were people mobilized through similar mobilizing structures in the different countries? Was there a comparable degree of organizational embeddedness of protesters across all countries?

About seven out of ten F15 protesters were active members of one kind of organization or another, with Spain and Germany falling below average and the US well above average. Globally, new social movements, social organizations (charities, religious and cultural) and interest representation groups (political parties and trade unions) were all more or less equally represented, closely followed by transnational organizations, youth organizations and, to a very small degree, peace groups. The last were firmly represented in the American protests (with more than a quarter of the demonstrators being an active peace group member). When we take a look at the columns of Table 8.6, we see that, leaving aside peace and youth groups, no specific kind of organization was able to dominate the streets in Germany, Belgium, Switzerland and the Netherlands. In Italy and Spain there were very few new social movement members protesting; and in the UK and the US, interest representation and social organizations predominated.

The relatively high numbers of first timers in the UK, US and the Netherlands are not the result of a lesser organizational embeddedness. On the contrary, organizational membership among British and Dutch protesters was about average, and in the US membership was in fact the highest of all, with American demonstrators more than averagely actively involved in all types of organizations. The low and average membership levels in Spain and Italy confirm the finding that organizational embeddedness is not related to protest frequency. Italians were the most likely to be mobilized through an organization rather than through websites and other media, and they were most likely to attend the demonstration with fellow-members of their organization. They were also most likely to be members of organizations directly involved in organizing the action (nearly one in three); which may also be part of the explanation for radical profile of the Italian protestors.

Conclusion and discussion: an inside view on transnational mobilizing

In this chapter we have been scrutinizing the mechanisms by which the 15 February protests came into being, and how they were translated into the different national contexts. Our analyses show that a transnational protest event like F15 by and large mobilizes the same kind of people throughout the West. Yet, it is also clear that there were many differences between protesters from different countries. How can we explain these phenomena?

Let us start with the American and British protesters. Americans were the oldest and the most highly educated of all the protestors, with the highest proportion of women. British protestors were scored second highest on all three of these dimensions. They shared beliefs about the war (not all war, but *this* war was wrong and could only be justified if all diplomatic means had run out) and they had a relatively high number of newcomers among their ranks. The American protesters most closely resembled the socio-demographic profile of a typical new social movement. Their high degree of organizational embeddedness supports and explains this finding. Only this specialized group was able to pass the high participation threshold set by the lack of a supportive domestic political environment in the USA. The British and the Dutch[6] protesters match those of the Americans on many socio-demographic characteristics, on anti-war attitudes and on organizational affiliations. In all three countries, especially in the Netherlands, the number of new protestors was very high. In the UK and the Netherlands[7] this latter observation is not all that surprising, given the fact that protest had reached an absolute low, so that large mobilizations inherently presuppose newcomers. This low protest cycle stage and consequently the high number of first-time protesters may have led similar people onto the streets in both countries. Furthermore, there was a similar political context of divided elites in both countries, with the Dutch government dissolved and an internally divided governing party in the UK, which can be assumed to have a similar effect on protestors' perception of their political efficacy.

The Italian story was very different. The Italians' leftist views and voting, as well as their lack of support for the political system in Italy, could point to the fact that the Italian demonstration was more than just an anti-war demonstration, but served equally to vent the protestors' discontent with the Berlusconi government. The Italian protesters had the most experience with all kinds of (radical) action repertoires. This could be explained by the protest cycle in Italy which produced a high national level of protest experience, and by the fact that the Italian demonstrators were the most likely of all to be recruited through organizations. The Spanish protesters followed a similar pattern, with strongly increasing protest experience (albeit lower than the Italians). Yet, socio-demographically they were more diverse than the Italians, and organizational embeddedness was relatively low in Spain. These were protesters who were surfing the national protest wave, in a climate where protest is an obvious way of displaying discontent. The conflict between the Spanish Government and the opposition over the war was plainly reflected in the demonstrators' political beliefs and behaviour (left voting), but combined with a relatively high level of support for their domestic political system shows that these were anti-government protesters not anti-state protestors. Once again the Spanish protest seems to have gone beyond anti-war feelings and is just as much aimed at national government *tout court*.

The Swiss protesters' profile matched that of the Spanish on many variables, yet we do not have a ready explanation for that. It seems as if the Swiss government's silent opposition to the war provoked the same mobilizing mechanisms as did the overtly pro-war attitude of the Spanish government. Belgium and Germany display a less distinctive profile, but their protesters' lack of clear, national targets, and their contentment with their national governments' positions on the war, had no effect on their own perception of the protest's political efficacy. It appears that the demonstrations in Belgium and Germany were not merely collective signs of solidarity, but in fact transnational efforts for true change in a pressing issue in international relations.

The 15 February 2003 protests were the largest transnational and coordinated surge of simultaneous demonstrations around the world. If there has ever been a transnational mobilization, this was the one. If there has ever been something as transnational civil society at work, it was on 15 February and the weeks and months before that. We have seen how it was carefully planned and initiated, first as a European initiative, then later crossing the Atlantic, and eventually pervading the world. With the extensive use of the Internet, and building on the dynamics of the European and World Social Fora, social movement and civic organizations from all over the world joined their forces to mobilize as many people as possible on this same day, all using the same banners and promoting the same slogans. The results of these efforts were unique, with millions of people taking to the streets in what seemed to be one global demonstration. Yet, in each country, the position taken by the government and the opposition on the war, as well as the stage of the national protest cycle, had their effects on the kinds of people who demonstrated. Thus, transnational protest is profoundly shaped by national circumstances.

Notes

1 This chapter is based on three congress papers, respectively presented in Marburg (ECPR General Conference 2003) Corfu (CAWM, 2003) and Uppsala (ECPR, Joint Sessions of Workshops 2004).
2 Respectively coordinated by Stefaan Walgrave, Bert Klandermans, Dieter Rucht, Michelle Beyeler, Manuel Jímenez, Mario Diani and Donatella della Porta, Wolfgang Rüdig and Lance Bennett.
3 Non-published personal interview by the authors, December 2004.
4 The only exceptions were the Greek demonstrations in Athens and Thessalonica, where a more violent atmosphere and drastic police intervention set a far more dramatic tone.
5 ESF 2001–2002; WVS 2001. We lack US data on the second variable (actual protest experience in the past 12 months).
6 With the exception of their score on education.
7 We lack data for the US.

References

Barnes, S. and Kaase, M. (1979) *Political Action: Mass Participation in Five Western Democracies*, London, SAGE publications.
Cortright, D. (2004) *A Peaceful Superpower*, Indiana, The Fourth Freedom Forum.
della Porta, D. and Kriesi, H. (1999) 'Social Movements in a Globalizing World: an Introduction', in D. della Porta, H. Kriesi and D. Rucht (eds), *Social Movements in a Globalizing World*, Hampshire, MacMillan Press, pp. 3–22.
della Porta, D., Kriesi, H. and Rucht, D. (eds) (1999) *Social Movements in a Globalizing World*, Hampshire, MacMillan Press.

Duyvendak, J. and Koopmans, R. (1995) 'The Political Construction of the Nuclear Energy Issue', in H. Kriesi, R. Koopmans, J. Duyvendak and M. Giugni (eds), *New Social Movements in Western Europe*, London, UCL Press, pp. 145–164.

Epstein, B. (2003) 'Notes on the Antiwar Movement', *Monthly Review*, 55, 3 (Summer 2003).

Favre, P., Fillieule, O. and Mayer, N. (1997) 'La fin d'une étrange lacune de la sociologie des mobilisations: L'étude par sondage des manifestants: fondaments théoriques et solutions techniques', *Revue Française de Science Politique*, 47, 3–28.

Koopmans, R. (1999) 'A Comparison of Protests against the Gulf War in Germany, France and the Netherlands', in D. della Porta, H. Kriesi and D. Rucht (eds), *Social Movements in a Globalizing World*, Hampshire, MacMillan Press, pp. 57–70.

McCarthy, J. (1997) 'The Globalization of Social Movement Theory', in J. Smith, C. Chatfield and R. Pagnucco (eds), *Transnational Social Movements and Global Politics: Solidarity Beyond the State*, Syracuse, New York, Syracuse University Press, pp. 243–259.

Norris, P. (2002) *Democratic Phoenix*, Cambridge, Cambridge University Press.

Norris, P., Walgrave, S. and Van Aelst, P. (2004) 'Who Demonstrates? Anti-state Rebels or Conventional Participants? Or Everyone?' *Comparative Politics*, 2, 251–275.

Oberschall, A. (1996) 'Opportunities and Framing in the Eastern European Revolts of 1989', in *Comparative Perspectives on Social Movements*, Cambridge, Cambridge University Press, pp. 93–121.

Rochon, T. (1988) *Mobilizing for Peace: The Antinuclear Movements in Western Europe*, London, Adamantine Press Ltd.

Ruzza, C. and Bozzini, E. (2003) Anti-Americanism, European Identity and the Second Persian Gulf War Peace Movement, Paper for the ECPR 2003 general conference in Marburg, Germany, 18–21 September.

Smith, J. and Johnston, H. (2002) *Globalization and Resistance: Transnational Dimensions of Social Movements*, London, Rowman and Littlefield Publishers.

Smith, J., Pagnucco, R. and Chatfield, C. (1997) 'Social Movements and Global Politics: A Theoretical Framework, in J. Smith, C. Chatfield and R. Pagnucco (eds) *Transnational Social Movements and Global Politics – Solidarity Beyond the State*, Syracuse, New York, Syracuse University Press, pp. 59–80.

Tarrow, S. (1998) *Power in Movement: Social Movements and Contentious Politics*, Cambridge, Cambridge University Press.

Tarrow, S. (2002) *The New Transnational Contention: Organizations, Coalitions, Mechanisms*, prepared for the Panel on 'Social Movements and Transnational Social Movements', APSA Annual Meeting, Chicago, September.

Van Aelst, P. and Walgrave, S. (1999) 'De Stille revolutie op straat. Betogen in België in de jaren '90', *Res Publica*, 41, 41–64.

Van Aelst, P. and Walgrave, S. (2001). 'Who is that (Wo)man in the Street? From the Normalisation of Protest to the Normalisation of the Protester' *European Journal of Political Research*, 39, 461–486.

Verhulst, J. and Walgrave, S. (2007) 'Politics, Public Opinion and Media on the War on Iraq', in S. Walgrave and D. Rucht (eds), *Protest Politics: Antiwar Mobilization in Advanced Industrial Democracies*, Minneapolis, MN, University of Minnesota Press.

Part III

Social capital and trust within different democratic systems

9 On the externalities of social capital

Between myth and reality

Luigi Curini

Introduction

One of the most intriguing issues in the social capital debate is civic engagement as a (possible) collective good. The claim is that in social contexts with dense networks of voluntary associations, there is an externality effect from membership which contributes to the development of generalized trust that cannot be reduced to individual effects. How exactly this externality occurs – the causal mechanism behind this relationship – is still largely a puzzle. The aim of the present chapter is to offer a way to disentangle individual and aggregate effects of civic engagement from both a theoretical and a statistical point of view. Theoretically, we will introduce a game of incomplete information where the beliefs of the players about the type of actor they are expecting to face matter for producing different kinds of equilibria. Empirically, we will use a multilevel model to link the micro- and the macro-levels of analysis. Our aim is to test three hypotheses. First: are *members* of associations more trusting than *non-members*? Second and third: are *members* (and similarly, *non-members*) of associations more trusting when they live in areas with dense associational networks? A selection of data from the database of the World Values Survey of 1990 is examined: the micro-level is constituted by individuals; the macro-level by regions of different (European) countries.

The theory

Although authors define it in various ways, social capital is, at its core, a set of institutionalized expectations that other social actors will reciprocate co-operative overtures (Boix and Posner 1998). These expectations generate co-operation by making otherwise unco-operative actors willing to undertake those overtures in the first place. In this sense, social capital refers to trusting attitudes of individuals in a community (Fukuyama 1995). It is often argued that one of the main sources of social capital is civic engagement, that is, membership in networks and voluntary associations (Putnam 2000). We can identify two channels through which civic engagement may have an impact on individual trust – the "monitor channel" and the "diffusion channel" (Curini 2004). In the *monitor channel* individuals learn trust and co-operation through involvement in civic groups and organizations where a pattern of repeated interactions allows self-enforcing agreements to be reached by reinforcing norms of reciprocity. This dynamic leads to more trust of fellow members, yet it does not contribute on its own to more generalized trust outside the group.

The *diffusion channel* consists of how this learned trust and co-operation is transferred to other contexts, that is, how these group experiences can be generalized. To better clarify this, two ideas must be introduced. The first one is underlined by Tocqueville in "Democracy in America": the French philosopher noted that people who learn the "advantages of combination" through associating with others used to transfer their attitudes from commerce to politics and vice versa (Jordana 1999). In a similar fashion, Elster (1997) recognizes that every time a person learns concrete behaviour in a specific aspect of life, she will probably transfer this behaviour to other fields.

The second idea is the acknowledgement of the bounded rationality of individuals. That is, where the individual strives consciously to achieve some goals, but does so in a way that reflects cognitive and computational limitations (Kreps 1990). As a result, individuals do not calculate a complete set of strategies for every situation they face. In normal situations, individuals are inclined to use heuristics – "rules of thumb" – which they have learnt over time regarding responses that tend to give them good outcomes in particular kinds of situations. Needless to say, individuals are also able to learn and use norms. The behavioural implications of assuming that individuals acquire norms do not vary substantially from the assumption that individuals learn to use heuristics (Ostrom 1998). Indeed, one may think of norms as heuristics that people adopt from a moral perspective, in that these are the kinds of actions they wish to follow in living their life. As a consequence, individuals will attach an internal valuation – positive or negative – to taking particular types of actions.

In this regard, it is interesting to note that many norms about the behaviour that is expected in particular types of situations are learnt from interactions with others in diverse communities (Coleman 1987). Whenever this is the case, the change in preferences represents the internalization of particular moral lessons from life. Thus institutions (or a particular structure of interaction) may induce specific behaviours – self-regarding, opportunistic or co-operative – which then become part of the behavioural repertoire of the individual.

Summing up: an actor, after having experienced repeated benefits from other people's co-operative actions (as a by-product of the monitor channel), may resolve that she should always initiate co-operative actions in the future (the impact of the diffusion channel). As stressed by Putnam, associations "instill in their members habits of co-operation, solidarity, and public-spiritedness" (Putnam 1993: 89–90). Indeed, when individuals interact frequently, it seems that moral norms justifying patterns of behaviour tend to evolve spontaneously (Platteau 1994). As a result, developing an individual "taste for co-operation" – as the indirect outcome of the mutual (and fruitful) interplay between the monitor and the diffusion channel – implies both acting in a trustful as well as in a trustworthy way *even* in a one-shot game.[1]

"Civic actors", nevertheless, remain conditional actors: as the popular adage reminds us, "fool me once, shame on you; fool me twice, shame on me". Any heuristic or norm is just part of the individual perception of the costs and benefits of a given action; it does not mechanically determine the outcome in any given situation. The assumption is that expressing preferences (i.e. through actions) and not simply holding preferences (i.e. values) is costly. As a consequence, personal preferences matter only when the costs of expressing preferences are low (North 1991). That said, a more realistic code of moral behaviour seems the principle of reciprocal fairness: according to this code, "you behave the way which you would like the others to behave, but only if they actually meet this expectation" (Sugden 1984: 774–777). In other words, civic actors may not only become more trustful and trustworthy, but morally aggressive *too*; i.e. people want to be kind to those who have been kind to them (the positive reciprocity aspect) and to hurt those who have hurt them (the negative reciprocity aspect). This latter point is precisely the indirect effect of civic participation.

This is sufficient to capture an important feature of reality: that in most cases people have the option of making trouble for someone who has upset them. This option can then be utilized to affect the opponent's decision strategically ex-ante. However, retaliation can be quite costly – so costly that actual retaliation may render its executor even worse off than if her opponent was simply allowed to cheat. As a consequence, due to this excessive cost, any self-commitment to retaliate – especially in one-shot interaction – should not be credible to potential exploiters (Dixit and Skeath 1999). Why could the commitment be nevertheless convincing?

Co-operative behaviours can be promoted and sustained if, instead of incurring a cost for the punishment of defectors, agents are rewarded for such an act, implying that they feel some sort of a gain from punishing (Axelrod 1986). People can thus be motivated to sanction fraudulent practices because they feel morally shocked or outraged, sparked by observations of cheating on the part of other individuals. To relieve their feeling of indignation and anger, they are then apparently willing to incur personal costs. Or, to put it in another way, when a person is motivated by indignation, his act of punishment will give him the "pleasure of revenge" (Elster 1989: 69), so that the cost of punishment is compensated for by a pleasurable emotion. Compelling evidence for the existence of what is called "strong reciprocity" comes from controlled laboratory experiments, particularly the study of public goods, common pool resources and other games (Fehr and Gächter 2000), from historical accounts of collective action (Scott 1976) as well as from everyday observation. Our idea is that civic participation can "cradle" these strong reciprocators. This conclusion, as we will show in the next section, has important consequences for the spread of trusting attitudes in a given community.

A game of social capital

In order to bring out the essential points, let us assume a non-repetitive inter-action. Two agents meet for the first time and decide to engage in a single trans-action which requires them to deliver independently something of a certain quality which can only be assessed after delivery. They do not explicitly set out the mutual obligations in a written contract but tacitly expect that the transaction will be correctly completed (this framework can be generalized to any situation involving a Prisoner's Dilemma).

The game is presented in Figure 9.1. In this game, Nature moves first. With a probability of α player X is a SC type (i.e. a social capital player: to be defined below). With a probability of $1 - \alpha$, player X is *not* a SC type. While the value of α is known to both the first mover and the second one, the actual choice of Nature is only revealed to player X. After Nature moves, player X must decide whether to co-operate (C1) or to defect (D1). After making this choice, player Y must then decide whether to co-operate (C2) or to defect (D2). This decision is made with knowledge of the actions of the incumbent but without knowledge of Nature's choice, that is, the X type. Now consider the situation where individual X decides on C1 – for whatever reason – whereas individual Y chooses D2. Agent X then gets the sucker's pay-off while agent Y does well. The former is presumably upset by this and may well decide spontaneously to look out for retaliatory action. Since people are quite inventive, when motivated, in finding ways to get back at others, agent X will usually have the power to spoil things for agent Y. The problem is that agent X can achieve this effect only by himself suffering additional losses in time, energy and resources. In this respect, and according to what we stressed above, we are assuming that only player X_{SC} is able to effectively punish a cheating Y (the decision to punish is not explicitly reported in Figure 9.1. However, it is assumed in the payoffs of the players).

Concerning the preference ordering of the game, some annotations are useful. First, the fact that $(M + S) > S$ means that for X_{SC} punishing someone who cheated her produces a psychic benefit (the pleasure of revenge) that will tend to neglect, or compensate for, a considerable part of the material costs caused by retaliation. This setup is meant to capture the notion of "moral aggressiveness" as a possible strategy for the game. As a consequence, her payoff in terms of utility will be higher than the one expected when only the material impact is considered (i.e. $M > 0$). The high psychic attraction of retaliation for social capital cheated people is what makes the self-commitment to punish a defector a credible move. These benefits have nevertheless a limit: indeed, the fact that $(M + S) < L$ shows that X_{SC} would prefer to defect from the beginning instead of choosing to co-operate and then punishing a cheating Y. Second, cheating imposes a subjective cost on X_{SC} – equal to (G) – which reduces the utility she draws from the mere material outcome of this strategy. Finally, when Y decides to cheat, her payoff (t) decreases as a function of the level of punishment (p) faced. We only require that $r > (t - p)$.

This game has two Bayesian equilibria in pure strategy (see Curini 2004 for

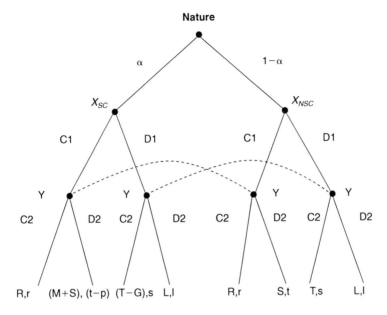

Figure 9.1 A game of social capital.

X_{SC}: $R > L > (M + S) > (T - G) \approx S$; X_{NSC}: $T > R > L > S$; Y: $t > r > (t - p) > l > s$

Notes
T (t) = temptation to defect; R (r) = reward for mutual cooperation; L (l) = loss from mutual defection; S (s) = sucker's payoff; M = pleasure for moral aggressiveness; G = feeling of guiltiness; p = punishment.

the proofs and a discussion). In the first one, all players choose to co-operate. Formally: see Case I.

Case I

(1) player X chooses	(a) C1 if Nature chooses A
and	(b) C1 if Nature chooses B
(2) player Y chooses	(a) C2 if X chooses C1
and	(b) D2 if X chooses D1
(3)	$\alpha \geq \dfrac{t - r}{p}$

This strategy combination is an equilibrium only for a certain set of beliefs: namely, if $\alpha \geq \frac{t-r}{p}$. In other words, for the virtuous equilibrium to emerge, α must increase when the "temptation of defection" (the difference between t and r) increases. However, when the value of p gets higher, even a small chance of meeting an X_{SC} player can be enough to discourage player Y from cheating. When $\alpha < \frac{t-r}{p}$ we have the second perfect Bayesian pooling equilibrium in pure strategies. Now all the players defect. Formally: see Case II.

Case II

(1) player X chooses	(a) D1 if Nature chooses A
and	(b) D1 if Nature chooses B
(2) player Y chooses	(a) D2 if X chooses C1
and	(b) D2 if X chooses D1
(3)	$\alpha < \dfrac{t-r}{p}$

The results above reveal some interesting points. Beliefs and uncertainty play a big role in the game: under certain conditions this uncertainty, coupled with Y's beliefs about X, will lead Y to co-operate. Indeed, the virtuous equilibrium (Case I) is characterized by a X_{NSC} player who bluffs and by a player Y who is unable to discover it. When this happens, player X_{SC} provides to all players a collective good: her ability to punish the one who cheats. This is precisely the *externality* generated by civic engagement: even actors who do not belong to any association are induced to behave in an honest way, given that this behaviour benefits them.

Through this dynamic, past events can play an important role in explaining the success (or the failure) of present and future co-operation. As shown, this is a game of incomplete information. In other words, player Y does not know the true type of player X she is facing; she bases her judgement on a subjective probability before the game begins, but from where do these initial subjective probabilities come? It is reasonable to assume that the beliefs at the beginning of the game about α will be heavily influenced by what player Y observes in her everyday life (Does she observe a lot of civic actions by other players?). She will also be influenced by what she knows about the history of co-operation of a given community (Is her community known to be civic?).

As a result, for a X_{NSC} player, trusting others is safer in a context rich in civic engagement or with a tradition of civic engagement. Vice versa, in communities with a low density of civic associations (Case II), everybody will trust less as an equilibrium response to a low trust civic environment. The final outcome, in both cases, is the result of human action, but not of human design (Hayek 1967).

A comparison between the two cases – I and II – tells us something about X_{SC} player's strategy too. Indeed, she will choose to co-operate only when Y's beliefs are consistent with a virtuous equilibrium. This seems reasonable: the propensity to trust others (to co-operate in a one-shot game) is never an unconditional strategy even for virtuous players. At the beginning of a game, individuals do or do not initiate co-operative behaviour based on their own norms, how confident they are that others are reciprocators (based on any information they glean about one another) and how structural variables affect their own expectations and their expectation of others' behaviour. In this scenario, then, a trustful behaviour is encouraged by an "optimism over the level of optimism" (Seabright 1993), but it is hampered by a generalized pessimism about the chance to meet virtuous players in a given context.

Moreover, the virtuous equilibrium (Case I) is sensitive to shifts in the composition of the population. Once the frequency of individuals who have adopted a co-operative attitude falls below a critical level, the increasingly destructive losses they have to bear in the interactions with defaulting individuals will induce them to reorient themselves. This could be due, for example, to the quickly increasing retaliation costs making the punishment a rather self-defeating strategy (Witt 1986). Given this result, the final outcome will be the equilibrium outlined in Case II. On the contrary, in Case I, X_{SC} player sees her expectations of co-operation confirmed. This process is self-enforcing, since the higher readiness for retaliation and the lower tendency to defect will decrease the probability that retaliation would indeed take place. In turn, this will increase the readiness to retaliate, whenever necessary, and it will reduce, as a consequence, the costs for X_{SC} players to express their conviction.

The research design

From the previous sections we can infer three main hypotheses that would be interesting to test. The first one works at the individual level and the other two hypotheses work through an externality effect.

- The higher the civic engagement of an agent, the stronger her attitude of (generalized) trust should be.
- *Members* of associations (i.e. X_{SC} players) should be more trusting when they live in areas with dense associational networks.
- *Non-members* (i.e. X_{NSC} players) should be more trusting when they live in areas with dense associational networks.

A selection of data from the large database of the World Values Survey (WVS) 1990 is examined to conduct the empirical part: the entire sample comprises 10,571 respondents living in 67 regions. The choice of regions as our macro-level of analysis is a direct consequence of our theoretical assumptions: as stressed, we noted that actors can be influenced by their beliefs about the behaviour of other people. As a result, it seems reasonable to assume that an actor will be especially influenced by the "history of co-operation" of a territorial unit closer to her for two simple reasons: she will probably know much more about it (compared to the history of co-operation of some higher territorial unit); and she will interact more often with other people living in the same region.

In order to ensure the highest degree of comparativeness, only EU European regions with a sufficient number of respondents were selected (i.e. more than 50). The WVS are door-to-door cluster samples (Van der Meer 2003), which means that a sample may be representative for a certain country, but that it is not a random sample on a regional level. The minimum level of respondents per region has then been chosen to minimize this problem. In spite of these omissions, the selection still results in a large regional database (see Appendix).

One option for testing our three hypotheses is to conduct the analysis only at the individual level (Stolle and Rochon 1998). Though an individual level of analysis is useful to answer our first hypothesis (i.e. the relationship between individual civic participation and trust), this approach is unable to take account of the externality of civic engagement at aggregate level. In other words, individual-level analysis cannot capture the external effects of group membership on the trusting attitudes of individuals.

The danger, here, is to commit an atomistic fallacy, since no attention is paid to the context in which human behaviour actually occurs. This context can be defined as the family environment in which the individual lives, or more generally, as a "contact circle" of varying size organized around the individual. In fact this context does have an influence on individual behaviours, and it seems fallacious to consider individuals in isolation from the constraints imposed (and opportunities created) by the society and milieu in which they live (Courgeau 2003).

A second option is to conduct an aggregate analysis, taking the region as our unit of analysis. The main problem, here, is that now we discard all the within-group (i.e. within-regions) variation, which could well mean that a huge share (usually the majority) of the percentage of the variation could be thrown away before the analysis begins. Often, as a result, relations among the aggregate variables are much stronger, and could thus be different from their relationships at the individual level. We cannot therefore rely on a simple aggregate level analysis to disentangle individual and societal relations between civic engagement and generalized trust. In our effort to verify whether an externality actually occurs, we will instead perform a multilevel analysis.

The logic of a multilevel framework

In the social sciences, concepts and data structures can be – and often are – hierarchical. By this, we mean situations in which our dependent variable describes behaviours of individuals; but *where* the individuals are grouped into larger units, such as families or neighbourhoods, and so forth (Bryk and Raudenbush 2002). If our theory (as in the current chapter) states that the outcome behaviour will be influenced by both the person's characteristics and those of the context, then the covariates we are interested in employing should refer to the characteristics of both the individuals and the higher order units.

As noted by Steenbergen and Bradford (2002), comparative researchers in political science have commonly sought to model multilevel data with "dummy variable models", i.e. contextual units such as countries, states, or, in the present context, regions, are assigned dummy variables to capture the entire unit-specific heterogeneity. Though dummy variable models can account for macro-heterogeneity, they contain no substantive explanation of this heterogeneity.

On the contrary, a multilevel model involves performing regressions of regressions. Regressions are done at the lowest – or individual – level (i.e. level-1) in order to predict a level-1 outcome as a function of other level-1 characteristics. These equations are done separately for the various level-2 units, and are referred to as within-unit models. The parameters estimated from the first level (i.e. intercepts and slopes) are then used as outcome variables in the level-2 analysis in which they are modelled as a function of group level variables. At this point, the level-2 units are the units of analysis, and other level-2 character-istics are the independent. These regressions are called between-unit models. Doing this, the "variance around each parameter from the first level is also taken into account in the regression at the next level" (Arnold 1992: 61).

Measurement issues

According to our previous discussion, we are interested in (generalized) trust: in other words, trust towards other people whom we have not known before. To measure this form of trust (our dependent variable) we refer to the question traditionally employed, i.e. "Generally speaking, would you say that most people can be trusted or that you can't be too careful in dealing with people?". On an individual level, the respondents who gave a positive answer in the WVS to this question, stating that most people can be trusted, get a value of 1; 0 other-wise.

Respondents in the WVS were also asked whether they belonged – and if yes, if they were active or inactive members – to any of the following types of organizations: (a) sport or recreation organization; (b) religious organization; (c) art, music or educational organization; (d) labour union; (e) political party; (f) charitable organization; (g) environment organization; (h) professional associ-ation; and (i) any other voluntary organization. As a result, we computed two different sets of indicators of civic engagement at both individual and regional level.

At the individual level, we computed the following variables: $GROUP\_A_{ij}$, i.e. the number of organizations to which respondent i living in region j is an *active* member; $GROUP\_W_{ij}$, i.e. the number of organizations to which respon-dent i is an *inactive* member (this last indicator is computed *only* for respondents who belong as inactive members to at least one association, without being an active member in any of them). We treat differently the two measures of indi-vidual civic participation, because we assume that those who actively participate are somehow more likely to take part in the body of knowledge that is transmit-ted by the organization's activities and, as a result, are more likely to learn to co-operate.

In the present analysis, we also use the distinction made by Knack and Keefer (1997): in other words, groups a, b, c, f, g and i are identified as Putnam-esque groups, i.e. groups with mainly social goals and with a mostly horizontal organi-zational structure; while groups d, e and h are identified as Olsonian groups, i.e. they are deemed representative of groups with mainly political goals and with a mostly vertical organizational structure. The idea behind this distinction is that different kinds of social interactions could also have different consequences for the building of trusting habits. As above, we computed the following variables: $PUTNAM\_A_{ij}$, $PUTNAM\_W_{ij}$, for Putnam-esque type of groups; $OLSON\_A_{ij}$, $OLSON\_W_{ij}$, for Olsonian type of groups.

For each indicator of civic engagement identified at the individual level, we computed a corresponding indicator at regional level, as:

$$M_j = \sum_{i=1}^{n} \frac{M_i}{n},$$

where M_i is the number of associations to which actor i belongs; M_j is the density of civic associations in region j; and n is the number of people living in j (in our case, the respondents in the sample for region j). Substituting M_i for the different indicators of civic engagement, we obtained: $GROUP_j$; $GROUP\_A_j$; $PUTNAM_j$; $PUTNAM\_A_j$; $OLSON_j$; $OLSON\_A_j$. As a result, $GROUP_j$ constitutes a reasonable approximation of Putnam's notion of the density of horizontal networks in a society.[2] In a similar fashion, $GROUP\_A_j$, can be considered as the "strong" density of civic engagement (i.e. the density of people who actively participate). The same applies to Olsonian and Putnam-esque groups.

The statistical results

The background

There appears to exist a large non-random amount of clustering in our data; i.e. there is a significant difference among regions about trusting attitudes of individuals (model A, Table 9.1).[3] Indeed, converting the log-odds to probabilities shows that the plausible interval value lies between (0.203, 0.589) with respect to the probability to answer "yes" to the trust question, an indicator of large variation among regions. One can ignore this aspect of the data only at the peril of drawing incorrect statistical inferences.

Testing hypothesis 1

Belonging to one or more civic organizations – especially if a respondent participates in an active way – matters for trusting attitudes. For example, one

Table 9.1 Trust variance among regions (entire sample)

	Model A
Fixed	
Level 1	
CON	−0.505**
Random	
Level 2	
μ_{0j} (intercept)	0.195**

Notes
*: $p < 0.05$; **: $p < 0.01$.
All estimates are on a logit scale.

standard deviation increment in *GROUP_S$_{ij}$* increases *ceteris paribus* the probability to trust others by 4.4 per cent (from 37.8 to 42.2 per cent: model C, Table 9.2). The difference among the kinds of associations involved appears only when we consider the inactive members. In this latter case, being a member of a Putnam-esque group matters, while being a member of an Olsonian group does not significantly increase the probability to trust others.[4]

Another interesting point, given our sample, is that the variance for each random slope is never statistically significant (this is another added value of using a multilevel model). In other words, the impact of (individual) civic engagement upon trust does not show any change due to a contextual effect. To take an example, whether an active (or inactive) member of a civic group is located in Sicily or in Scotland does not seem to affect the strength of the relationship between individual civic engagement and the trusting attitudes of an actor. This relationship is fixed (unconditional) regardless of macro-variations and contextual changes.[5]

Testing hypothesis 2

As we have already discussed, there exists a significant difference among regions concerning trusting attitudes of individuals. Regional differences, however, are not the same as differences due to contextual factors. Indeed, regional differences may be an artefact: they occur because people living in a region differ from those in other regions. By taking individual characteristics into account, we expect the level-2 variance to decline substantially. If this were the case, we would not need to look for additional contextual factors. In our case, once individual characteristics have been taken into account, the analysis reveals just a slight decrease in level-2 variance (model C, Table 9.2; model H, Table 9.3). In other words, trusting is done by individuals, but they do so in particular contexts, and those contexts influence respondents in their own right. Thus the findings presented here further support the case that similar people living in different types of place tend to trust differently. If trusting attitudes vary significantly at both levels, how should we account for this variance?

For an active civic actor (i.e. an individual who participates as an active member to at least one civic group), living in a civic region seems to matter. That is, she appears to be more trusting than an active civic actor living in a less civic region. Indeed, for our stereotypical respondent in Table 9.2, living in a region with a density of (strong) civic engagement one standard deviation higher than the average value for the sample increases the probability to trust others by 5 points (from 36.6 to 41.6 per cent).

The difference between the encompassing indicator of civic density (*GROUP$_j$*) and the density of strong participation (*GROUP_A$_j$*) is slight, whereas both models including these macro-variables explain a large portion of variance at level-2 (46.8 and 53.6 per cent respectively). Finally, the type of groups matters at level-2: only the density of Putnam-esque groups is significant (model F, Table 9.2). In other words, it seems that regional civic engagement

Table 9.2 The externality of civic engagement on active members

	Model B	Model C	Model D	Model D – bis	Model E	Model F	Model F – bis
Fixed							
Level 1							
CON	−0.116	−0.499**	−0.548**	−0.563**	−0.502**	−0.545**	−0.575**
$GROUP\_S_{ij}$	—	0.204**	0.201**	0.202**	—	—	—
$OLSON\_S_{ij}$	—	—	—	—	0.177*	0.184*	0.196*
$PUTNAM\_S_{ij}$	—	—	—	—	0.213**	0.209**	0.206**
LOW_MID_{ij}	—	0.327*	0.316*	0.317*	0.327**	0.315*	0.314*
$HIGH\_MID_{ij}$	—	0.529**	0.544**	0.563**	0.529**	0.539**	0.566**
AGE_{ij}	—	0.001	0.001	0.001	0.001	0.001	0.001
HK_{ij}	—	0.060**	0.057**	0.046*	0.060**	0.058**	0.045*
SEX_{ij}	—	0.010	0.009	0.022	0.015	0.013	0.021
Level 2							
$GROUP\_S_j$	—	—	1.394*	—	—	—	—
$GROUP_j$	—	—	—	0.398**	—	—	—
$OLSON\_S_j$	—	—	—	—	—	1.945	—
$PUTNAM\_S_j$	—	—	—	—	—	1.312*	—
$OLSON_j$	—	—	—	—	—	—	1.551
$PUTNAM_j$	—	—	—	—	—	—	0.149
PPP_j	—	—	−0.001	−0.001	—	−0.001	−0.001
L_UNEMP_j	—	—	−0.028	−0.018	—	−0.027	−0.004
$PEOPLE_j$	—	—	0.001	0.001	—	0.001	0.001
Random							
Level 2							
μ_{0j} (intercept)	0.140**[a]	0.118**	0.075*	0.064*	0.118*	0.080*	0.061*
Proportional decrease of variance of σ_{00}	—	15.7	46.8	53.6	15.9	42.7	56.7

Notes

*: $p < 0.05$; **: $p < 0.01$.

All estimates are on a logit scale; our sample consists of 2.085 respondents at level-1.

AGE_{ij}, HK_{ij}, $GROUP\_S_{ij}$, $OLSON\_S_{ij}$ and $PUTNAM\_S_{ij}$ are centred around the grand mean.

All level-2 variables in the models have been centred around the grand mean.

a This variance estimate is the basis for calculating the proportional decrease of variance in subsequent models.

Table 9.3 The externality of civic engagement on inactive members

	Model G	Model H	Model I	Model I – bis	Model L	Model M	Model M – bis
Fixed							
Level 1							
CON	−0.316**	−0.643**	−0.636**	−0.679**	−0.677**	−0.687**	−0.705**
GROUP_W_{ij}	–	0.192**	0.193**	0.182**	0.041	0.040	0.041
OLSON_W_{ij}	–	–	–	–	0.270**	0.273**	0.260**
PUTNAM_W_{ij}	–	–	–	–	0.199	0.213	0.212
LOW_MID_{ij}	–	0.192	0.192	0.196	–	–	–
HIGH_MID_{ij}	–	0.504**	0.520**	0.537**	0.512**	0.536**	0.541**
AGE_{ij}	–	−0.005*	−0.005*	−0.005*	−0.005*	−0.005*	−0.005*
HK_{ij}	–	0.034*	0.035**	0.031*	0.034*	0.033**	0.031**
SEX_{ij}	–	0.022	0.016	0.021	0.078	0.072	0.072
Level 2							
GROUP_S_{j}	–	–	0.486	–	–	–	–
GROUP_{j}	–	–	–	0.252*	–	–	–
OLSON_S_{j}	–	–	–	–	–	0.715	–
PUTNAM_S_{j}	–	–	–	–	–	−0.725	–
OLSON_{j}	–	–	–	–	–	–	−0.025
PUTNAM_{j}	–	–	–	–	–	–	0.256
PPP_{j}	–	–	−0.001	−0.001	–	−0.001	−0.001
L_UNEMP_{j}	–	–	−0.005	0.006	–	−0.010	−0.002
PEOPLE_{j}	–	–	0.001	0.001	–	0.001	−0.001
Random							
Level 2							
μ_{0j} (intercept)	0.106**a	0.080**	0.079*	0.060*	0.083**	0.074*	0.065*
Proportional decrease of variance of σ_{00}	–	24.4	25.3	42.5	21.3	29.6	38.2

Notes

*: $p < 0.05$; **: $p < 0.01$.

All estimates are on a logit scale; our sample consists of 2,678 respondents at level-1.

AGE_{ih}, HK_{ij}, GROUP_W_{ij} OLSON_W_{ij} and PUTNAM_W_{ij} are centred around the grand mean.

All level-2 variables in the models have been centred around the grand mean.

a This variance estimate is the basis for calculating the proportional decrease of variance in subsequent models.

must be strong (i.e. it must present a high level of activism among its members) and must be rich in Putnam-esque groups to be able to generate the highest externality.[6] The impact of regional civic density is statistically significant *even* when we consider the inactive members (Table 9.3), but in this case only the level of the encompassing indicator of civic density is able to generate a significant and positive externality.[7]

Figure 9.2 compares the impact of the encompassing indicator of regional civic density ($GROUP_j$) for both active and inactive members,[8] differentiated by belonging to the working or to upper-middle class. In every possible situation, active members are more likely than inactive members to trust another. Second, the probability of trusting others increases when the civic density increases, regardless of being an active or inactive member. Third, belonging to a considerable number of associations, even if in an inactive way, is a stronger indicator of trust than belonging to fewer associations but in an active way (i.e. the quantity of participation matters more than the quality of it, *ceteris paribus*). Nevertheless, this difference decreases when we move along the *x*-axis (i.e. when the civic density grows). Finally, in regions rich in civic density, being a highly

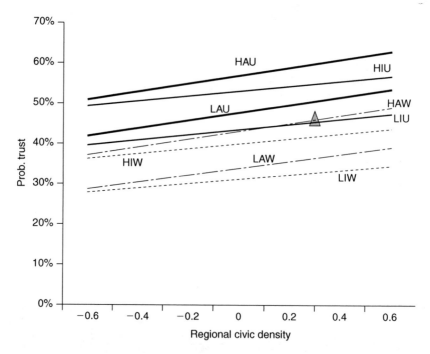

Figure 9.2 The externality of civic engagement on active and inactive members.

Notes
HAU: high activist – upper class; LAU: low activist – upper class; HIU: high inactivist – upper class; LIU: low inactivist – upper class; HAW: high activist – working class; LAW: low activist – working class; HIW: high inactivist – working class; LIW: low inactivist – working class.

active member seems, at least in one case, to be a stronger indicator of trust than belonging to the upper-middle class (see the triangle in Figure 9.2).

Testing hypothesis 3

The externality effect of civic engagement does not seem to hold for non-member respondents, in spite of a significant variance of trusting attitudes among regions (Table 9.4). No macro-indicator of social capital is statistically significant (although always with the expected sign). This result suggests the need to look for other relevant (macro) variables. For example, a major source of (interpersonal) trust is government's credible commitment to uphold property rights and to protect constituents from each other (Hooghe and Stolle 2003), which is, of course, the traditional Hobbesian explanation.

As a result of our analysis, we are left with a puzzle. How to explain the fact that there is an externality effect just for civic actors (both active and inactive)? Here we can only offer some clues for future research. First of all, if (a) the trust question employed by the WVS largely measures the experiences people have in dealing with other people; if (b) there is a direct relationship between belonging to a civic group and trusting attitudes (as seems the case); and if (c) "social capital actors" (the X_{SC} players in the game) are somehow able to discriminate among individuals (Frank 1988), then we have a first idea to build upon. Alternatively, we can suppose that civic actors are able to form clusters of homogeneous subpopulations where they mainly interact with people like themselves (Witt 1986). Both options would add a layer of complexity to the game introduced previously.

Conclusion

The main question of this chapter was whether civic engagement had aggregate effects on generalized trust that could not be explained by the sum of individual level effects. In the first part we proposed a theoretical model to explain why learning to co-operate in a civic organization can have external consequences. The idea was that an actor, through his/her civic engagement, becomes not only trustful and trustworthy, but even, and at least under certain conditions, morally aggressive. With regard to this we employed a simple game where the uncertainty of a player regarding the true type of her opponent could lead to a virtuous equilibrium of mutual co-operation.

In the empirical part of the chapter we introduced a multilevel model based on the database of the World Values Survey of 1990 to investigate the interaction between the micro-level (i.e. the respondents) and the macro-level (i.e. the regions) without incurring the usual problems of ecological – and atomistic – fallacy. Although we estimated rather limited models, these results lead us to the conclusion that participation in at least some kinds of voluntary associations has indeed some externality effects on the level of individual trust. However, our results are not entirely conclusive given our theory.

Table 9.4 The externality of civic engagement on non-members

	Model N	Model O	Model P	Model Q	Model R	Model S
Fixed						
Level 1						
CON	−0.774***	−0.852**	−0.848**	−0.847**	−0.845**	−0.844**
LOW_MID_{ij}	–	0.063	0.058	0.056	0.060	0.061
$HIGH\_MID_{ij}$	–	0.211*	0.212*	0.210*	0.219*	0.219*
AGE_{ij}	–	0.005*	0.005*	0.005*	0.005*	0.005*
HK_{ij}	–	0.056 **	0.056**	0.056**	0.054**	0.054**
SEX_{ij}	–	−0.075	−0.074	−0.074	−0.072	−0.072
Level 2						
$GROUP\_S_j$	–	–	0.196	–	–	–
$OLSON\_S_j$	–	–	–	0.877	–	–
$PUTNAM\_S_j$	–	–	–	0.088	–	–
$GROUP_j$	–	–	–	–	0.151	–
$OLSON_j$	–	–	–	–	–	−0.133
$PUTNAM_j$	–	–	–	–	–	0.224
PPP_j	–	–	−0.001	−0.001	−0.001	−0.001
L_UNEMP_j	–	–	−0.019	−0.018	−0.014	−0.017
$PEOPLE_j$	–	–	0.001	0.001	0.001	0.001
Random						
Level 2						
μ_0(intercept)	0.135 **	0.142**	0.148**	0.151**	0.146**	0.149**

Notes
*: $p < 0.05$; **: $p < 0.01$.
All estimates are on a logit scale; our sample consists of 5.808 respondents at level-1.
AGE_{ij} and HK_{ij} are centred around the grand mean.
All level-2 variables in the models have been centred around the grand mean.

Indeed, a higher density of associations (especially of a Putnam-esque type, i.e. the kind of associations reasonably richer in terms of weak ties) seems to sustain the diffusion of trust within a given community. Nevertheless, this effect appears to be largely *one-sided*: it is felt only by those who belong (as active or inactive members) to at least one organization. As a result, a public good – in terms of a more "trusting atmosphere" – is produced and consumed by everyone, even by those who (like the non-members) do not seem to be (directly) influenced by the above dynamic. The interesting point is that non-members keep showing a significant variance at regional level in regard to their trusting attitudes. Finding a more comprehensive answer should be one of the most interesting challenges ahead for the social capital debate.

Appendix: list of regions

Austria
Wien
Niederösterreich
Burgenland
Steiermark
Kaernten
Oberösterreich
Salzburg
Tirol
Vorarlberg
Belgium
Antwerpen
Liege
Reg.Bruxelles-Cap./
   Brussels Hfdst.Gew.
West-Vlaanderen
Oost-Vlaanderen
Limburg
Hainaut
Namur
France
Ile de France
Germany
Bayern*
Hessen*
Niedersachsen*
Nordrhein-Westfalen*
Rheinland-Pfalz*

Schleswig-Holstein*
Italy
Piemonte
Liguria
Lombardia
Veneto
Emilia-Romagna
Toscana
Umbria
Marche
Lazio
Campania
Puglia
Basilicata
Calabria
Sicilia
Netherlands
Overijssel
Gelderland
Utrecht
Noord-Holland
Zuid-Holland
Noord-Brabant
Limburg
Portugal
Algarve
Madeira

Spain
Andalucia
Comunidad Valenciana
Extremadura
Galicia
Madrid
Murcia
Navarra
Pais Vasco
Aragon
Asturias
Baleares
Canarias
Cantabria
Castilla-La Mancha
Castilla-Leon
Catalana
United Kingdom
Wales*
Scotland*
East Anglia
North Ireland

*= NUTS 1; NUTS 2 otherwise (The Nomenclature of Territorial Units for Statistics [NUTS] is a geocode standard developed by the European Union for referencing the administrative division of countries for statistical purposes).

Notes

1 The widely discussed relationship between bonding associations and personalized trust on one side, and bridging associations and generalized trust on the other side, is clearly related to the distinction between the monitor and the diffusion channels of civic engagement. Indeed, persons who participate in bridging associations, i.e. associations rich of weak ties, are presumably even the ones who can benefit most from the mutual (and fruitful) interplay between the two channels as discussed in the text, compared with people who join just bonding associations (i.e. associations rich of strong ties). See Curini (2004) for details.

2 In more detail, $GROUP_j$ measures the average number of civic associations present in a region, *regardless* of the quality of individual participation (active or inactive membership). We call it the "encompassing indicator of civic density".

3 Model A shows a reliability estimate for the intercept of 0.829, which indicates that the sample means tend to be quite reliable as indicators of the true regional means on trusting attitudes. A similar result applies to all the other models employed.

4 Among the control variables, education (HK_{ij}: age in years at which the respondent completed her highest education), income (operationalized by two dummy variables: LOW_MIDDLE_{ij} and $UPPER\_MIDDLE_{ij}$, according to whether the respondent describes herself as belonging to the lower/middle class or to the upper middle class/upper class) and, to a lesser extent, age (AGE_{ij}), matter. Controlling for gender (SEX_{ij}) is never significant.

5 The same result applies to every model we fitted. For simplicity we do not report the coefficients for the random slopes in the tables.

6 Besides the civic engagement variables, we controlled for the impact of three other macro-variables: the power purchasing parity per capita (variable: PPP_j), the rate of (long term) unemployment (L_UNEMP_j) and the number of residents in a given region ($PEOPLE_j$). No control variable shows a significant impact. Source: *Panorama of EU's Countries and Regions 1987–1996*, About Beyond 20/20, cd-rom release 4. All data are referred to 1990.

7 Once we split between Olsonian and Putnam-esque groups (i.e. model M and M-bis), the regional civic density does not show a significant impact on the trust variable. This could be due to a partial collinearity effect between the two independent variables. Indeed, $PUTNAM_j$ alone consistently presents a significant impact on trust.

8 "High active" and "high inactive" means belonging to the respective averaged higher quartiles of the distribution in the sample. Vice versa, "low active" and "low inactive" means belonging to the respective averaged lower quartiles of the distribution in the sample.

References

Arnold, C. (1992) An Introduction to Hierarchical Linear Models, *Measurement and Evaluation in Counseling and Development*, 25: 58–90.

Axelrod, R. (1986) An Evolutionary Approach to Norms, *American Political Science Review*, 80 (4): 1095–1111.

Boix, C. and Posner, D. (1998) Social Capital: Explaining Its Origins and Effects on Government Performance, *British Journal of Political Science*, 28 (4): 686–693.

Bryk, A. and Raudenbush, S. (2002) *Hierarchical Linear Models*, Newbury Park: SAGE.

Coleman, J. (1987) *Norms as Social Capital*, in G. Radnitzky and P. Bernholz (eds), *Economic Imperialism: The Economic Approach Applied Outside the Field of Economics*, New York: Paragon, pp. 135–155.

Courgeau, D. (2003) From the Macro-micro Opposition to Multilevel Analysis in

Demography, in D. Courgeau (ed.), *Methodology and Epistemology of Multilevel Analysis*, Dordrecht: Kluwer, pp. 43–91.

Curini, L. (2004) *Il dilemma della cooperazione*, Milano: V&P Università.

Dixit, A. and Skeath, S. (1999) *Games of Strategy*, New York: W.W. Norton & Company.

Elster, J. (1997) *Egonomics*, Barcelona: Gedisa.

Elster, J. (1989) Social Norms and Economic Theory, *Journal of Economic Perspectives*, 3 (4): 99–117.

Fehr, E. and Gätcher, S. (2000) Cooperation and Punishment, *American Economic Review*, 90 (4): 980–994.

Frank, R. (1988) *Passions Within Reasons*, New York: W.W. Norton & Company.

Fukuyama, F. (1995) *Trust*, London: Hamish Hamilton.

Hayek, F. (1967) The Results of Human Action but Not of Human Design, in *Studies in Philosophy, Politics and Economics*, Chicago: Chicago University Press, pp. 96–105.

Hooghe, M. and Stolle, D. (2003) *Generating Social Capital*, New York: Palgrave Macmillan.

Jordana, J. (1999) Collective Action Theory and the Analysis of Social Capital, in J.W. Van Deth *et al.* (eds), *Social Capital and European Democracy*, London: Routledge, pp. 45–71.

Knack, S. and Keefer, P. (1997) Does Social Capital have an Economic Payoff? A Cross-country Investigation, *Quarterly Journal of Economics*, 112: 1251–1288.

Kreps, D. (1990) *A Course in Microeconomic Theory*, New York: Harvester.

North, D. (1991) *Institutions, Institutional Change and Economic Performance*, Cambridge: Cambridge University Press.

Ostrom, E. (1998) A Behavioural Approach to the Rational Choice Theory of Collective Action, *American Political Science Review*, 92 (1): 1–22.

Platteau, J. (1994) Behind the Market Stage Where Real Societies Exist: Part I, *Journal of Development Studies*, 3: 533–577.

Putnam, R. (1993) *Making Democracy Work: Civic Traditions in Modern Italy*, Princeton, NJ: Princeton University Press.

Putnam, R. (2000) *Bowling Alone*, New York: Simon & Schuster.

Scott, J. (1976) *The Moral Economy of the Peasant: Rebellion and Subsistence in Southeast Asia*, New Haven, CT: Yale University Press.

Seabright, P. (1993) Is Cooperation Habit-Forming?, in P. Dasgupta and K. Maler (eds), *The Environment and Emerging Development Issues*, Oxford: Clarendon Press, pp. 283–307.

Steenbergen, M. and Bradford, S. (2002) Modeling Multilevel Data Structures, *American Journal of Political Science*, 46 (1): 218–237.

Stolle, D. and Rochon, T. (1998) Are All Associations Alike?, *American Behavioural Scientist*, 42 (1): 47–66.

Sugden, R. (1984) Reciprocity: The Supply of Public Goods Through Voluntary Contributions, *The Economic Journal*, 94: 772–787.

Van der Meer, J. (2003) Rain or Fog? An Empirical Examination of Social Capital's Rainmaker Effects, in M. Hooghe and D. Stolle (eds), *Generating Social Capital*, New York: Palgrave Macmillan, pp. 133–152.

Witt, U. (1986) Evolution and Stability of Cooperation without Enforceable Contracts, *KYKLOS*, 39: 245–266.

10 Creating social capital and civic virtue

Historical legacy and individualistic values – what civil society in Spain?

Rafael Vázquez García

Introduction

Since the restoration of democracy, Spain seems to have become a modern capitalist economy, a liberal democratic state and a tolerant, pluralist society, based in principle on respect for values common to other Western societies, including individual freedom and human rights. This has been the result of a deep institutional and cultural transformation of which the most exceptional aspect has been the democratic transition (Pérez-Díaz, 1993). However, it is not so clear that the set of values, attitudes and feelings that constitute political culture has been transformed in the same positive direction. In this chapter we argue that current Spanish political culture still contains many elements of subjection.

While a flourishing market economy may make a liberal democracy stable (Lipset, 1959), what makes a truly civil society, and not only liberal and formally democratic, is a wider range of aspects than the market economy (Diamond, 1997). We can observe the outcomes of a successful transition to democracy in Spain in many aspects: political and governmental stability, a reasonable party system developing towards a moderate two-party system without extremist parties, low poverty levels and so on (Pérez-Díaz, 1996). But what about civil society? What is the degree of political and social engagement in Spain? How strong is civic democracy in Spain? How much civic culture can we find in Spain?

Hypothesis

We argue that the return of democracy has not produced a largely more engaged and civic civil society in Spain. We have to take into account historical consequences and obstacles and current structural difficulties, related to the individualistic values that shape the features of civil society in Spain, in terms of both social capital and civic virtue. This involves reviewing both historical forces and contemporary factors and their effects on civil society. We believe that both factors are necessary and complementary in order to obtain a clear and accurate description of civil society at the present time. Some scholars maintain that the capability of a society to make cooperation among its members possible is determined by its historical experience. In the light of this approach, we will try to test three hypotheses:

1   Despite the increase in social capital since the restoration of democracy in Spain, it still remains in low intensity equilibrium. Some elements of political culture (interest in politics, satisfaction with democratic performance, institutional and social distrust, etc.) have remained stable, with similar attitudes and values over time. This seems to be due to a certain cultural legacy of norms and values, transmitted from generation to generation by political socialization.
2   There is a lower level of social involvement in Spain. Although the membership and participation in voluntary associations and intermediary organizations are relatively similar to most other Western nations, the extent of involvement is always lower. Spaniards are less likely to belong, participate, donate money or work in voluntary organizations than citizens in any of the other countries.
3   At the micro-level those who are explicitly involved in associations present more civic virtues, such as more interest, higher capability to understand political issues, greater participation in politics or being more informed (Morales, 2004: 498). On the other hand, at least at aggregate level, private and individualistic values play a role in creating civic virtue, which implies a greater social and political engagement, since earlier politicization encouraged people to relate to each other.

We will divide our chapter into two main sections. We start with a theoretical framework exploring Spanish political culture since the 1970s. We demonstrate the main features that define the historical evolution of Spanish society, tracing the continuity from the period of dictatorship through to the period of political transition. We identify variables and indicators pointing to the presence of a set of elements which determine the success in developing a stable democracy (Inglehart, 1988; Diamond, 1998) and a more participative civic society (Diamond, 1997). At the same time, we seek to mark theoretically existing connections between civil society, social capital, civic organizations and civic virtues, connections which make it possible to improve the quality of democracy.

In the second part, our three hypotheses will be tested against our empirical findings. First, we will give an analysis of the main features of political culture in the last decades. Second, we will describe socio-political participation in Spain, comparing it with the rest of Europe, and analysing the type and degree of involvement. Finally, we will try to find substantive ties between several socio-political indicators and voluntary social engagement. This chapter is based on survey data, most of which comes from the World Values Survey (WVS), the European Social Survey (ESS) (2002–2003) and the CIS (*Centro de Investigaciones Sociológicas*).

Theoretical framework

Historical legacy and political culture in Spain

Our point of view is that, as we will see later, historical tradition is very important in the understanding of the present political culture (Almond and Verba,
1963; Putnam, 1993). The Francoist legacy, political transition and the first
years of democracy are undoubtedly necessary for looking at present day
Spanish society. As has been said

> there is a kind of historical singularity made out of a vast array of beliefs,
> customs and attitudes that are the legacy of a set of other historical tradi-
> tions and that could be considered a reflection of historical backwardness
> and inconsistent with the rules and values of an open society.
>
> (Pérez-Díaz, 1990: 26–27)

Following López-Pintor, Spanish political culture is determined by five
important phenomena (López-Pintor, 1982: 74):

1   Civil war (1936–1939): people who lived through it, have transmitted it as
    an experience of victory or defeat. As a result ideological cleavages
    (left/right, secular/religious) have marked the years that followed (Pérez-
    Díaz, 2003).
2   Authoritarian regime: the Francoist regime promoted anti-democratic and
    anti-partisan values and customs, thereby demobilizing any open and free
    civic society (Gracia García and Ruiz Carnicer, 2001; López and
    Aranguren, 1976; López-Pintor and Buceta, 1975). Dictatorship left a
    legacy of disinterest in politics, apathy, political scepticism, a terrible lack
    of confidence in political elites and an estrangement from the decision-
    making process. Political and social circumstances in Spain over the last
    150 years have hardly promoted the development of voluntary associations.
    Political life has been characterized by an extraordinary discontinuity.
    "These problems were aggravated by systematic electoral fraud, the exten-
    sive functioning of *caciquismo*, and the increasingly widespread feeling of
    alienation from the political system" (Torcal and Montero, 1999: 178).
3   The process of industrialization in the 1970s produced deep changes in eco-
    nomic activity, incomes policy, urbanization, social stratification, and in
    education and lifestyles.
4   Since the early 1960s the political breakdown of the regime emphasized its
    limited legitimacy and popular support.
5   The gradual and peaceable installation of democracy expanded freedom and
    civil rights, and confirmed the new political rules.

Once democracy came into existence, however, political culture was characterized by:

1   The legitimacy of a rule-bound political system, but dissatisfaction with its performance. That is, the result of the divergence between generally positive values towards the political system, and negative perceptions of the way it works.
2   Political disaffection. This can be considered to be the result of a distrusting and suspicious vision of all human relations, acquired at an early stage of the socialization process (Montero *et al.*, 1997: 18).
3   Disinterest and lack of knowledge about politics.
4   Low political involvement.
5   Ideological moderation.

To sum up, we can say that the general lack of interest in politics does not affect the legitimacy of democracy and democratic institutions, giving support to Almond and Verba's theory that democratic systems with high legitimacy and stability are compatible with a citizenry scarcely involved in political and social action (Almond and Verba, 1963).

Civic society, social capital and civic virtue

Warren places civil society halfway between political society and the public sphere on the one hand, and "intimate spaces" on the other hand, where family and friendship are the dominant elements (Warren, 2000: 57; Table 10.1). Civil society is the domain of social organization where voluntary associative relations are dominant, and political mediating associations are excluded.

What makes civil society "civil" is the fact that it is a sphere within which citizens may freely organize themselves into groups and associations at various levels. We also use the concept here because of its great explanatory potential for the theory of the political, as well as for the theory of the transition and consolidation of democracies. Most theorists since Tocqueville have focused on the importance of civic society, and specially, voluntary associations as vital to the performance and life of democracy (Selle and Stromsnes, 2001: 135). For current political theorists

> typical face-to-face deliberative activities and horizontal collaboration within voluntary associations far removed from the political sphere, such as sports clubs, agricultural cooperatives, or philanthropic groups, promote interpersonal trust, fostering the capacity to work together in future, creating the bonds of social life that are the basis for civil society and democracy.
>
> (Norris, 2002)

In addition, civic society based on associations makes citizens themselves stronger, in a democratic way, by providing them with civic and political skills, and improving their sense of efficacy. "Associations work as schools of democracy, and their development should, therefore, be promoted for their positive consequences for democracy as a whole" (Morales, 2002: 498). Civic virtue

Table 10.1 Locating civil society

Closeness of social relations	Means of social coordination		
	Legal coercion	*Social (norms and communication)*	*Money*
Distant	States	Mediating spaces: publics	Markets
	Mediating associations: "political society"		Mediating associations: "economic society"
Intermediate		Civil society. Pure associative relations	
Intimate		Families, friendship	

Source: Warren (2000: 57).

transcends the concept of social capital and combines some more elements, related to democratic theory and the republican tradition (Barber, 1984). As Warren notes "the list of potential civic virtues is a long one: attentiveness to the common good and concerns for justice; tolerance of the views of others, trustworthiness, willingness to participate, deliberate and listen; respect for the rule of law, and respect for the right of others" (Warren, 2000: 73).

Social involvement is frequently associated with the concept of social capital (Putnam 1993, 1995, 2000). At the core of the conventional definition of social capital is membership in voluntary associations, which may be dedicated to a variety of purposes ranging from the recreational or social to the religious or political. Social capital refers to the stock of active connections among people: trust, mutual understanding, and shared values and behaviours that bind the members of human networks and communities and, particularly, members of socio-political associations and groups (Cohen and Prusak, 2001: 4).

Are all associations alike in their democratizing effects or are there elements of group life which are specifically beneficial for generating these norms of reciprocity and trust? In this sense, we can distinguish, following Putnam (2002) and Zmerli (2002) among others, between bonding and bridging social capital. The former refers to the value assigned to social networks between homogeneous groups of people and the latter to that of social networks between socially heterogeneous groups (Putnam, 2000: 22–23). The distinction is useful in highlighting how social capital may not always be beneficial for society as a whole. Horizontal networks of individual citizens and groups that enhance community productivity and cohesion are said to be positive social capital assets, whereas self-serving gangs and hierarchical patronage systems that operate at cross purposes to societal interests can be thought of as negative social capital burdens on society. What is clear is that the development of civic attitudes is mostly seen as being located in several forms of social interactions, of which membership in voluntary organizations could be the most important (Hooghe and Stolle, 2003: 3).

Empirical evidence

Hypothesis 1: historical legacy and political culture

As discussed above, the Spanish tradition of political culture can be explained as a function of several elements, which can be summed up as follows: democratic cynicism, political dissatisfaction, disinterest and low levels of involvement. Linz refers to legitimacy as the belief that existing political institutions, in spite of their faults and defects, are better than any alternative system (Linz, 1988: 65).

Spaniards who agree with the statement "democracy is the best system for a country like ours" are constantly increasing. Even though democracy as an ideal was not absolutely fixed in Spanish public opinion in the early 1980s, democratic legitimacy has been completely consolidated since the end of the decade and, even more, since the middle of 1990s. Support for democracy rose from two-thirds to more than three-quarters by 2002, affirming the superiority of democracy over any other political system. Levels of support for democracy in Spain are, in fact, similar to those found in other Western societies. The indicator "satisfaction with democratic performance" measures a felt discrepancy between democratic norms and the actual democratic process. Satisfaction with democratic praxis is always lower than legitimacy. In 2002 only 56 per cent of citizens declared that they were very or quite satisfied with democratic performance. Almost 20 years before, the percentage was not that much lower at 43 per cent. This combination of legitimacy and dissatisfaction is a phenomenon that Maravall has called "democratic cynicism", which seems to be common to other Mediterranean countries as well (Montero and Morlino, 1993). People put a high rating on the attractiveness of democracy as a form of government, but at the same time place a low rating on the performance of their particular democratic regime.

On the other hand, interest in politics is the most frequently used indicator to measure the level of subjective political implication. According to the data, Spaniards generally speaking are less likely to be interested in politics than the inhabitants of most other European countries. Levels of political interest have been extremely low in Spain, despite the enormous political, economic and institutional changes witnessed over the last 25 years. The only relative increase took place during the first two years of the transition (Sastre García, 1997: 79). Since the early 1980s around 50 to 60 per cent of Spaniards declared that they had no (or not very much) interest in politics. Only between 15 and 20 per cent of citizens were "very" or "quite" interested in politics. The continuity of the figures over time is also evident. In 1960, during the dictatorship, 21 per cent people were "very" or "quite" interested in politics, 20 per cent in 1971, 27 per cent in 1980, 22 per cent in 1989 and 24 per cent in 1990.

This low level of interest in politics is accompanied by a relatively low electoral turnout. Abstention levels have gone above 30 per cent in general elections and 40 per cent in some European elections, with electoral participation rates remaining relatively stable over the last two decades. As in other countries, local and regional elections tend to be considered less important than national ones. Citizens perceive central government to be the core decision-making process, which poses a difficulty for the development of a genuine civic society, which is associated by many authors with local initiatives.

In addition, and when asked about their confidence in institutions, Spanish citizens expressed less confidence in those related to the public sphere, such as political parties, trade unions, the national government or the parliament. On the other hand, some traditional institutions such as the church and the police have held their ground, with social movements making strong late appearances (ecology 58 per cent and women's movement 39 per cent). Even though political parties are perceived, for the most part, as necessary in order to make democracy work, particularly as the main channels for representation and participation, their performance is strongly criticized by public opinion. They are often seen as disturbing elements in political life because of corruption, their rude and vulgar criticisms, and their exclusive search for votes and partisan interest. So, it is clear that politics generally, and politicians specifically, generate negative feeling in most of the citizens. Distrust of politics and politicians is the best way to define relations between the political elites and the ordinary people (Uriarte, 2001).

Finally, we find that levels of interpersonal trust have not changed to a great extent across generations, due to a certain cultural legacy transmitted from generation to generation. The level of interpersonal trust is resistant to the great economic, social and political changes that have taken place in the last 30 years and this is a shared aspect with other Southern European democracies like Italy, Greece and Portugal (Magone, 2003). A mutual and reciprocal suspicion has become one of the historical and most important features in these countries, as a distinctive attribute (Inglehart, 1988: 51). We again find how pre-democratic values continue during the democratic period; 72 per cent who declared to not trust each other in 1971 is almost the same as that (68 per cent) more than 25 years later.

Hypothesis 2: civic engagement and individualistic values

We have also tried to discover the existence of a set of values, which can be defined as private or individualistic values linked to the historical legacy of dictatorship, that obstruct the creation of social capital and civic virtue. With this purpose we carried out an analysis of the most important aspects of everyday life. In addition, starting from Warren's typology of associations, we specifically analysed the Spanish situation in order to make a sketch of the more prevalent organizations to see how they affect the development of civil society.

Table 10.2 presents a detailed overview of the 17 countries taken into consideration. They are analysed in relation to the most important aspects that people consider to be necessary to be a good citizen. Across all countries participation in voluntary associations, which is more closely linked to generating social capital, is seen to be more important for citizenship than exclusive political involvement. This situation does not mean, necessarily, that there is massive participation in associations, but at least associations are considered important for democratic life. It is paradoxical to observe that in Spain, which presents a relatively low level in participatory politics, being active in politics appears as an important consideration – again, "democratic cynicism". Table 10.2 proves that the existing civic virtue of interest in politics is related to legalism only, not to active participation. This is a common feature for all the countries. In addition, the importance of forming independent opinion stands out and supports the predominance of a liberal vision and an individualist conception of political life, where having personal and exclusive ideas is more important that forming opinions by socialization in groups and deliberation in associations. Data show that individualist values, such as exclusive confidence in familiar spheres, are a constant factor in Spanish political culture.

A bigger picture of this phenomenon of mistrust and lack of solidarity is presented in Table 10.3. In Spain, the possibilities of collaboration run into

Table 10.2 Most important aspects to be a good citizen

	Support people who are worse off than themselves	Vote in elections	Always obey laws and regulations	Form their own opinion, independently of others	Be active in voluntary associations	Be active in politics
Germany	7.31 (6,940)	7.55 (6,912)	7.54 (6,961)	8.81 (6,968)	4.84 (6,968)	4.25 (6,946)
Norway	7.94 (346)	8.19 (348)	8.18 (347)	8.62 (347)	5.95 (347)	4.75 (346)
Finland	8.02 (417)	7.59 (417)	8.56 (417)	8.51 (415)	5.5 (416)	4.43 (415)
Netherlands	7.41 (1,303)	7.48 (1,306)	7.28 (1,302)	8.19 (1,307)	5.82 (1,303)	4.24 (1,302)
Switzerland	7.4 (600)	7.37 (599)	7.28 (603)	8.68 (601)	5.68 (600)	4.4 (601)
Ireland	7.67 (303)	7.7 (303)	8.35 (303)	8.16 (297)	5.78 (299)	3.82 (300)
Luxembourg	7.55 (35)	8 (35)	8.43 (35)	9.14 (35)	6.72 (35)	3.77 (35)
Denmark	7.56 (426)	8.07 (430)	7.69 (432)	8.78 (427)	5.28 (423)	4.89 (424)
United Kingdom	6.82 (4,743)	7.16 (4,761)	8.31 (4,758)	8.25 (4,743)	5.17 (4,744)	3.48 (4,738)
Israel	8.46 (455)	7.98 (454)	8.91 (456)	8.47 (452)	6.8 (453)	4.41 (454)
Spain	7.76 (3,115)	6.43 (3,083)	7.12 (3,101)	7.52 (3,039)	5.85 (3,044)	3.52 (3,044)
Belgium	6.95 (398)	6.56 (840)	7.43 (841)	7.81 (832)	5.35 (834)	3.41 (835)
Italy	7.84 (4,825)	7.51 (4,854)	8.48 (4,877)	7.98 (4,751)	6.43 (4,759)	3.99 (4,752)
Czech Republic	6.15 (827)	6.16 (841)	8.16 (849)	7.98 (843)	4.45 (838)	2.93 (839)
Hungary	6.71 (791)	8.26 (794)	9.1 (801)	7.93 (782)	4.51 (769)	3.66 (781)
Poland	7.48 (3,093)	7.65 (3,075)	8.99 (3,131)	8.16 (3,019)	5.54 (3,042)	5.11 (3,018)
Greece	8.37 (859)	8.12 (856)	8.75 (862)	8.54 (853)	6.01 (847)	5.42 (848)
Europe	7.58 (31,616)	7.61 (31,596)	8.13 (31,776)	8.41 (31,384)	5.62 (31,383)	4.24 (31,339)

Source: ESS, 2002–2003.

Notes
Mean scores in a scale 0–10.
(n) in brackets (only valid cases).

Table 10.3 Interpersonal relations – Spain in comparative perspective

	A8	A9	A10
Germany	6.99 (6,968)	7.33 (6,961)	6.12 (6,956)
Norway	6.64 (348)	7.01 (347)	6.09 (348)
Finland	6.46 (420)	6.88 (419)	5.68 (419)
Netherlands	5.71 (1,310)	6.19 (1,306)	5.26 (1,309)
Switzerland	5.64 (604)	6.2 (603)	5.32 (603)
Ireland	5.47 (305)	6 (305)	5.95 (305)
Luxembourg	5.18 (35)	5.5 (35)	4.54 (35)
Sweden	5.13 (722)	5.62 (720)	5.19 (724)
Denmark	5.13 (434)	5.62 (434)	5.19 (434)
United Kingdom	5.05 (4,771)	5.56 (4,758)	5.41 (4,755)
Israel	4.89 (457)	5.36 (455)	4.51 (458)
Spain	4.89 (3,162)	5.23 (3,147)	4.4 (3,143)
Belgium	4.81 (847)	5.61 (843)	4.44 (843)
Italy	4.52 (4,898)	4.59 (4,859)	4.07 (4,869)
Czech Republic	4.29 (855)	5.11 (838)	3.95 (853)
Portugal	4.16 (829)	5.27 (827)	3.91 (820)
Hungary	4.08 (804)	4.64 (796)	4.16 (804)
Slovenia	3.98 (165)	4.68 (165)	4.24 (166)
Poland	3.69 (3,142)	4.53 U(3,084)	3.16 (3,134)
Greece	3.63 (865)	3.69 (860)	3.01 (864)
Europe	5.05 (31,942)	5.61 (31,761)	4.79 (31,841)

Source: ESS, 2002–2003.

Notes
Mean scores in a scale 0–10.
(*n*) in brackets (only valid cases).
Questions in questionnaire:
A8: Interpersonal trust (Question: "Would you say that most people can be trusted (maximum 10), or that you can't be too careful in dealing with people (maximum 0)?" (scale 0–10)
A9: (Question: "Do you think that most people would try to take advantage of you if they got the chance (maximum 0), or would they try to be fair (maximum 10)?"
A10: (Question: "Would you say that most of the time people try to be helpful (maximum 10) or that they are mostly looking out for themselves (maximum 0)?"

difficulties and obstacles related to interpersonal trust (A8), the search for personal advantages (A9) and individualism and the lack of solidarity (A10). As we have already pointed out, these values are shared by all the Mediterranean nations and some Eastern Europe nations, such as the Czech Republic, Hungary, Slovenia and Poland.

In this situation, where privacy and mistrust predominate, the most important aspect in people's life is the family. It is the most intimate space, where they often find protection and security. Economic security is the second most important aspect of everyday life. Inside the same private area we have to take into account friendship and leisure time, normally spent with friends. This leaves politics as the least important aspect in Spanish everyday life. Most people do not spend a lot of time engaging themselves in organizational activities nor in political involvement compared with the time they spend in school, work or the family, with friends or in leisure time. These are likely to be more important spaces for the generation of trust and security than voluntary associations and the political sphere.

Reviewing the forms of socio-political involvement represented in Table 10.4 may question whether interactions such as signing petitions or taking part in lawful public demonstrations can be considered as social capital. These events are sporadic and usually do not require social trust and there is no continuity between these events. In most cases, these are discrete events, which only enjoy a short life and quickly disappear. They produce neither strong ties nor lasting networks. Most importantly, they do not create reciprocity: rather in most cases, these actions are driven by individualistic and hedonistic values, with no idea of a wider common good and have consequences which are limited to a very small group. As can be observed in Table 10.4, the greater the costs of involvement, the lower the level of participation. While signing a petition does not carry too many costs, participating in political or non-political associations, strike action or illegal protest activities do, with personal costs in terms of leisure time, money and physical integrity. Spain scores above the European average in relative terms, but is located far below the leading countries. If we look at the extent of activity within associations, the percentage decreases as the costs of involvement go up. In general terms, the survey data show that the levels of membership and other types of participation in voluntary associations (e.g. donating money and offering voluntary work) or in intermediary organizations in Spain are relatively low compared with most other Western democracies (Table 10.5).

As can be seen in Table 10.6, Spanish citizens are less likely to belong to, participate in, donated money to or work in voluntary organizations than citizens in any of the other countries in the table. This is not only true of political parties and trade unions but of all the organizations of civil society that depend on the voluntary participation of citizens.

Different types of association produce different results for generating civic virtue among their members and deepening the quality of democracy. Some of them generate more collaborative efforts but other ones promote a high individualism and hedonist lifestyle. Spain falls below the European average for all types of involvement (Table 10.6). In relative terms as well as global terms, the figures are very low and are not propitious for the creation of social commitment.

Hypothesis 3: creating social capital and civic virtue

Most empirical as well as theoretical studies on the effect of voluntary associations, since The Civic Culture (Almond and Verba, 1963), have shown that members of organizations exhibit more democratic and civic attitudes, as well as more active forms of political participation, than non-members (Billiet and Cambré, 1996) (Table 10.7).

Table 10.4 Socio-political involvement during the last 12 months

	Worked in a political party or action group	Worked in another organization or association	Signed a petition	Taken part in a lawful public demonstration	Participated in illegal protest activities
Denmark	4.1 (435)	17.3 (435)	28.2 (435)	8.3 (435)	1.1 (435)
Sweden	5 (725)	24.6 (725)	40.8 (718)	6.4 (724)	0.8 (725)
Norway	9.2 (348)	28.2 (348)	36 (347)	8.5 (348)	0.7 (348)
Netherlands	3.4 (1,309)	23.1 (1,309)	22.4 (1,305)	2.9 (1,307)	0.4 (1,309)
Finland	3.5 (420)	30.7 (420)	24 (420)	2 (420)	0.3 (420)
Belgium	5.4 (848)	23.2 (847)	33.9 (843)	8.4 (845)	2.4 (846)
Germany	3.9 (6,983)	17.8 (6,983)	30.5 (6,968)	10.6 (6,983)	1.1 (6,978)
United Kingdom	3.4 (4,774)	9.2 (4,771)	40 (4,765)	4.4 (4,774)	0.8 (4,772)
Ireland	4.7 (302)	13.8 (299)	27.6 (300)	7.1 (299)	0.8 (301)
Israel	5.7 (457)	7.4 (457)	18.4 (455)	9.9 (456)	1.4 (456)
Slovenia	3.5 (165)	2.3 (164)	11.8 (164)	2.7 (164)	0.8 (164)
Czech Republic	4.7 (850)	15.1 (849)	16.1 (849)	4.6 (846)	1.4 (849)
Spain	6.1 (3,159)	16.7 (3,153)	24.2 (3,155)	17.5 (3,157)	1.7 (3,131)
Italy	3 (4,882)	7.6 (4,886)	17.4 (4,858)	11 (4,882)	1.8 (48,82)
Portugal	4.2 (824)	4.2 (824)	7.3 (825)	4.3 (825)	0.3 (825)
Hungary	2.9 (807)	2.9 (807)	4.2 (806)	3.7 (807)	0.8 (807)
Greece	4.8 (864)	5.7 (862)	4.8 (862)	4.5 (863)	1.5 (863)
Poland	2.9 (3,147)	5.9 (3,146)	6.9 (3,144)	1.3 (3,146)	0.2 (3,146)
Europe	5 (31,937)	15.1 (31,923)	23.8 (31,855)	7.3 (31,921)	1.2 (31,894)

Source: ESS, 2002–2003.

Notes
Percentages
(n) in brackets (only valid cases).

Table 10.5 Associational involvement (Spain in Europe)

	None		Member		Participated		Donated money		Voluntary work	
	Spain[a]	Europe[b]	Spain	Europe	Spain	Europe	Spain	Europe	Spain	Europe
Sports club	81.2	68.7	12.4	23	10.2	14.6	3.1	5.4	1.3	6.6
Cultural/hobby activities	83.4	78.2	11	14.6	7.5	10.7	2.9	3.6	2.3	4.5
Trade union	91.8	76	5.5	22	1.8	3.7	2	2.2	0.5	1.1
Business/professional organization	93.6	88.9	4.7	9.1	1.9	3.3	0.8	1.2	0.1	1.1
Consumer	94.7	80.7	3.7	18.1	1.4	1.2	1	1.1	0.1	0.2
Humanitarian aid/human rights	88.7	83	4	5.8	4	2.6	5.9	11.6	1.4	1.9
Environmental protection	93.9	87.3	1.8	6	2.1	2.2	1.9	6.7	0.3	0.9
Religious	88.9	80.7	6	13.6	4.4	6.2	3.2	7.3	1.3	3.1
Political party	95	92.6	2.8	5.3	1.8	2.2	0.6	1.4	0.8	1.2
Science/education/teachers/parents	88.6	89.9	7.5	6.7	3.9	4.1	2.2	1.9	1.3	2
Young/elderly/women	88.6	83.5	7	11.5	5.4	6.9	1.6	2.6	1.4	3.2
Any other voluntary organization	92.7	89.4	3.4	6.6	1.4	2.9	1.7	2.5	0.8	2.4

Source: ESS, 2002–2003.

Notes
Percentages.
a n: 3,198 (only valid cases).
b n: 30,593 (only valid cases).

Table 10.6 Type of involvement in associations (Spain in Europe)

	Member	Participated	Donated money	Voluntary work
Denmark (437)	92	48	34	28
Sweden (725)	90	47	44	35
Norway (348)	84	47	44	38
Netherlands (1,311)	84	41	43	29
Finland (420)	76	36	19	12
Belgium (850)	71	49	26	23
Germany (6,983)	71	44	34	26
United Kingdom (4,775)	70	49	39	23
Ireland (307)	68	38	32	16
Israel (461)	55	27	13	7
Slovenia (166)	52	26	31	19
Czech Republic (864)	43	19	13	8
Spain (3,198)	36	25	15	7
Italy (4,910)	35	22	12	5
Portugal (831)	29	18	16	6
Hungary (808)	27	20	6	9
Greece (867)	25	13	9	6
Poland (3,161)	21	11	12	5
Europe (30,593)	54	34	25	17

Source: ESS, 2002–2003.

Notes
Percentages
(*n*) in brackets (only valid cases).

Table 10.7 Volunteers and civic virtue (Spain)

	Worked in an association in the last year	
	Yes	*No*
Interest in politics	39 (0.258**)	18
Facility to understand politics[a]	40 (0.160**)	21
Capability of forming an opinion[b]	49	23
Active role in the future[c]	28	7
Voted in the last election	81	71
Member of political party	7 (0.107**)	2
Provide help for people	26 (0.097**)	20
Discussing politics	47 (0.263**)	24

Source: ESS, 2002–2003.

Notes
Percentages.
a Question: How often does politics seem so complicated that you can't really understand what is going on?
b Question: How difficult or easy do you find it to make your mind up about political issues?
c Question: Do you think that you could take an active role in a group involved in political issues?
In brackets, Pearson's correlation coefficient **Significant at $p < 0.01$. *Significant at $p < 0.05$.

The Spanish case does not appear to be distinctive. At the micro-level we have found that people who worked in an association during the last year are more politically active across all the dimensions tested. That is, they are more interested in and more likely to discuss politics, are more likely to vote and have higher membership of political parties and voluntary organizations. They are more sanguine about their ability to affect political life (facility and capability to understand politics) and more inclined to help other people. Nevertheless, global rates of membership and work in associations, as we have shown, are low, which means that these effects only relate to very few people.

Factors producing voluntary participation

If we run a correlation analysis to check the influence of some indicators of political culture, private values and socio-demographic factors, as explicative variables for voluntary participation, the result can be observed in Table 10.8, which contains the result of a correlation analysis (Spearman's rho). In relation to political culture, civic engagement in associations increases with interest in politics. That is, the greater the presence of interest in politics, the greater the probability of using any voluntary organizations. Associational involvement is significantly related to the importance of politics in everyday life, (and, of course, to the importance assigned voluntary organizations) and negatively related to the importance assigned to family. Most respondents who declared that family is one of the most important aspects in life tend to be less involved in social networks, such as voluntary organizations. Private values play an impor-

Table 10.8 Correlations between non-political associational involvement and interest in politics, most important aspects in life, solidarity and socio-demographic factors

	Interest in politics	0.236**
Importance in life of:	Family	−0.145**
	Friends	−0.003
	Leisure time	0.022
	Politics	0.169**
	Work	−0.026
	Religion	0.061*
	Voluntary organizations	0.091**
	Help others (Solidarity)	0.123**
Socio-demographic variables	Gender	−0.118 **
	Age	−0.099**
	Education	0.247**
	Ideology	−0.078**

Source: ESS, 2002–2003.

Notes
Spearman's rho.
**Significant at $p < 0.01$. *Significant at $p < 0.05$.

tant role in understanding the obstacles to a more dynamic civic society. With regard to the socio-demographic variables included in the analysis, the relation with education and gender should be noted. These coefficients reveal that less educated citizens and women are least likely to engage in non-political forms of association. Up to a point, age and ideology also play a role, with intermediate age cohorts and left ideology indicating increased civic engagement.

Conclusion: the nature of civil society in Spain

In summarizing the empirical evidence, we might conclude as follows. The values of Spanish political culture show a society with strong legitimacy, but very low level use of participatory rights and liberties. We have more or less liberal citizens, but not civic citizens. Democracy exists, but in a formal way, without active citizenship. The historical evolution of Spanish society may help us to understand the path dependency of the current situation of a rather weak civil society in Spain.

As Morales has shown, we cannot argue about a retreat of citizens to the private sphere (Morales, 2003: 28). If that is true, we must add that levels of social engagement at the end of 1970s were quite low, compared with other nations and, in some cases, similar to those during the Franco regime. It was hoped that levels of social engagement would increase with democratic consolidation, but strong economic growth and the legitimacy of the democratic system have not produced a much more engaged civil society, which on the contrary continues to be immersed in the private realm of the family, leisure time, friendship and work. The possibilities of increasing social activities and, therefore, civic virtue are associated positively with public variables such as interest in politics, and negatively with private values such as the importance of family.

In Spanish civil society some elements, such as legitimacy and support for the rule of law, are completely established, but at the same time private relations, generally within the family or the circle of friends predominate, with a dose of *clientelism*. In Spain

> the situation should be defined as that of a field in which we find two competing cultural traditions, that of an open society and that of the tribal [closed and *neo-clientelistic*] societies of the past.
>
> (Pérez-Díaz, 1990: 30)

This situation could be defined as *liberal privatism*,[1] where citizens are conceived as legal persons but not as neighbours, bounded together by contract but not by a common participatory activity, and among others considerations, a representative democracy with a mistrustful and passive political style. This is not a strong democracy, which would have a cooperative and active pattern of political and social transactions (see Barber, 1984).

Not all types of associations create reciprocity. In the absence of strong traditions of group loyalty, as in Spain and other Mediterranean countries (Magone,

2003), it seems likely that many individuals would use most organizations and patron–client networks in an instrumental fashion, and that they would give primacy to a narrow definition of individual (or family) self-interest (Pizzorno, 1966). So, they may be led to play the game of exchange among themselves and with the public authorities in the spirit of exacerbated hyper-individualism, which is typical of those who are proud of outsmarting everybody else. The growing emphasis on individual achievement may have sharpened the sense that opportunism is an important dimension of social advancement and a pervasive feature of society. This trend obviously could readily lead to some decline in overall levels of social trust and, what is most important, of civic engagement.

As Habermas has demonstrated, a real public sphere requires more than the institutional guarantees of the constitutional state since it also needs "the supportive spirit of cultural traditions and patterns of socialization, of the political culture, of a populace accustomed to freedom" (Habermas, 1992: 453). However, socialization in Spain has perpetuated an apolitical culture that has not allowed civil society to emerge fully. Contemporary theories of democracy suggest that, in fact, most current democratic systems are representative democracies, but they, too, remain far from being participative democracies. In addition, and what is more important, associations by themselves do not make societies more democratic, but most democratic societies have more and better associations than Spain does (Rossteutscher, 2002: 525; Marinetto, 2003: 117). It seems that beyond formal and liberal democracy, there are not yet genuine democratic *mores*, the "habits of the heart" of "strong democracy" (Barber, 1984).

Acknowledgements

I gratefully acknowledge professor Miguel Jerez's comments on the early version of this chapter and Jaime Andreu and Fundación Centra de Estudios Andaluces, and Mannheimer Zentrum für Europäische Sozialforschung (MZES, University of Mannheim) for letting me use the data bank: mainly, European Social Survey and World Values Survey. Special gratitude goes to Derrick Purdue and Mariano Torcal, for all their comments and suggestions.

Note

1 That is, the social position of being non-committal to or uninvolved with anything other than one's own immediate interests and lifestyle.

References

Almond, G. and Verba, S. (1963) *The Civic Culture: Political Attitudes and Democracy in Five Nations*. Princeton University Press, Princeton.
Barber, B. (1984) *Strong Democracy: Participatory Politics for a New Age*. University of California Press, Berkeley.
Billiet, J. and Cambré, B. (1996) "Social Capital, Active Membership in Voluntary

Organizations and Some Aspects of Political Participation". Paper presented at Conference on Social Capital and Democracy, Milan, October, 3–6.

Cohen, D. and Prusak, L. (2001) *In Good Company: How Social Capital Makes Organizations Work.* Harvard Business School Press, Cambridge.

Diamond, L. (1997) *Civil Society and the Development of Democracy.* WP, 101 (CEACS, Juan March Institute), Madrid.

Diamond, L. (1998) *Political Culture and Democratic Consolidation.* WP, 118. CEACS (Juan March Institute), Madrid.

Gracia García, J. and Ruiz Carnicer, M. A. (2001) *La España de Franco (1939–1975): cultura y vida cotidiana.* Síntesis, Madrid.

Habermas, J. (1992) "Further Reflections on the Public Sphere", in C. Calhoun (ed.) *Habermas and the Public Sphere.* MIT Press, Cambridge, Massachusetts.

Hooghe, M and Stolle, D. (2003) "Introduction: Generating Social Capital", in M. Hooghe and D. Stolle (eds) *Generating Social Capital: Civil Society and Institutions in Comparative Perspective.* Palgrave Macmillan, New York.

Inglehart, R. (1988) "Cultura politica y democracia estable". *Revista de Española de Investigaciones Sociológicas*, 42: 45–65.

Linz, J. J. (1988) "Legitimacy of Democracy and Socioeconomic System", in Mattei Dogan (ed.) *Comparing Pluralist Democracies.* Westview Press, Boulder.

Lipset, S. M. (1959) "Some Requisites on Democracy: Economic Development and Political Legitimacy". *American Political Science Review*, 53: 69–105.

López Pina, A. and Aranguren, E. (1976) *La cultura política de la España de Franco.* Taurus, Madrid.

López-Pintor, R. (1982) *La opinión pública española: del franquismo a la democracia.* CIS, Madrid.

López-Pintor, R. and Buceta, R. (1975) *Los españoles de los años 70.* Tecnos, Madrid.

Magone, J. M. (2003) *The Politics of Southern Europe: Integration into the European Union.* Praeger, Westport.

Marinetto, M. (2003) "Who Wants to be an Active Citizen? The Politics and Practice of Community Involvement". *Sociology*, 37 (1): 103–120.

Montero, J. R. and Morlino, L. (1993) "Legitimidad y democracia en el sur de Europa". *Revista Española de Investigaciones Sociológicas*, 64: 7–40.

Montero, J. R., Gunther, R. and Torcal, M. (1997) *Democracy in Spain: Legitimacy, Discontent, and Disaffection.* Working Paper, 100. CEACS (Juan March Institute).

Morales, L. (2002) "Associational Membership and Social Capital in Comparative Perspective: a Note on the Problems of Measurement". *Politics & Society*, 30 (3): 497–523.

Morales, L. (2003) *Ever Less Engaged Citizens? Political Participation and Association Membership in Spain?* ICPS, WP, 220, Barcelona.

Morales Diez De Ulzurrun, L. (2004) *Institutions, Mobilisation, and Political Participation: Political Membership in Western Countries.* Instituto Juan March de Estudios e Investigaciones, Madrid.

Norris, P. (2002) *Democratic Phoenix: Reinventing Political Activism.* Cambridge University Press, New York.

Perez-Díaz, V. (1990) *The Emergence of Democratic Spain and the "Invention" of a Democratic Transition.* Working Paper, 1. CEACS (Juan March Institute), Madrid.

Pérez-Díaz, V. (1993) *The Return of Civil Society.* Harvard University Press, Cambridge.

Pérez-Díaz, V. (1996) *España puesta a prueba, 1976–1996.* Alianza, Madrid.

Pérez-Díaz, V. (2003) "De la guerra civil a la sociedad civil: el capital social en España entre los años treinta y los años noventa del siglo XX", in R. D. Putnam (ed.) *El declive del capital social. Un estudio internacional sobre las sociedades y el sentido comunitario.* Círculo de Lectores/Galaxia Gutenberg, Barcelona.

Pizzorno, A. (1966) "Amoral Familism and Historical Marginality". *International Review of Community Development*, 15.

Putnam, R. D. (1993) *Making Democracy Work.* Princeton University Press, Princeton.

Putnam, R. D. (1995) "Bowling Alone: American's Declining Social Capital". *Journal of Democracy*, 6 (1): 65–78.

Putnam, R. D. (2000) *Bowling Alone: The Collapse and Revival of American Community.* Simon & Schuster, New York.

Putnam, R. D. (2002) *Democracies in Flux: The Evolution of Social Capital in Contemporary Society*, Oxford University Press, Oxford.

Rossteutscher, S. (2002) "Advocate or Reflection? Associations and Political Culture". *Political Studies*, 50: 514–528.

Sastre García, C. (1997) *Transición y desmovilización política en España.* Universidad de Valladolid, Valladolid.

Selle, P. and Stromsnes, K. (2001) "Membership and Democracy", in P. Dekker and E. M. Uslaner (eds) *Social Capital and Participation in Everyday Life.* Routledge/ECPR, London.

Torcal, M. (2003) *Political Disaffection and Democratization History in New Democracies*, Kellogg Institute. WP, 308.

Torcal, M. and Montero, J. R. (1999) "Facets of Social Capital in New Democracies: The Formation and Consequences of Social Capital in Spain", in J. van Deth, M. Maraffi, K. Newton and P. H. Whiteley (eds) *Social Capital and European Democracy.* Routledge.

Uriarte, E. (2001) "La crisis de la imagen de la política y de los políticos y la responsabilidad de los medios de comunicación". *Revista de Estudios Políticos*, 111: 45–64.

Warren, M. E. (2000) *Democracy and Association.* Princeton University Press, Princeton.

Zmerli, S. (2002) "Bonding and Bridging Social Capital: A Relevant Concept for Political Participation?" Paper presented at the ECPR Joint Sessions. Turín, Italy.

11 Social capital and political trust in new democracies in Asia

Ingredients of deliberative communication and democratic governance

Ji-Young Kim

Introduction: communitarian perspectives on political participation

Political participation is not a transitory whim. It has been a public concern since the concept of democracy was formulated because it is the route to the democratic ideal. Citizen participation in politics is, on the one hand, a means to make representative systems function properly, and, on the other hand, it has as its purpose grassroots politics which embrace voices of all shades (Parry *et al.* 1992). While political participation may have been a long-standing issue of human history, why and how it has absorbed public attention has taken different forms over time in accordance with political environments. The latter half of the twentieth century, in particular, has seen vigorous professional endeavours to improve citizen participation in politics, as indicators have emerged to signal that representative institutions are in danger. One of those indicators was electoral participation, from which it can be seen that voting turnout has consistently decreased over the last few decades (Putnam, 1993, 2000).

Whereas earlier studies on political participation focused primarily on voting behaviour, more recently scholars have started to pay attention to a variety of other modes of political participation, which involve diverse action repertoires, ranging from protest activities such as going on demonstration marches and signing petitions, to discussing political affairs with neighbours and friends and wearing buttons. In fact, some studies have demonstrated that participation in political activities, in a broad sense, inclusive of these various modes, has not actually decreased, despite voting participation being in a decline. Drawing on these observations, the scholars concerned argue against the popular contention that citizens' political participation has been eroded. Indeed, some evidence of political engagement cautions against the widely accepted view of political alienation (Bennett, 1998: 745; Cain *et al.* 2003; Norris, 2002).

A part of the reason for the emergence of these conflicting views is attributable to the multifaceted dimensions of political participation. Recent scholarly debates have tended to converge on the role of community involvement in revitalizing participatory democracy, or 'communitarian participation'. Namely, one's motivation to participate in politics comes from a concern for his or her community. Although emphasis is in general given to a citizen's involvement in the geographically confined local community, in the 'socially mobile' modern world, a variety of groupings based on common interests and a shared sense of identity (i.e. job, ethnicity, hobby and leisure) are the sources of communitarian participation (Parry *et al.* 1992).

Dimensions of political participation are distinguished by the values they embody, types and aims of action, and functions, and one of the dimensions is called 'participation as interaction':

> [It] stresses the idea of public membership, of citizens 'sharing' justice and orienting their actions toward a 'public' or 'common good'. It is closely associated with a view of politics as the set of activities and relationships concerned with maintaining community, fostering cooperation among individuals and groups, and encouraging settlement of disputes through public communication.
>
> (Scaff, 1975: 454)

This notion of participation rather puts aside the core political character of voting in representative institutions of the state in favour of concerns with justice and community. In the end, both concepts – 'participation as interaction' and 'communitarian participation' – draw our attention to civil society as a subject to explore in investigating political participation. Civil society is a public sphere beyond the boundary of the state, where citizens take collective action to pursue their public interests and common goods. It is the self-organization of society characterized as independent and autonomous from the state power and co-operative for social benefits (Diamond, 1994; Dryzek, 1996; Foley and Edwards, 1996; Habermas, 1989; Keane, 1988). Community involvement is a building block of vibrant civil society and a country's political development rests on the extent to which civil society penetrates citizens' political lives and drives its influence on the political process.

Yet, it is important to keep in mind that civil society involves a wide spectrum of political characteristics as will be explained in the next section. While civic political organizations have driven political development and democratization across many countries, the current debates on civil society tend to 'devalue' such political aspects, as Foley and Edwards (1996: 43) argue. One of the prominent examples would be found in Putnam's social capital theory, which emphasizes the role of apolitical associational life in promoting political participation. The theory conceptualizes social capital as having two principal components: one, social networks, and the other, social trust. In particular, Putnam's social capital is inclusive of a wide range of civic organizations, drawing significant political implications from apolitical social networks. While social capital is believed to be an important element in revitalizing civil society, however, a growing body of criticism has raised a question about its direct relationship with political participation (Foley and Edwards, 1996; Navarro, 2002; Newton, 1999, 2001; Uslaner, 2002). Given the fierce debates regarding the political consequences of social capital, it is worthwhile to examine how social capital is related to citizen engagement in the political process.

Civil society and social capital in new democracies

The role of civil society in the political process has become increasingly important not only in established democracies, but also in emerging societies. Since civil society is hardly a tangible concept, it has taken different shapes and forms depending on where researchers place emphasis. The concept of civil society was defined in opposition to the state (Keane, 1988), and the concept of civil society has been used to describe historical opposition to the state, from civil rights movements in North America, to new social movements in Western Europe, and to democratization movements in Eastern Europe, Asia and Africa – political waves which were propelled by strong dissent against established state institutions (Dryzek, 1996). The growth of civil society advances democracy by resisting authoritarian regimes and reforming corrupt governments (Bellah *et al.* 1985; Seligson, 1999; Weigle and Butterfield, 1992). As such, the performance of representative institutions directly reflects how civil society reacts. The relationship between the state and civil society has, therefore, been an effective indicator of how the polity concerned works.

While civil society is apparently an important concept in investigating political participation, contemporary debates on the subject have prompted further theoretical refinement of the concept because it involves a wide spectrum of political characteristics. Foley and Edwards (1996) suggest that there are two types of civil society. The first model emphasizes associational life as a lubricator of reciprocal norms between citizens and civic co-operation for mutual benefits. This model is formulated in the liberal democracy tradition, as distinctively outlined in De Tocqueville's (1969) work. On the contrary, the second model sheds light on civil society 'as an organized counterweight to the state' (Foley and Edwards, 1996: 39). Prominent examples of this model include the cases of Latin America and Eastern Europe, that is, those who resisted authoritarian regimes (Foley and Edwards, 1996). The distinction between the first and the second models is important because it leads us to consider the fact that the essence of civil society is affected by the political system and its political environments, and thus to attend to cross-national variations.

Furthermore, another important implication of this conceptualization relates to how to characterize the political nature of civil society. As Foley and Edwards argue, a significant distinction between the two models is that the first model tends to rather devalue the political character of civil society. This apolitical tendency in the characterization of civil society has become more prominent in recent years as a result of a series of works produced by Robert Putnam, who is considered an exponent of the first model of civil society, and who has given rise to the heated debates over social capital (Foley and Edwards, 1996).

Putnam's (1993, 2000) theory of social capital is based on the idea that associational life is an essential building block that establishes vibrant civil society and facilitates political revitalization. According to him, civic associations garner reciprocal norms and social trust, which he believes are the core antecedents of political regeneration and economic development. Putnam illuminates a positive aspect of civic associations by suggesting that most of them are 'bridging' networks that connect heterogeneous social groups, which are distinct from 'bonding' networks of which groupings are based on homogeneity. What makes his theory unique is the focus on associational life in non-political organizations and groups, and also his reliance on the political implications of generalized social trust. As illustrated by his catchy phrase 'bowling together', civic associations in Putnam's theory encompass a wide range of social groups including hobby groups and leisure societies, and even such strong ties as family and friends. Putnam's approach to civil society reveals that the capacities of social capital in his arguments are too broad, including personal networks and social trust at their core. As a consequence, controversy converged on this apolitical character of civil society (Navarro, 2002; Newton, 1999, 2001; Uslaner, 2002). Foley and Edwards clarify a paradoxical aspect of Putnam's conception of civil society as follows:

> In order to foster a genuine spirit of 'wider cooperation,' his argument suggests, such associations must not be 'polarized' or 'politicized.' They must 'bridge' social and political divisions and thus, presumably, be autonomous from political forces. These caveats echo a long tradition of 'pluralist' analysis. Yet how can such associations shape political participation and 'civic engagement' without engaging in specifically political issues and without representing compelling social interests?
>
> (Foley and Edwards, 1996: 41)

As such, a currently popular account of civil society seems rather to exclude the political nature it might involve, and it is this point that raises a question of how such apolitical civil society is related to political participation – especially participation in the political process of representative institutions. Certainly, the matter of which model of civil society more closely approximates to the context of a country depends on a variety of factors, notably including the level of democratic development. The question of political consequences of apolitical social capital seems to be more appropriate to ask in the case of established democracies because civil society in consolidating democracies, such as the countries in Eastern Europe, Latin America and Asia, is likely to be closer to the second model – 'a counterweight to the state' (Foley and Edwards, 1996: 39) – which fosters political activism. However, civil society in those consolidating democracies might be in transition from the second to the first model of civil society, and therefore, it is still important to inquire, in those countries as well, into the relationship between apolitical social capital and political engagement.

The relationship between social capital and political trust

The rationale behind raising the question about the political consequences of social capital is concerned with how such a non-political character of social capital is related to participation in institutional politics. Among various predictors of political participation in institutional politics, political trust has drawn much scholarly attention in recent decades. Political trust is an 'evaluative orientation', drawing upon people's expectations of the performance of institutions (Hetherington, 1998: 791; see also, Miller and Listhaug, 1999). Political trust – in other words, trust or confidence in political institutions – matters because it generates political participation. In recent years, a series of survey studies have demonstrated the matching trends between the gradual erosion over time of political trust and the consistent decline of public participation in the political process, notably in elections (Almond and Verba, 1963; Finifter, 1970; Stokes, 1962; see Levi and Stoker, 2000: 486). Alternatively, some scholars focused on political trust as a motivational force for oppositional political action. In this case, low political trust – in other words, high political distrust – facilitates political discontent, which engages citizens in unconventional modes of alternative political activities (Gamson, 1968; Kaase, 1999). In any event, political trust is a significant antecedent of citizens' political engagement.

The reason why political trust is frequently dealt with in recent scholarly debates is because the studies of social capital have highlighted the concept of trust. A major reason why social capital theory gave rise to persistent debates is likely to be because the theory brought trust to the forefront in explaining the operation of social capital. As described earlier, Putnam's social capital theory places greater emphasis on social trust – generalized trust between citizens – as a condition for democratic development (Putnam, 1993, 2000). The problematic aspect of generalized trust in relation to associational involvement and political participation in social capital theory is that the complicated nature of trust is being oversimplified. The bulk of criticisms were, therefore, centred on the extent to which social trust influences political participation. Those criticisms suggest that political trust, rather than social trust, is a necessary condition for political revitalization. They claim that the former is quite distinctive from the latter in terms of its formation and political consequences, and that the political implications of social trust are limited (Foley and Edwards, 1999; Kaase, 1999; Kim, 2005; Levi, 1996; Navarro, 2002; Newton, 1999, 2001; Newton and Norris, 2000; Uslaner, 2002). The reason for making a distinction between social and political trust is not just for conceptual elaboration, but also because it involves differential behavioural mechanisms, which yield different predictions in terms of anticipating political revival.

Political trust is clearly distinct from social trust in terms of its origins and nature. Unlike interpersonal and social trust, which is based on direct contacts with close persons – kin, family, friends and those in direct social relations – trust in political institutions and politicians is formed through indirect learning, especially via the mass media (Kaase, 1999: 3, 12–13; Newton, 1999: 179,

2001: 205). Nevertheless, an array of cultural theories suggests that political trust is also fundamentally grounded on, and generated by, interpersonal trust, which is formed by socialization early in life and by cultural norms. These theories emphasize the importance of social trust in generating co-operative relations between individual citizens, eventually yielding vibrant civil society and political reanimation (Almond and Verba, 1963; Inglehart 1990; Putnam, 1993; see Mishler and Rose, 2001, for a discussion of cultural theories). By assuming this, and particularly connecting its positive role to the political domain, social trust, more often than not, was regarded as inclusive of political nature, without being properly discriminated from political trust (Foley and Edwards, 1999; Levi, 1996; Mishler and Rose, 2001).

While social trust is contingent upon social variables such as income, education and social position, and closely linked to individuals' life satisfaction (Whiteley, 1999), many studies have identified that political trust does not necessarily have social causes, and is likely to be randomly distributed throughout social groups, encompassing variant socio-demographic factors (Lawrence, 1997; Newton, 1999; Orren, 1997). Political trust is, instead, more strongly associated with such political variables as partisanship (King, 1997), the Left–Right political ideology (Kaase and Newton, 1995) and participation in political organizations, not social ones (Flanders *et al.*, 1996, cited in Newton, 1999: 184).

Given these distinctive mechanisms of generating political trust, it becomes imperative to investigate how social capital is related to political trust. Some studies have demonstrated that engagement in voluntary organizations is negatively associated with electoral participation (Barnes *et al.*, 2004) and with political trust (Brehm and Rahn, 1997). Furthermore, specifically focusing on South Korea, it has been found that the two components of social capital – associational involvement and social trust – are negatively related to political trust (Kim, 2005). Interestingly, this finding is endorsed by a different set of survey data – the World Values Surveys – conducted in South Korea, which is analysed in this chapter. Moreover, it is quite compelling that a consistent pattern is also observed in Taiwan, another Asian new democracy. As Table 11.1 shows, in both countries, associational involvement has turned out to be negatively related to political trust, and social trust does not have a significant relationship with it. Furthermore, engagement in the non-political civic associations, regardless of types of associations, was negatively associated with trust in political institutions. The categories of civic organizations in Table 11.1 are identical with the 'bridging' social networks in Putnam's theory, but their political consequences are found to be somewhat negative in the two countries unlike what Putnam expected them to be. Put differently, whereas engagement in civic organizations plays the role 'bridging' individuals and heterogeneous groups of society, the bridging social capital has little to do with *political* revitalization in the cases of Asian new democracies.

This result warrants some modification of Putnam's contention that social capital creates a high level of political trust, and encourages a search for a rationale for the negative relationship. A possible explanation for the negative rela-

Table 11.1 Correlations between social capital and political trust in Korea and Taiwan

Social capital	Political trust	
	Korea	Taiwan
Social trust	0.02	−0.03
Associational involvement	−0.10**	−0.19**
Religious organizations	−0.04*	
Sports/recreation organizations		−0.16**
Arts organizations	−0.12**	−0.16**
Environmental organizations	−0.04*	−0.19**
Professional associations	−0.06**	−0.19**
Charitable organizations	−0.06**	

Source: The World Values Surveys 1995–1997.

Notes
*$p < 0.05$, **$p < 0.01$. The figures represent bivariate correlation coefficients. Associational involvement is the aggregated value of the levels of involvement in the organizations illustrated in the table.

tionship between social capital and political trust comes from citizen expectations, which are regarded as a significant factor in evaluating government performance and generating trust and distrust in political institutions. Distrust of government correlates with a high level of citizen expectations of government performance (Miller and Listhaug, 1999). Since citizens have high democratic ideals for how government should perform, they tend not to trust government when they perceive it as not satisfying their democratic ideals. This account is particularly applicable to the politics of new democracies, as citizens in new democracies are likely to have higher expectations regarding the performance of political institutions because they have undergone dramatic political transformation such as regime alteration and party realignment, and this situation often engenders idealistic expectations of newly established regimes and institutions (Miller and Listhaug, 1999). In turn, these high expectations are likely to create a gap between citizens' political ideals for the workings of political institutions and the reality of how those institutions perform politically (see also, Rose *et al.*, 1999). How social capital might be involved in this causal relationship is that associational participants are more likely to be exposed to public life and political stimuli, which lead to a greater likelihood of perceiving poor institutional performance. The increasing gap between high expectations of government performance and political perceptions of the harsh political world among associational participants is seen to account for the negative relationship of social capital to political trust (Kim, 2005).

Another possible cause of the negative relationship of social capital to political trust is concerned more specifically with the political contexts of new democracies. Although it is widely believed that associational involvement stimulates political participation in a way that improves citizens' political qualities by providing members with more frequent chances to engage in public life, this line of argument has been formulated primarily by observing the circumstances of established democracies. Associational life in new democracies might not involve such a lubricating political character as that embedded in established democracies for two reasons:

- Civil society may be divorced from any concern with politics.
- Civil society may take the form of 'counterweight to the corrupt state' mentioned earlier in relation to Latin America.

In relation to the first of these possibilities, several studies on associational life in the former Soviet Union encourage the consideration of this different political context according to the level of democracy. These studies argue that, in undemocratic regimes such as the former Soviet Union, social networks of trusted acquaintances function to isolate members from distrusted institutions, resulting in a negative relationship between the two (Mishler and Rose, 2001: 35; Rose, 1995; Shlapentokh, 1989). A consideration of this political context provides an explanation for the negative relationship between social capital and political trust in South Korea and Taiwan.

Lastly, the negative relationship also draws our attention to Woolcock's configuration of two dimensions of social capital: one is called 'integration' that connotes 'intra-community ties', and the other 'linkage' indicating 'extra-community networks'. (These equate to 'bonding' and 'bridging' social capital (Putnam, 2000)). Positive outcomes of social capital such as democratic co-operation for social benefits are achieved when levels of both integration and linkage are high. However, when linkage – in other words, a community's external networks – is low while the level of integration – that is, the degree of internal ties – is high, the likely result of this configuration is 'amoral familism' (Woolcock, 1998: 172). Although it is not certain that the current result showing the negative consequences of associational involvement in terms of political trust can be qualified as 'amoral familism', Woolcock's configuration, in any event, provides a valid framework to approach associational life in Korea and Taiwan. It might be the case that associations in those countries have strong internal ties but their external links with other communities and society in general are more or less weak. The low political trust among associational participants is explained along the same line. Namely, one's strong involvement in a non-political association does not contribute to expanding one's trust towards political institutions but is more likely to reinforce only one's attachment to the association, strengthening internal integration of the association. Although the strong internal integration of an association is not deemed as amoral familism, it is in any event exposed to the risk of yielding such negative patterns of social relationship.

The second possibility is that civil society takes the form of a critical counterbalance to the state and claims allegiance denied the state, as has been suggested in parts of Latin America and Africa. It is, in fact, important to pay attention to the negative political consequence of apolitical associational life given that one might argue that the current result is nothing but a reflection of deeply rooted

Table 11.2 Citizen engagement in civic associations

	Korea	*Taiwan*
Religious organizations	378	
Sports organizations		64
Arts organizations	146	75
Labour unions	48	137
Political parties	70	74
Environmental organizations	113	21
Professional organizations	119	35
Charitable organizations	184	

Source: The World Values Surveys 1995–1997.

Note
The figures represent the number of respondents who identified themselves as active participants in the associations. $n = 3,263$.

political cynicism prevalent in the two countries. In other words, it might be plausible to assert that the negative association between social capital and political trust is highly susceptible to political contexts such as prevalent political cynicism, and therefore, it will not be observed if political cynicism is not present. However, observations of the trends of political participation in the two countries render such speculation tenuous. In actual fact, the patterns of political cynicism are not identical between Korea and Taiwan, and rather, contrasting patterns of political participation are observed between the two. First of all, whereas the eroding membership in such traditional political organizations as trade unions and political parties is witnessed in Korea, citizen engagement in those types of organizations is on the rise in the case of Taiwan. As Table 11.2 shows, the levels of involvement in labour unions and political parties are higher than those of the other types of associations in Taiwan, while the opposite is observed in Korea.

The second indicator of the contrast between the two countries is voting turnout. As Figures 11.1 and 11.2 demonstrate, while voting participation in parliamentary elections in Korea for more than three decades has been consistently decreasing with slight upturns in the middle of the period, there is no sign of declining participation in elections in Taiwan. Especially during the 1990s, Korea shows the waning trend of electoral participation, in contrast to the case of Taiwan showing no obvious indication of consistent decline. More obviously, voting turnout in presidential elections in the two countries shows a stark contrast: the level of participation in Taiwanese presidential elections has increased between the two points of time, in contrast to the substantial decrease in the case of Korea (see Figure 11.3).

Given these circumstances, it is notable that the finding that social capital is negatively related to political trust has been observed even in the midst of the rising trend of political participation as shown in the case of Taiwan. The negative relationship of social capital to political trust is not simply anchored in the political context of prevalent political apathy but appears to be cross-contextually consistent.

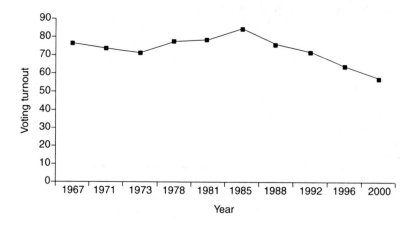

Figure 11.1 Voting turnout in parliamentary elections in Korea (source: International
IDEA (Institute for Democracy and Electoral Assistance)).

Note
Voting turnout is a percentage of the total number of votes divided by the number of names on the
voters' register (refer to www.idea.int for more details).

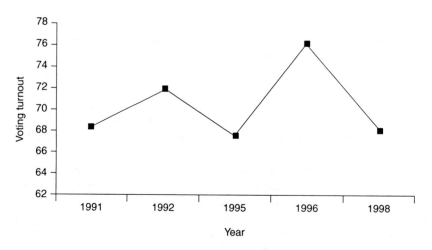

Figure 11.2 Voting turnout in parliamentary elections in Taiwan (source: International
IDEA (Institute for Democracy and Electoral Assistance)).

Note
Voting turnout is a percentage of the total number of votes divided by the number of names on the
voters' register (refer to www.idea.int for more details).

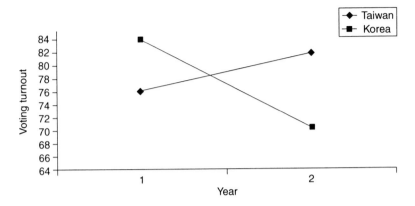

Figure 11.3 Voting turnout in presidential elections in Korea and Taiwan (source: International IDEA (Institute for Democracy and Electoral Assistance)).

Notes
For Taiwan, year 1 indicates 1996 and year 2 is 2000. For Korea, year 1 indicates 1997 and year 2 is 2002. Voting turnout is a percentage of the total number of votes divided by the number of names on the voters' register (refer to www.idea.int for more details).

Implications for local governance

Towards the promotion of political capital

Putnam's theory of social capital has invigorated scholarly debates on communitarianism, leading many to believe that social networks based on community involvement are a key determinant of political regeneration. However, we find that non-political, and exclusively social, activities of civic associations hardly enhance civic engagement in institutional politics. The popular debates on civil society, such as Putnam's (1993, 2000), appeared to leave out its political character, without which the facilitation of political engagement is not plausible. In the face of this apolitical characterization of civil society, some argue that political aspects of civicness need to be separately termed as political capital in order to be distinguished from social capital. Political capital – i.e. associational involvement in civic political organizations and their political activities, and relevant political qualities – is more directly related to political participation. Booth's and Richard's (1998) study on the case of Central America is a good example of the differentiation between social and political capital. These researchers have tested Putnam's theory in that region and have found that political capital is a significant antecedent of democratic development whilst social capital is not.

The attempt to promote political capital requires further refinement of the concept in order to distinguish it from social capital. For example, one easy way is to discriminate according to the types of participating associations since the different effects on political participation can be clearly discerned between non-political and political associations. Whereas non-political organizations have a limited impact on political participation, political associations are expected to promote citizen engagement in the political process. Nevertheless, civil society involves a multitude of normative dimensions, and thus we need to further differentiate between social and political capital in that regard. While there are only a few studies that directly deal with political capital, the work of Sørensen and Torfing (2003) elaborates the concept in the course of differentiating it from social capital. As they note:

> While social capital refers to trust-building through social interaction in civil society, political capital refers to individual powers to act politically that are generated through participation in interactive political processes linking civil society to the political system.
>
> (Sørensen and Torfing, 2003: 610)

Based on this idea, Sørensen and Torfing identified three dimensions of political capital: 'endowment', 'empowerment' and 'political identity'. Endowment indicates the level of accessibility to the decision-making process. Empowerment concerns the capability to affect the political process. Finally, political identity deals with the extent to which citizens perceive themselves as political actors. In their case study in Denmark, participation in networked politics in local communities has been found to be positively associated with these three dimensions of political capital (Sørensen and Torfing, 2003).

To generalize the three dimensions further, crucial components of political capital are, in the end, concerned with overall political qualities and efficacy. In this vein, the Internet draws our attention as it provides several implications in terms of how to build political capital. In fact, a number of social capitalists have suggested that the Internet can be an effective means of enhancing political engagement (see Coleman and Gøtze, 2001), given that online deliberation was found to enhance significantly citizen engagement in political activities (Dahlgren, 2001). Political deliberation over the net enhances individual citizens' political qualities, contributing to an invigoration of normative aspects of political capital. Again, it is important to distinguish online political activities from non-political ones, given that a study has shown that the involvement in non-political online communities – which are regarded as a form of social capital – is not conducive to the facilitation of political engagement (Kim, 2006). According to the study, online social networks themselves are not sufficient to promote political participation, rather deliberative activities on public issues are a necessary condition for civic engagement in politics. Therefore, it is important to develop a variety of web-based deliberative features of the Internet and apply them to civic activities and the political process. For instance, the efforts to regenerate local politics via ICT applications have emerged as a desirable aspiration from the perspectives of political capital and communitarianism

(Margetts, 2000), which may offer citizens and civil society better opportunities for engagement in democratic governance and consequently an increase in political capital. At a macro-level, this in turn indicates towards an increasing role played by civil society in the political process.

Improving institutional performance

Although we concur with the argument that associational engagement is a critical component of developing vibrant civil society and regenerating civic political life in one degree or another, it is not apparently a sufficient condition for revitalizing institutional politics. It is citizens' evaluation of institutional performance that exerts a more direct impact on political trust and their engagement in the political process, particularly institutional politics (Kim, 2005; Newton, 1999, 2001). Although representative institutions have the authority to implement policies and to control society, they gain their legitimacy from public support. Whether political institutions are accountable and how citizens evaluate them are crucial determinants of participation in voting and institutional processes.

In new democracies institutional performance has particular resonance given that the dramatic regime changes from authoritarian to democratic government have swept away the regimes in which citizens' political attitudes were formed based on early-life socialization and created high expectations of institutional performance, which together renders the performance impact on civic political engagement greater (Kim, 2005; see also, Miller and Listhaug, 1999). It is therefore important to develop effective avenues to improve institutional performance so as to enhance political trust of citizens.

Representative democracy and local governance

Although this study focuses on political participation, the intent of this work is to extract implications for contriving how to advance representative democracy. A country's level of democracy could be optimal when the two models of democracy – participatory and representative – are properly balanced. Indeed, those two models are supplementary rather than in competition with each other. Representative institutions require grassroots participation, and civic engagement in the political process is hardly feasible without accountable institutional devices in the representative system. One of the factors disengaging citizens from the political process is the way that citizens perceive representative institutions distant and indifferent to the citizens' own needs and wishes. Citizens are less motivated to participate in national affairs unless strong incentives are given, and in turn, this often results in free-rider problems.

In this vein, a promising alternative to both enhance political capital and improve institutional performance comes from local governance. Local governance has become a focal subject in recent scholarly debates, and one of the reasons for this rise is a growing body of interest in civic participation (Teune,

1995): the proximity of local government to its constituents leads them to become attentive to local affairs (Parry *et al.*, 1992). Furthermore, there are more occurrences of direct contacts between citizens and local representatives, and more systematic avenues by which citizens take part in local affairs (Newton, 1976; Sharpe, 1970). In fact, proponents of participatory democracy have paid much attention to local community involvement as they believe that it regenerates political participation (Parry *et al.*, 1992). The process of local democracy is attractive because the role of local government goes beyond service delivery, drawing ordinary citizens into local political life. As Stoker states, 'local democracy can rest its claim on being the most accessible avenue for political participation. It is in local politics that people feel most competent and are most immediately engaged' (Stoker, 1996:188).

In this regard, Cochrane (1996) points out that, to realize local democracy, empowerment emerges as the most critical issue to be dealt with. While a top-down process of empowering – i.e. state authorities empower local groups and citizens to handle particular local issues – might be one way to attain local democracy, demands and action from below can be a more effective driving force to achieve that political end. The concept of 'associative democracy' suggests a bottom-up process where 'the role of local government in such a model of democracy is to provide the framework in which the associations can develop and interact most fruitfully' (Cochrane, 1996: 206; see also, Hirst, 1994). Although the associative model is too idealistic, neglecting substantive matters such as power relationship, its theoretical underpinnings are intended to bridge participatory and representative democracy (Burns *et al.*, 1994).

Apart from the matter of the theoretical validity of possible models of local democracy, practical attempts to reflect public opinion on the local political process have been made. In fact, a few examples including local referenda, application of citizen surveys and market research, and citizen juries for decision-making have been made use of in some countries, or suggested as an alternative for possible implementation. Yet, it is important to keep in mind that those models involve loopholes of simple majority rules, with detailed gradations of a multitude of minority opinions being ignored (Cochrane, 1996). Perhaps, in order to cope with the challenges, lessons can be learned from studies of electoral systems which draw attention to how to represent better the wishes of the public, thereby becoming 'the cogs that keep the wheels of democracy properly functioning' (Farrell, 2001: 2). As long as the models are equipped with proper methods to represent local citizenry fully, the harmonization of participatory and representative democracy will be more easily attained. In effect, jury-type models for decision-making are deemed slightly different from the other two alternatives in that they weigh on political deliberations between citizen jurors to arrive at a policy recommendation (Margetts, 2000; see also, Smith and Wales, 1999). Attention should be given to this sort of example so that more responsive and representative governance can be embodied in localities so as to enhance political trust of citizens.

The efforts to create practical methods to engage citizens in the political process refer us back to the Internet, which offers new opportunities for democratic participation in local governance. Although there are challenges to the development of ICTs in the political process, the democratic potential of the Internet in revitalizing local governance should not be ignored. A prominent example is shown by the Amsterdam Digital City, which signalled an explosive proliferation of digital cities in the Netherlands and provided 'a platform for a number of well-supported public discussion groups on a wide range of issues' (Margetts, 2000: 198). Although there remains a question of whether these websites go beyond deliberative spheres to engage the citizenry in the decision-making process, the localized ICT initiatives provide significant implications for democratic development in South Korea and Taiwan. The successful cases of electronic local governance such as those of the Netherlands provide good examples for those countries to follow in an attempt to bridge participatory and representative democracy. The point here is that although the Internet has failed so far to deliver effective participation in local governance, it does have potential as a tool for widening participation.

Attending to the fact that responsive and accountable performance of representative institutions is achieved on the premise of grassroots participation in the political process, social capital, which is a controversial subject associated with political participation, has been examined in the contexts of the Asian new democracies. Future scholarship is encouraged to shed light on further cases showing variations in the relationship of social capital to political participation so that an ideal form of social capital is implemented in the political process to attain democratic governance.

References

Almond, G. and Verba, S. (1963/1989). *The Civic Culture: Political Attitudes and Democracy in Five Nations*. Newbury Park, CA: Sage Publications.

Barnes, M., Stoker, G. and Whiteley, P. (2004). 'Delivering Civil Renewal: Some Lessons from Research', ESRC Seminar Series: Mapping the Public Policy Landscape, available at www.esrc.ac.uk/esrccontent/downloaddocs/CivilPamphletFinal.pdf (accessed on 23 October 2004).

Bellah, R., Madsen, R., Sullivan, W., Swidler, A. and Tipton, S. (1985). *Habits of the Heart: Individualism and Commitment in American Life*. Berkeley, CA: University of California Press.

Bennett, W. (1998). 'The Uncivic Culture: Communication, Identity, and the Rise of Lifestyle Politics', *PS: Political Science and Politics*, 31 (4): 740–761.

Booth, J. and Richard, P. (1998). 'Civil Society, Political Capital, and Democratization in Central America', *The Journal of Politics*, 60 (3): 780–800.

Brehm, J. and Rahn, W. (1997). 'Individual-Level Evidence for the Causes and Consequences of Social Capital', *American Journal of Political Science*, 41 (3): 999–1023.

Burns, D., Hambleton, R. and Hoggett, P. (1994). *The Politics of Decentralisation: Revitalising Local Democracy*. London: Macmillan Press.

Cain, B., Dalton, R. and Scarrow, S. (2003). *Democracy Transformed? Expanding Political Opportunities in Advanced Industrial Democracies*. Oxford University Press.

Cochrane, A. (1996). 'From Theories to Practices: Looking for Local Democracy in

Britain', in D. King and G. Stoker (eds), *Rethinking Local Democracy* (pp. 193–213). London: Macmillan Press Ltd.

Coleman, S. and Gøtze, J. (2001). 'Bowling Together: Online Public Engagement in Policy Deliberation', available at www.hansardsociety.org.uk.

Dahlgren, P. (2001). 'The Public Sphere and the Net: Structure, Space, and Communication', in W. Bennet and R. Entman (eds), *Mediated Politics: Communication in the Future of Democracy* (pp. 33–55). Cambridge University Press.

De Tocqueville, A. (1969). *Democracy in America*. Garden City, NY: Anchor Books.

Diamond, L. (1994). 'Rethinking Civil Society: Toward Democratic Consolidation', *Journal of Democracy*, 5 (3): 4–17.

Dryzek, J. (1996). 'Political Inclusion and the Dynamics and Democratization', *American Political Science Review*, 90 (1): 475–487.

Farrell, D. (2001). *Electoral Systems: A Comparative Introduction*. New York: Palgrave.

Finifter, A. W. (1970). 'Dimensions of Political Alienation', *American Political Science Review*, 64: 389–410.

Foley, M. and Edwards, B. (1996). 'The Paradox of Civil Society', *Journal of Democracy*, 7 (3): 38–52.

Foley, M. and Edwards, B. (1999). 'Is It Time to Disinvest in Social Capital?', *Journal of Public Policy*, 19 (2): 141–174.

Gamson, W. (1968). *Power and Discontent*. Homewood, IL: Dorsey.

Habermas, J. (1989). *The Structural Transformation of the Public Sphere: An Inquiry into a Category of Bourgeois Society* (T. Burger, Trans.). Cambridge, MA: MIT Press.

Hetherington, M. (1998). 'The Political Relevance of Political Trust', *American Political Science Review*, 92 (4): 791–808.

Hirst, P. (1994). *Associative Democracy: New Forms of Economic and Social Governance*. Cambridge: Polity Press.

Inglehart, R. (1990). *Culture Shift in Advanced Industrial Society*. Princeton, NJ: Princeton University Press.

Kaase, M. (1999). 'Interpersonal Trust, Political Trust, and Non-institutionalised Political Participation in Western Europe', *West European Politics*, 22 (3): 1–21.

Kaase, M. and Newton, K. (1995). *Beliefs in Government*. New York: Oxford University Press.

Keane, J. (ed.) (1988). *Civil Society and the State*. London: Verso.

Kim, J. (2005). 'Bowling Together Isn't a Cure-All: The Relationship between Social Capital and Political Trust in South Korea', *International Political Science Review*, 26 (2): 193–213.

Kim, J. (2006). 'The Impact of Internet Use Patterns on Political Engagement: A Focus on Online Deliberation and Virtual Social Capital', *Information Polity*, 11 (1).

King, D. (1997). 'The Polarization of American Political Parties and Mistrust of Government', in J. Nye, P. Zelikow and D. King (eds), *Why People Don't Trust Government*. Cambridge, MA: Harvard University Press.

Lawrence, R. (1997). 'Is It Really the Economy, Stupid?', in J. Nye, P. Zelikow, and D. King (eds), *Why People Don't Trust Government*. Cambridge, MA: Harvard University Press.

Levi, M. (1996). 'Social and Unsocial Capital: A Review Essay of Robert Putnam's *Making Democracy Work*', *Politics & Society*, 24 (1): 45–55.

Levi, M. and Stoker, L. (2000). 'Political Trust and Trustworthiness', *Annual Review of Political Science*, 3: 475–507.

Margetts, H. (2000). 'Political Participation and Protest', in P. Dunleavy, A. Gamble, I.

Holliday and G. Peele (eds), *Developments in British Politics 6* (pp. 185–202). London: Macmillan Press.

Miller, A. and Listhaug, O. (1999). 'Political Performance and Institutional Trust', in P. Norris (ed.), *Critical Citizens: Global Support for Democratic Government*. New York: Oxford University Press.

Mishler, W. and Rose, R. (2001). 'What Are the Origins of Political Trust?: Testing Institutional and Cultural Theories in Post-Communist Societies', *Comparative Political Studies*, 34 (1): 30–62.

Navarro, V. (2002). 'Politics, Power, and Quality of Life: A Critique of Social Capital', *International Journal of Health Services*, 32 (3): 423–432.

Newton, K. (1976). *Second City Politics: Democratic Processes and Decision-Making in Birmingham*. Oxford University Press.

Newton, K. (1999). 'Social and Political Trust in Established Democracies', in P. Norris (ed.), *Critical Citizens: Global Support for Democratic Government*. New York: Oxford University Press.

Newton, K. (2001). 'Trust, Social Capital, Civil Society, and Democracy', *International Political Science Review*, 22 (2): 201–214.

Newton, K. and Norris, P. (2000). 'Confidence and Public Institutions: Faith, Culture, and Performance?' in S. Pharr and R. Putnam (eds), *Disaffected Democracies: What's Troubling the Trilateral Countries?* Princeton, NJ: Princeton University Press.

Norris, P. (2002). *Democratic Phoenix: Reinventing Political Activism*. New York: Cambridge University Press.

Orren, G. (1997). 'Fall from Grace: The Public's Loss of Faith in Government', in J. Nye, P. Zelikow and D. King (eds), *Why People Don't Trust Government*. Cambridge, MA: Harvard University Press.

Parry, G., Moyser, G. and Day, N. (1992). *Political Participation and Democracy in Britain*. New York: Cambridge University Press.

Putnam, R. (1993). *Making Democracy Work: Civic Traditions in Modern Italy*. Princeton, NJ: Princeton University Press.

Putnam, R. (2000). *Bowling Alone: The Collapse and Revival of American Community*. New York: Simon & Schuster.

Rose, R. (1995). 'Russia as an Hour-Glass Society: A Constitution without Citizens', *East European Constitutional Review*, 4 (3): 34–42.

Rose, R., Doh, C. and Munro, N. (1999). 'Tensions between the Democratic Ideal and Reality: South Korea', in P. Norris (ed.), *Critical Citizens: Global Support for Democratic Government*. New York: Oxford University Press.

Scaff, L. (1975). 'Two Concepts of Political Participation', *The Western Political Quarterly*, 28 (3): 447–462.

Seligson, A. (1999). 'Civil Association and Democratic Participation in Central America: A Test of the Putnam Thesis', *Comparative Political Studies*, 32 (3): 342–362.

Sharpe, L. (1970). 'Theories and Values of Local Government', *Political Studies*, 18: 153–174.

Shlapentokh, V. (1989). *Public and Private Life of the Soviet People*. New York: Oxford University Press.

Smith, G. and Wales, C. (1999). 'The Theory and Practice of Citizens' Juries', *Policy and Politics*, 27 (3): 295–308.

Sørensen, E. and Torfing, J. (2003). 'Network Politics, Political Capital, and Democracy', *International Journal of Public Administration*, 26 (6): 609–634.

Stoker, G. (1996). 'Redefining Local Democracy', in L. Pratchett and D. Wilson (eds),

Local Democracy and Local Government (pp. 188–209). London: Macmillan Press Ltd.

Stokes, D. (1962). 'Popular Evaluations of Government: An Empirical Assessment', in H. Cleveland and H. Lasswell (eds), *Ethics and Bigness: Scientific, Academic, Religious, Political, and Military* (pp. 61–72). New York: Harper.

Teune, H. (1995). 'Local Government and Democratic Political Development', *Annals of the American Academy of Political and Social Science*, 540: 11–23.

Uslaner, E. (2002). *The Moral Foundations of Trust*. New York: Cambridge University Press.

Weigle, M. and Butterfield, J. (1992). 'Civil Society in Reforming Communist Regimes: The Logic of Emergence', *Comparative Politics*, 25 (1): 1–23.

Whiteley, P. (1999). 'The Origins of Social Capital', in J. van Deth, M. Maraffi, K. Newton and P. Whiteley (eds), *Social Capital and European Democracy* (pp. 25–44). London: Routledge.

Woolcock, M. (1998). 'Social Capital and Economic Development: Toward a Theoretical Synthesis and Policy Framework', *Theory and Society*, 27: 151–208.

12 Creating social capital through deliberative participation

The experience of the Argentine popular assemblies

Julien D. Talpin

Introduction

Social capital and deliberative democracy theories share a crucial assumption: political participation can have – under certain specific conditions – positive developmental effects on individuals. Participation in deliberative institutions or voluntary associations could create "better citizens". Social capital is defined here as the ties linking individuals through the creation of formal (e.g. associations) or informal (e.g. friends or family) networks. The question of the norms of trust and reciprocity is therefore deliberately excluded from this conceptual definition, their analysis being postponed to the interpretation of the sources and effects of social capital, which can only be drawn from empirical research. Generally, two types of democratic outcomes of social capital are distinguished: micro- and macro-effects. At the individual level – on which this chapter focuses – networks of civic engagement are believed to have positive effects on their members; they socialize them into democratic culture and teach them trust, cooperation and tolerance, making them better citizens. At the institutional level, these networks lubricate institutional settings, making them more legitimate and efficient. As Robert Putnam puts it, they make democracy work better by increasing institutional performances (Putnam 1993). The same kind of argument can be found, more or less explicitly, in the deliberative democracy literature. The transformative power of deliberation indeed underlies its definition. Joshua Cohen is perhaps the clearest on the political relevance of this process of collective will formation (Cohen 1997: 69): "Democratic politics [. . .] shapes the identity and interests of citizens in ways that contribute to the formation of a public conception of the common good". Participation in deliberative institutions, as they foster processes of mutual information and conviction, would enlighten and enlarge individuals' preferences and interests, making them more tolerant, other-regarding and aware of the public good.

One crucial question for the self-transformation assumption is whether values appearing at the local level, within small-scale institutions or associations containing close-knit individuals, can be generalized to the rest of society? It has indeed been underlined that social capital generated within groups at the local level could sometimes lead to stronger parochial communities rather than to generalized trust and reciprocity (Levi 1996; Bell 1998). There is no clear evidence that repeated face-to-face interactions in small networks increase the level of trust in a society. It could, on the contrary, fragment it between different small groups with high levels of internal trust, but distrustful of and antagonistic to outsiders. This question is directly addressed in this chapter that evaluates the necessary conditions for the development of a certain type of social capital that allows for the generalization and bridging of civic virtues formed within groups of personal acquaintances. Are the deliberative procedures adopted by some associations or social movement organizations enough to avoid parochialism? Under which circumstances can social capital lead to stronger parochial communities and sometimes, on the contrary, to generalized trust and reciprocity? How and when can bonding social capital lead to or on the contrary impede the development of bridging and linking social capital?

As outlined in the introduction to this volume, social capital is now usually split into three types: bonding, bridging and linking. Bonding consists of dense ties within a group and therefore corresponds to issues such as "community cohesion" and social movement identity. Bridging refers to the "strength of weak ties", i.e. the value of connections between groups within wider civil society. Linking concerns the ability of civil society actors to link to institutions in order to acquire access to resources and influence decisions in their favour. So not only does the strength of social ties matter, but also their content, the type of actors with whom one relates. It is not the same to interact with a neighbour, a member of a different ethnic or cultural community or an institution. The identity of the actors has therefore to be taken into account to understand the dynamic of social capital creation. A special type of actor is investigated in this chapter: a deliberative social movement in a context of conflict with the State.

Accordingly, deliberative procedures militate much more in favour of openness, pluralism and universalism than of strengthening the strong social bonds of a closed community and should thus avoid the risks of parochialism. It can therefore be hypothesized that the deliberative organization of a voluntary association should allow for the generalization of the civic virtues generated internally and thus foster the reciprocal development of bridging and linking social capital. The best way to test this theoretical assumption is to confront it with an empirical case study that fulfils the requirements of both social capital and deliberative democracy theories. It should, consequently, be a voluntary association organized along deliberative procedures.

The Argentine popular assemblies, which appeared in the wake of the December 2001 crisis in the neighbourhoods of the capital city Buenos Aires and then spread all over the country, seem to fulfil such conditions. As a social movement organized along deliberative procedures, they should have internal democratic effects on participants. It is certainly not the only case to fulfil the conditions necessary for the development of civic virtues among members. Some European SMOs among the "new global" movement also share such characteristics, and especially the deliberative emphasis (see Andretta *et al.* 2002). The study of the Argentine popular assemblies could, nevertheless, offer an interesting and refreshing insight on these theoretical questions. First, it might be illuminating to study the construction of social capital in times of crisis and conflict with the State. Times of high contention and dispute can reveal hidden aspects that are often not visible under more "normal" conditions. Then, the Argentine popular assemblies as they are organized on a local territorial basis – the neighbourhood – brought together people from heterogeneous social, political and ideological backgrounds, fostering the creation of cross-cutting social networks. This heterogeneity, not so common among social movements, should have, according to most social capital and deliberative theorists, important effects on participants. Especially, a significant number of participants were new to politics and activism; as such, it has been easier to evaluate the specific effect of participation on these individuals, in comparison with more politicized ones. The sociological study of Argentine popular assemblies was therefore used to test the hypothesis about the creation of social capital in deliberative organizations. This chapter is split into four sections, the first presents the Argentine context, the second evaluates the school of democracy hypothesis, the third scrutinizes the role of deliberative interactions in the creation of a bonding social capital and the final section examines the conflictive relationship between bonding and bridging social capital in the Argentine context.

A deliberative institution in a contentious context

Within the few months between October 2001 and January 2002 the Argentine people moved from silence to noise and then to political mobilization. The October 2001 legislative elections already embodied the growing legitimacy crisis of Argentine democracy: even though voting is compulsory in this country, almost 40 per cent of the electorate did not participate; the lowest electoral turnout in Argentina's democratic history. This was called the "*bronca* vote", symbolizing Argentine citizens' defiance towards their representatives. From the beginning of December 2001 onwards tension increased in the country, with multiple lootings of stores and demonstrations in response to the deteriorating economic and social situation. The crisis reached its climax on the 19th and 20th of December. Hundreds of thousands of Buenos Aires' inhabitants went down the streets banging pots and pans – hence its label of the "*Cacerolazo* night" – to protest against the state of siege proclamation by President Fernando de La Rua. The following morning, his authority weakened, the President had to resign. But the mobilization did not stop there, new *cacerolazos* were organized on the following Fridays. Inhabitants of most of the capital city's neighbourhoods met at the corners of their district's main streets to demonstrate together. Rapidly, however, these informal gatherings, which were originally aimed at mobilizing people for protest, transformed themselves into local assemblies. Through this form of organization citizens managed to move away from noise and protest to make their voice heard and express new forms of political discourses. Somewhat surprisingly, they organized themselves in a deliberative way, the principle of "horizontality" being central to their mobilization. We will try to understand here to what degree the Argentine popular assemblies fit the social capital and deliberative democracy criteria.

To put Putnam's perspective in a nutshell, one could say that three conditions are necessary to reach the internal democratic transformation of individuals engaged in secondary associations: (1) relationships among networks of civic engagement should allow direct face-to-face interactions among participants; (2) these relationships should take a horizontal shape; and (3) associations should cut across social and cultural cleavages. Argentine popular assemblies seem to fit in this general framework. As local institutions, they are based on face-to-face interactions among their members. Argentine popular assemblies generally did not bring together more than 100 members, which meant that everybody knew each other and physical proximity was facilitated. Then, as examined below, the assemblies are formally ruled by horizontal procedures and interactions. Finally, as neighbourhood organizations, they cut across social, cultural and political cleavages. Even if the middle classes were over-represented, low-income people also represent a significant number of the members. They were also politically very diverse, since the popular assemblies did not have any fixed ideology or programme. They thus gathered together very heterogeneous people from anarchists to Christians, "a-political citizens" to Trotskyst militants.

Argentine popular assemblies seem therefore to fulfil Robert Putnam's voluntary associations' criteria and, as such, should have positive developmental effects on participants. The analysis of their procedural organization reinforces this assumption. Not only did the Argentine popular assemblies emerge, but they also immediately organized along "deliberative rules". The identity of Argentine popular assemblies is indeed directly linked to the concept of "horizontality". The deliberative organization was generally discussed and voted on in the first sessions of most popular assemblies, in January 2002. Discussion in popular assemblies was made in an argumentative way, which means that participants made propositions that were then discussed and criticized by others. This does not mean that only rational arguments were voiced within popular assemblies, since very often personal testimonies, opinions or emotional accounts were stated. Popular assemblies' sessions were public. They took place in public spaces: in the streets, in municipal or associative meeting rooms, and sometimes in squatted buildings. Popular assemblies' sessions were also inclusive. Formally, no one could be excluded from the discussions. Any participant was free to speak up, to make propositions, to criticize others' propositions and to vote for or against these propositions at the end of the session. Finally, even if the assemblies generally attempted to reach a consensus, it was often hard to do so in a limited amount of time. They therefore had to take decisions on majority votes. In these cases, a formal equality was attributed to every participant, each one having a vote.

These procedural norms, which were usually not written but respected by custom, seem – from a formal point of view – to correspond to the defining criteria of deliberative democracy. Even if their number varies from one scholar to the next, four formal criteria are generally considered to characterize a fair deliberative procedure: (1) *rationality*, deliberation being a collective decision-making process ruled by the force of the best argument (Manin 1987; Cohen 1997); (2) *publicity*, arguments have to be justified in front of all the participants (Elster 1998; Gutmann and Thomson 1996); (3) *inclusion* (Bohman 1996; Young 2000); and (4) the regulatory ideal of the discussion should be the largest possible agreement amongst participants, i.e. a *consensus* (Habermas 1996).

As it has been shown how the Argentine popular assemblies fit the social capital and deliberative paradigms, we can now evaluate whether their participants have been shaped by the deliberative interactions accordingly and thus built a special type of social capital.

Schools of democracy?

A widespread metaphor in the literature about deliberative democracy and social capital sees local participatory institutions and voluntary associations as "schools of democracy" (Pateman 1970; Barber 1984; Evans and Boyte 1986; Mansbridge 1999). The Argentine popular assemblies could be, given their adequacy with the procedural model of deliberative democracy, such schools. What would be learned in this type of institution? Generally, two types of developmental effects are put forward by proponents of participatory democracy: (1) democratic skills and (2) civic virtues. These categories are obviously very broad. By democratic skills, it is meant the ability to voice one's opinions, propositions or criticisms, and the capacity to listen to others' arguments. Civic virtues are defined here as internal solidarity, empathy and tolerance of differences (Warren 2001). How can these variables be tested? Purely qualitative methods have been used in this research, through an in-depth ethnographic study of the popular assemblies in 2002. Participant observation in various assemblies was aimed at understanding individuals' self-presentation strategies and vocabularies of motives in situation, related to the necessity of public justification and their potential effects on individuals' long-term values. Interviews were understood as means to grasp participants' narratives about their own identity and empowerment. Actors' narratives should help to understand their own personal trajectories and subjective changes in the course of political participation.

Concerning democratic skills, one could study objective improvements such as clarity of the arguments, logic of the propositions, inference capacities and so on. It seems, nevertheless, that when it comes to voicing one's opinions within a deliberative arena, other types of domination processes have also to be taken into account. Domination is not only a question of who speaks and how much, but also of how one speaks. Generally, members with fewer resources made shorter, less analytical and less articulate interventions in the Argentine popular assemblies. They were listened to less well and other members often started to talk to their neighbours when some interventions became too confused. Whereas speech is almost sacred within the Argentine popular assemblies – no one being allowed to interrupt someone else – the few exceptions to this rule always happened when members spoke up. They were sometimes cut short or even

interrupted. Some participants allowed themselves remarks that could destabi-
lize less confident speakers. Some examples are striking. Once, Oscar – one of
the most marginal members of the group, who was accused of causing "trou-
bles" in the assembly – spoke up to answer the criticisms addressed to him.
After only a few minutes, the reactions of the other *assembleistas* were rather
harsh: "Speed up! Go right to the point"; "You already said all that"; "what's
your point?" He never finished his intervention, and told me how frustrated he
felt about it: "They are accusing me, and I cannot even answer. It's unfair". The
public attention given to one's speech is indeed strong evidence of one's ability
to speak and convince others. In practice, not everyone is listened to equally.

These inequalities of treatment, which significantly influence individuals'
abilities to speak in public, are then internalized; so that some marginal individuals felt deeply that they were not entitled to speak. One could hypothetically
state that with the same "objective" argumentative skills some would speak
more than others, because they feel they have a legitimate right to do so.
Participants in deliberation have different "epistemological authority" (Sanders
1997); that is to say that some are seen as potentially more persuasive than
others. It is more likely to be men than women, whites than blacks, middle class
than working class. As such, the development of deliberative skills should not
only focus on individuals' objective abilities but also on the feeling of entitlement to speak (Young 1996).

The first thing to learn in a "school of democracy" should therefore be that,
independently of individuals' objective skills, everyone should feel entitled to
speak up. Teaching deliberative skills thus firstly implies bolstering the confidence of the most marginalized participants. This lack of self-confidence is
clearly stated in Diego's words, a 22-year-old participant from Villa Urquiza
popular assembly:

> At the start I didn't talk much. I do not talk much more today, but I am [. . .]
> when I want to say something, I go and I say it. But it is hard. In the middle
> of the assembly, when 100 persons are watching you, and that you have to
> pass in front of everybody to take the microphone and speak [. . .] It scares
> you, so that sometimes you say stupid things. [. . .] I'd like to change the
> organization: stop using the microphone, all sitting in circle, not using any
> speakers' list, etc. According to me it should just be like when you sit down
> to talk with *friends*.

He was obviously overwhelmed by the formality of the procedures of the
assembly. This example shows how participants can be symbolically excluded
from the start. It takes time to get integrated and thus to be "allowed" to speak
and to be potentially convincing. When certain participants make you feel that
you cannot speak, it has a performative power: you cannot. But even if integration can be difficult, it seems that an educative process took place within Argentine popular assemblies since, after a few months, participants felt much more
competent to speak up. Diego, for instance, feels more confident about speaking:

It is obviously easier to speak now than at the beginning. It is not easy still, but you feel that you know these guys, that they can criticize you without being nasty. Most people are friends now for me, and it is easier to speak with friends than with strangers.

He states that he talks more now than he used to. He may not be more convincing in public than he used to be, but at least he feels that he can speak, which is nevertheless an important achievement. Alejandro, a member of Corrientes y Medrano's assembly, also feels that he has changed:

Yes, I have changed. I was much more inhibited before. I couldn't speak in public, I thought it was reserved for educated persons. [...] And finally I realized that everybody here could speak up and say what he had to say. I feel that I can speak and disagree and criticize people which are much more "important' than me now.

These examples reflect subjective changes that can have tremendous democratic consequences. Participants to the Argentine popular assemblies felt both more entitled to speak up and more ready to listen to each other. Political participation seems able, under certain conditions, to foster a more competent and democratic citizenship. It seems also that a form of internal solidarity and sense of tolerance developed through time amongst the participants of the Argentine popular assemblies. They also learnt the value of certain civic virtues. Discourses about solidarity, tolerance or empathy might well be embedded in identity-building strategies and self-valorization attitudes, but they also evidence a process of (re)framing of one's values and behaviour that is worth studying.

Carlo, for instance, a member of Villa Urquiza popular assembly, feels that he has experienced an intimate and personal transformation through participation:

It changed me, that's for sure. Even in the most private and personal details. [...] I always thought that we were forming a real community, united, and that individual solutions didn't exist. But to live it, to experience it every day, in your personal life, thanks to the assembly [...] It is impressive and it gives you strength and self-confidence. [...] I have the impression that all that changed people a lot, the relationships between them, etc. To unite, in the neighbourhoods, and to rebuild a form of solidarity, it changes you.

The popular assemblies made the expression of a form of solidarity possible. The possibility to live one's commitments seems to carry a deep transformative power. Participation in Argentine popular assemblies not only spurred the development of a sense of solidarity but also of tolerance towards other members. It is especially true of leftist political party militants who participated in popular assemblies. As Andrea – activist in the Trotskyst party MST (*Movimiento Socialista de los Trabajadores*) and member of the Ayacucho y Rivadavia assembly – puts it:

Not so long ago, we [MST militants] would never have accepted to participate in such an ideologically heterogeneous environment. We would have
found people too "petit bourgeois" and reformist. We even thought about
leaving at the beginning. [...] But we finally realized that we had a lot to
learn from "lay people", i.e. from our neighbours. [...] I am myself sur-
prised at my own attitude. I can listen to arguments I wouldn't have even
accepted to hear a few months ago, for which I had no respect in the past. I
don't agree but at least I can understand what they feel.

Basilio's case is also very telling. A militant of the Argentine Communist
party since 1985, he defines himself as a "democratic Marxist", but also a "revolutionary". He acknowledges that he has a "strong personality", and that he can
sometimes be "authoritarian and aggressive" when he disagrees with someone.
For instance, he used to be part of a local newspaper in Villa Urquiza in the
1980s, but he left it after a few years because he felt the others were "too
reformist". His reaction to political disagreement was neither tolerance nor conviction but exit. Since then, he thinks he has changed: "Before, I couldn't talk
about politics seriously with a reformist or right-wing person. Now I can. [...] I
think I am more mature politically, thanks to the assembly. It taught me to be
more tolerant". The move from "exit", in the case of the local newspaper, to
"voice" (Hirschman 1970) and listening, within the assembly, is an expression
of a deep personal change.

It seems therefore that participation in the Argentine popular assemblies
could teach civic values to their members. By providing a feeling of empowerment and developing internal solidarity and tolerance, this deliberative social
movement seems to fulfil some of our theoretical assumptions. The identity discourses reflected in the interview excerpts reflect the deep personal and political
shifts many members of the popular assemblies underwent along with their participation. It did not happen overnight, but in the long run their identity changed,
making them – maybe – "better citizens". It is then necessary to understand why
such learning mechanisms developed in these institutional settings.

Socialization in a civic virtue environment: creating a bonding social capital

Procedures by themselves cannot explain the process of personal change undergone by most participants, nor the avoidance of parochialism. It is not the deliberative organization of the movement that directly created norms of empathy
and tolerance, but the progressive creation of a bonding social capital. When one
tries to understand this feeling of solidarity by referring to actors' motives, the
same reason is always invoked: direct encounters with the other. Participation in
the popular assemblies allowed strangers from diverse backgrounds to meet
face-to-face and to create ties of trust and reciprocity. Friendship and personal
relationships play an important role in the development of these types of values
and behaviours. As Sebastian – a young member of Corrientes y Medrano

assembly – says, you behave differently with people you know and you do not know:

> My relations with people changed. Before, I had a kind of truly individualistic vision of life. I was a cool computer engineer, earning money [. . .] the usual story. And all this happened, the crisis, the kids dying of hunger again in such a rich country. [. . .] So I decided to quit my job and I started to go to demonstrations, assemblies, etc. It was really new for me. [. . .] And when you start participating in an assembly, you meet people, you become more or less friends [. . .] So, when one of them has a problem, with his job, his rent or anything, I am going to help him. He is not a stranger to me, he is a neighbour.

Alejandro, for instance, completely changed his mind about the unemployed workers' movement, the *Piqueteros*, once he met some of them in his neighbourhood assembly. The direct encounter with them, facilitated by the assembly, is understood as the cause of his personal change: "At the beginning I saw that as a remote reality, through television or news [. . .] And I didn't understand them". But the face-to-face encounter changed his mind: "What marked me, is to have *met* them [. . .] To *see* them work, to *know* them in their daily life". He insists on the visual experience of a hard and different reality. He saw with his own eyes what was first mediated by the news. Alejandro's explanations can be found in most *asambleistas*' stories. The direct contact, the physical presence of the other, allows one to see, to observe and therefore to inform his/her own judgement. Preferences are thus not only formed through media information but by face-to-face interactions.

Norms of empathy and tolerance developed in the popular assemblies derived from the personal relationships between the members. Altruistic and tolerant behaviours became the norm, so that everybody had to adopt them. One of the main explanations of self-change lies in the emergence of a new collective identity within the popular assemblies. Individuals' identities underwent a process of alignment in keeping with the norms and values prevailing in the popular assemblies. This collective identity building was all the more powerful in that it took place in a context of conflict with the State. Ties between members had to be strong to provide power to the powerless. Faced with a powerful actor like the State, a social movement has to be highly organized and integrated to offer a credible challenge. Participants in the Argentine popular assemblies thus experienced a process of secondary (re)socialization. To integrate themselves, individuals had to accept certain norms and values prevailing in the popular assemblies. Understanding activism and social movement participation as a process of secondary socialization is not new however. Political parties, voluntary associations and most of civil society institutions fulfil a function of socialization for their members. By creating interactions between formerly anonymous citizens, these institutions create strong social ties and shape individuals' identities. However, the specificity of the Argentine popular assemblies lies in the type of norms and values they promoted. They valorized mutual listening and understanding, tolerance and altruistic behaviours.

As mentioned earlier, the deliberative and democratic frame visible in actors' discourses shaped the formal organization of the assemblies. Through mechanisms of sanction and gratification, Argentine popular assemblies could shape individuals' behaviours and values. To allow tolerance and listening, they were organized along a set of formal procedures: speakers' lists, interdiction to interrupting one another, a time limit of three minutes per intervention and voting at the end of the sessions. These norms had to be respected and followed by all the members, deviant behaviours being systematically sanctioned. For instance, an individual cutting somebody short in a middle of his/her intervention would immediately be interrupted by the other participants, who would ask him/her to remain silent and listen to the speaker. If this kind of behaviour was regularly reproduced, the individual acquired a bad *reputation*. He was labelled "authoritarian" or "anti-democrat", as in the case of Oscar, discussed above. On the contrary, the one who conforms perfectly to the norms of the assembly, being particularly open-minded, tolerant and ready to listen to others, was highly praised within the institution. The case of Ezequiel, a 33-year-old member of Cid Campeador assembly, offers a good example of this phenomenon. He was said to be "clever", "reflexive", "open-minded"; people believed he "thinks a lot before speaking up". His good reputation granted him respect from the other participants, who naturally listened to him when he spoke up.

Behind these concepts of reputation and respect lies the question of the integration of individuals into the assemblies. The more he/she respected the norms of the group, the more he/she was rewarded and integrated. On the contrary, as long as he/she was regarded as an outsider, transgressing the rules, he/she was penalized and excluded. Behaviours are shaped through these social interactions. Such mechanisms constitute a strong incentive to conform to the dominant norms and values of the group and therefore to internalize them. This phenomenon of individual transformation cannot therefore be analysed as a superficial change. Norms are not only respected, they are also internalized. It is not, of course, a linear and harmonious process, as the new norms and values very often contradict those previously inculcated during individuals' primary socialization. Actors have, nevertheless, the possibility to leave the game at any time.

This process of socialization does not only affect democratic behaviours but also altruistic ones. Empathetic attitudes were indeed highly valorized within the Argentine popular assemblies. An individual was all the more integrated if he/she had invested time and energy for others and for the group. The specific moment to express this gratification was the beginning of sessions, when each assembly commission announced its weekly activities. Individuals that had adopted "good" behaviours were symbolically rewarded through a kind of theatrical ritual. The speaker of the commission stood at the centre of the circle and, once his/her intervention was over, people clapped, made ritual jokes and sometimes sung traditional Argentine political songs or even their own anthem, "*Que se vayan todos!*".[1] These types of rituals fulfil a double function. They socialize and integrate individuals through a process of sanction/gratification. They also create a distinctive collective identity with its own symbols, rituals and memories.

The Argentine popular assemblies thus made self-change possible through the creation of a bonding social capital. The dense ties and the intimacy created among former strangers allowed the realignment of individual frames and behaviours. Through the dialectic articulation of new altruistic and democratic "habitus" (Bourdieu 1984) in a social environment where such behaviours were greatly encouraged, it seems that Argentine popular assemblies made deliberation and solidarity possible. The Argentine popular assemblies seem to be a favourable environment for the development of civic virtue. They make civic virtue worthy – i.e. profitable – for individuals.

Excluding outsiders? The difficult move from bonding to bridging social capital in times of conflict

Self-change was, in some sense, on the agenda of the popular assemblies. There was indeed a common hope among the members of the Argentine popular assemblies that they could embody a vanguard leading to a broad social and cultural change in the country. Their basic assumption was that Argentine political, but also economic and social, crisis stemmed from cultural biases carried on through the country's history. The twentieth century in Argentina has, indeed, been marked by authoritarianism and a profound political instability. The last dictatorship is considered to have deeply influenced Argentine's civic culture. Authoritarianism and political violence indeed seem to have reached their climax between 1976 and 1983, with the "disappearing" – i.e. murder – of about 30,000 people. The aim of the 1976 military coup d'état was to bring authority back into a country where "the Christian and liberal" order was jeopardized by leftist "subversives". Following Guillermo O'Donnell, the dictatorship seems to have fulfilled its task perfectly: "The street and the school, the work place and the public office became places of submission and fear, or, to use a concept from political science, of the complete loss of citizenship" (O'Donnell 1999). It is this civic culture that the Argentine popular assemblies' movement fought and tried to change. The "*no te mete*"[2] legacy was framed as one of the main causes of Argentine problems. Carlo, a member of the Villa Urquiza popular assembly, is very clear about this process:

> I think it is a personal problem, an internal struggle. One shouldn't forget that we were formatted by this system, that we have largely interiorized all these destructive behaviours and this authoritarian culture, which always tries to impose itself. To change things we have first to win this struggle against oneself.

However, the internal practices of the popular assemblies and the creation of a bonding social capital – that made self-change possible – impeded the achievement of this aim, as bridging social capital was never built by the movement. If the norms and values prevailing in the assemblies were generalized by the participants to the outsiders, this does not mean that outsiders themselves changed. It can be argued that since political participation – within a specific type of deliberative institution – is required to foster generalizable civic virtues, those who did not have the chance or the will to take part in this process remained unchanged. The values and norms held in the assemblies did not generalize outside the doors of the assemblies, as contacts with outsiders became more and more scarce. The move from bonding to bridging social capital seems to be far from being automatic.

According to Jean Cohen, trust or reciprocity cannot be transferred *naturally* from interpersonal relationships to others or to other contexts without a medium of exchange:

> One trusts particular people because of repeated interactions with them in specific contexts in which reciprocity is directly experienced. Interpersonal trust generated in face-to-face relationships is not an instance of a more general impersonal phenomenon. Nor can it simply be transferred to others or to other contexts. [. . .] Without mediations, there is no reason to expect that the forms of reciprocity or trust generated within small groups would extend beyond the group or, for that matter, that group demands would be anything other than particularistic.
>
> (Cohen 1999)

The metaphor of social "capital" would tend to imply that it is "generalizable". Capital accumulated in one situation can usually be invested in another. Financial capital, for instance, can be saved, accumulated, exchanged and transferred because there is a universal equivalent for it: money. As the medium of exchange and the equivalent for all forms of wealth and capital, money solves the generalization issue. However, interpersonal trust is, by definition, specific and contextual. Without any universal medium it cannot be generalized. Such a medium exists, it is simply overlooked by Putnam and most proponents of the neo-Tocquevillian approach. As defined, trust pre-supposes predictability and the assurance that others will perform as they said they would. In modern societies such predictability of individual behaviours is provided by the rule of law. Obligations and sanctions related to the rule of law foster the regularity and predictability of behaviours and, as such, develop universal trustworthiness. By limiting arbitrariness and favouritism, the law, as institutionalized cultural values and norms, provides everyone with the same amount of trust impartially.

However, in the Argentine case, the rule of law did not exist as such a medium of trust, since it is precisely the corruption and lack of trust in the judicial system – and especially the Supreme Court – that spurred the mobilization in the first place. The mass media could also be, by definition, one of these media of generalization (Newton 1999), by propagating the claims and values of social movements. However, Argentine popular assemblies did not have much media support. The popular assemblies only mobilized a few thousand people, and even if their influence was noticeable in many Buenos Aires neighbour-hoods, their audience in the media or on the political stage remained limited. But mediation can also be ensured through the role of "boundary spanners" – key actors who can act as network nodes and bridge different social networks. The Argentine popular assemblies progressively lost this kind of mediating actor. The crucial reason why the norms and values which appeared within the assemblies failed to be generalized to the rest of society is the progressive closure of the group on itself, that is to say its inability to create bridging social capital.

If collective identity building (re)socialized individuals, it also excluded some of them, thus impeding the creation of a bridging social capital. The exclusion process took two distinctive forms in the Argentine case: it made deviant members leave the assemblies and impeded the integration of newcomers. The bonding social capital created in the popular assemblies impeded the creation of bridging social capital and weakened ties with other actors and groups character-ized by different goals and identities. Indeed, for social movements the creation of bridging social capital – that is to say of loose networks of organizations – with other actors is crucial for the spread of mobilization, the fulfilment of their aims and their overall social and cultural impact (Polletta 1999).

To understand how this exclusionary process worked one has to turn to the emergence of the neighbourhood assemblies in Argentina. They were created in the wake of the crisis, following weeks of intense mobilization and contention. When created, they gathered together highly heterogeneous individuals, tied by a common anger against the government and the "failure of the political system". As such, the popular assemblies could be defined at the start as an "empty space", where any claim or ideology could be expressed. However, after only a few weeks, minority groups or excluded individuals left the assembly. As, very often, no consensus could be reached, decisions were taken by the majority, *de facto* excluding some of the members. This led many people to leave the assemblies. Those remaining thus created strong bonds between them-selves. Friendships appeared among them and the assembly was increasingly associated with the image of a family. Diego, a member of the Villa Urquiza assembly, states this very clearly: "Well, we are just like a great family. With all its problems, arguments, fights [...] all the things that are not said, and that come out at some point. I really feel I belong to the family of the assembly". These strong bonds allowed solidarity within the group but also discouraged dissent and criticisms. As Diego says:

> The assembly is like a family. And in a family the son is not going to tell the father what he thinks about him when he has a negative opinion. Just because he is afraid. It is not respect, it is fear. So you shut up.

The creation of bonding social capital thus seems to have closed the group on itself, either by making dissenters leave or by encouraging a silent loyalty over voicing criticisms. One anecdote of what took place at Corrientes y Medrano popular assembly is very telling about this problem. One night, during the weekly session of the assembly, a young female student showed up at the meeting. It was easy to identify her as a newcomer as nobody either knew her personally or had seen her before. Surprisingly, despite her young age, she had the courage to speak up. At first, most participants were rather enthusiastic about this already "active" newcomer. Unfortunately, she did not say the "right" thing. Once again, the debate was about how the assembly could spread in the neighbourhood, and every speaker was giving his/her own analysis of the limiting factors for the development of the assembly. The young student, as she felt entitled to speak in the name of those who did not dare to participate, started to criticize the sometimes "sectarian attitude" of the assembly. She especially focused her criticisms on the behaviour of some political parties, particularly active in this assembly. In a word, as an outsider, she said openly what the members could not say. The reaction was, however, immediate. Many older male participants and members of various leftist political parties felt directly attacked. They attacked her personally in response, arguing that despite all possible criticisms one could not deny the crucial mobilization and organizing role of most of the militants. New to these kinds of verbal battles she rapidly felt deeply embarrassed and ashamed. The result was rather straightforward: she never came back! This is only one example, but many others could be cited of the progressive closure of the popular assemblies following the formation of their collective identity.

A temporal distinction seems necessary to understand this phenomenon (see Table 12.1). In the short term strong ties, such as political parties' membership or personal friendship, were necessary for the emergence of the popular assemblies. Dense social networks and bonding social capital were crucial in the mobilization and organization of the people. As mentioned earlier, these strong ties helped to build up rather heterogeneous and open institutions like the popular assemblies. In the long term, however, the progressive silencing of dissenting "voices" led to the "exit" of most dissenters. The building of a strong collective identity closed the assemblies on themselves, impeding the diffusion of their protest through a wider constituency. It can therefore be concluded that social capital, i.e. networks of personal relationships, was necessary at the beginning but that its bonding nature produced by the mobilization worked as a barrier to the creation of bridging social capital and thus to the further development of the movement.

Table 12.1 Effects on social mobilization of social ties through time

Temporality	Strength of social ties	
	Weak	Strong
Short term	Apathy	Emergence
Long term	Diffusion	Closure

These conclusions seem in keeping with those of Francesca Polletta on the nature of "free spaces", who indirectly evokes a central debate of social capital theory (Polletta 1999). Her main point is that strong ties can limit rather than spur mobilization:

> Such networks [strong ties] may impede protest. This is partly because the absence of ties to outsiders may lead aggrieved people to interpret threats and conflicts in purely local terms [. . .] rather than in terms of the broader identities and ideologies that are necessary to mass mobilization. [. . .] Weak ties may facilitate it [mobilization], not only because they provide access to people and resources outside the community, but because potential insurgents may grant "known strangers" the authority to challenge the bonds of authority and deference within the community that have kept people from overt defiance.
>
> (Polletta 1999: 20)

She thus shows that "networks intersections" matter since the social *distance* of outsiders gives them the opportunity to adopt a critical attitude towards the group. Polletta takes, among others, the example of the women at the 1964 SNCC annual conference who, thanks to their status of outsiders – i.e. new members – could challenge the dominant patriarchal relationships within the movement. This can be compared with the anecdote we gave above about the young female student who, when she first participated in the Corrientes y Medrano assembly, challenged the closeness and the "sectarian attitude" of the group. Outsiders can therefore constitute powerful critical resources for a social movement, even if they often have to leave (as in the case of the SNCC feminists) to express themselves further against some dominant norms and values. Francesca Polletta argues in favour of the virtues of distance and therefore against the "free space" literature – but also against most of the social capital one – that focuses on the virtues of face-to-face interactions and strong social ties. It has, nevertheless, to be underlined that even if social distance might be a necessary condition for the growth of a social movement, the distance has to be put into presence to have any noticeable effect. Outsiders have to be brought face-to-face with insiders to have any significant effect on them. Criticisms and challenges to social movements from outsiders are plenty. However, they generally do not have any effect on them, as they are understood as "enemy discourses". To be efficient, the criticisms have to be made within the frame of the organization's discourse. Outsiders have to come towards the movement to influence it. The outsider cannot just be a stranger; he/she has to be a "known stranger" (Polletta 1999). Weak ties and bridging social capital are therefore to be understood firstly as social ties, i.e. as concrete physical interactions. Bridging social capital might be necessary for a social movement to achieve its goals, especially when in conflict with a powerful actor like the State, it still has to be understood as a physical interaction, without which social capital merely disappears.

Conclusion

The network of personal relationships created by the Argentine popular assemblies has had both a positive developmental effect on the participants and a negative effect in closing up the group on itself. Individuals became more empowered, tolerant and empathetic in their relations to each other, but it is uncertain whether they managed to expand these personal feelings outside the doors of the assemblies. The link between bonding and bridging social capital appears in this regard problematic. As the group developed stronger ties and progressively built a collective identity it made interaction with outsiders more conflictive, as it is largely in opposition to these strangers that the identity of the group had been formed in the first place.

The Argentine popular assemblies allowed their members to meet outsiders directly. They did not become insiders and the contacts were anyway too scarce to reach a true globalization of the movement. The tension between the globalization of protest and the development of a strong collective identity was never solved by the popular assemblies. However, these direct interactions with strangers allowed an enlargement of the members' judgements, a generalization of the values of solidarity, reciprocity and empathy born within the group. This self-transformation cannot directly be attributed to the deliberative procedures, since the actors are very clear on the fact that this generalization did not stem from a discursive process of mutual conviction, but rather through an emotional mechanism of empathy and reciprocity. It is more the face-to-face contact allowed by the local organization of the assemblies than the deliberative procedures themselves that created an emotional commitment of the members towards strangers, and especially the most marginalized of their compatriots. This emotional experience allowed, simultaneously, a cognitive process to take place, since the actors' judgements were informed by what they saw. Self-change was made possible by the type of norms and values put forward by the popular assemblies. Not only the procedures but the substance of the movement allowed this process to take place: as mentioned earlier, values such as altruism and tolerance were highly valorized within the popular assemblies. The ideology of the movement could not lead it to focus exclusively on local community interests. The type of behaviours that were valorized or punished through the deliberative rules of the assembly is therefore the main cause of self-change. More generally, it is the link between ideology and organization in social movements that has to be rethought, since the deliberative organization was a direct expression of the movement ideology and the prime marker of its identity.

Notes

1 Meaning "They all have to go!" in reference to the politicians and the cultural and financial elites of the country.
2 Means literally "Do not commit yourself".

References

Andretta, M., della Porta, D., Mosca, L. and Reiter, H. (2002) *Global, no global, new global: La protesta contro il G8 a Genova*, Roma: Laterza.

Barber, B. (1984) *Strong Democracy, Participatory Politics for a New Age*, Berkeley: University of California Press.

Bell, D. (1998) "Civil Society versus Civic Virtue", in A. Gutmann (ed.) *Freedom of Association*, Princeton: Princeton University Press, pp. 239–272.

Bohman, J. (1996) *Public Deliberation: Pluralism, Complexity and Democracy*, Cambridge, MA: MIT Press.

Bourdieu, P. (1984) *Distinction: A Social Critique of the Judgement of Taste*, London: Routledge

Cohen, J. (1997) "Deliberation and Democratic Legitimacy", in J. Bohman and W. Rehg (eds) *Deliberative Democracy: Essays on Reason and Politics*, Cambridge, MA: MIT Press, pp. 67–91.

Cohen, J. (1999) "Trust, Voluntary Association, and Workable Democracy: The Contemporary Discourse of Civil Society", in M. Warren (ed.) *Democracy and Trust*, Cambridge: Cambridge University Press, pp. 208–248.

Elster, J. (ed.) (1998) *Deliberative Democracy*, Cambridge: Cambridge University Press.

Evans, S. and Boyte, H. (1986) *Free Spaces*, New York: Harper and Row.

Gutmann, A. and Thomson, D. (1996) *Democracy and Disagreement*, Cambridge, MA: Harvard University Press.

Habermas, J. (1996) *Between Facts and Norms: Contribution to a Discourse Theory of Law and Democracy*, Cambridge, MA: MIT Press.

Hirschman, A. (1970) *Exit, Voice and Loyalty*, Cambridge, MA: Harvard University Press.

Levi, M. (1996) "Social and Unsocial Capital: A Review Essay of Robert Putnam's *Making Democracy Work*", *Politics and Society*, 24: 45–55.

Manin, B. (1987) "On Legitimacy and Political Deliberation", *Political Theory*, 15: 338–368.

Mansbridge, J. (1999) "On the Idea that Participation makes Better Citizens", in S. Elkin and K. Soltan (eds) *Citizen Competence and Democratic Institutions*, Philadelphia: The Pennsylvania University Press, pp. 291–325.

Newton, K. (1999) "Social Capital and Democracy in Modern Europe", in J. Van Deth, M. Maraffi, K. Newton and P. Whiteley *Social Capital and European Democracy*, London: Routledge, pp. 3–24.

O'Donnell, G. (1999) "Notes on Sociability and Politics in Argentina and Brazil", in *Ibid., Counterpoints, Selected Essays on Authoritarianism and Democratization*, Notre Dame: University of Notre Dame Press, pp. 79–94.

Pateman, C. (1970) *Participation and Democratic Theory*, Cambridge: Cambridge University Press.

Polletta, F. (1999) "Free Spaces in Collective Action", *Theory and Society*, 28: 1–38.

Putnam, R. (1993) *Making Democracy Work: Civic Traditions in Modern Italy*, Princeton, NJ: Princeton University Press.

Sanders, L. (1997) "Against Deliberation", *Political Theory*, 25 (3): 347–376.

Warren, M. (2001) *Democracy and Association*, Cambridge: Cambridge University Press.

Young, I. (1996) "Communication and the Other: Beyond Deliberative Democracy", in S. Benhabib (ed.) *Democracy and Difference: Contesting the Boundaries of the Political*, Princeton, NJ: Princeton University Press, pp. 120–135.

Young, I. (2000) *Inclusion and Democracy*, Oxford: Oxford University Press.

13 Conclusion

Civil society, governance, social movements and social capital

Derrick Purdue

Introduction

This book has been organized in three parts on civic organizations and governance, social movements from local to global, and social capital and trust. However, there are a number of connections between the work in each section; the approaches overlap – linking social capital corresponds to governance, civic organizations are hubs of social capital and often of social movements; networks and trust are features not only of social capital, but also of social movements and civil society. The concluding chapter aims to take four of the conceptual discussions contained in the preceding sections a little further. The first issue to address is whether civic organizations have an active role in governance or are simply drawn into the process of creating governable subjects for states. Linked to this is a second theme of competing conceptions of civil societies as (a) supportive to or (b) alternative power bases to states. The third theme we consider is the interplay of local, national and global spaces in social movement mobilization. The final theme concerns the balance of different types of social capital that were found in the case studies, and the forms of trust that underpin them.

Governance, governmentality and civil society

Civic organizations continue to play an important political as well as civil role integrating the public into a public sphere in relation to the state, and as vehicles for negotiation with state organs. 'The new governance' has come to indicate multi-organizational agency (Lowndes and Skelcher 1998), for example at the local level, but these chapters show that the ambivalent position of civic organizations as mediators between state forms and wider civil societies are further complicated by external funders and relatively dependent states in Eastern Europe, as well as by the tensions in central–local government relations in the UK (and other Western European countries).

This question is dramatized in the case of Community Empowerment Networks in England, which were set up by central government in order to establish civil society as an effective actor within Local Strategic Partnerships and other organs of local governance. Community engagement in governance involves a series of compromises, professional behaviour, accepting views and experience from state and business which is an anathema to many (Taylor 2006). Diamond (Chapter 4) is not alone in adopting a critical viewpoint on the requirement for civil society to oil the working of the state system. Other authors in Britain have criticized what they see as 'manufactured civil society' created by the state as a support for governmental power within the new governance (Hodgson 2004) and forms of community development (e.g. capacity building) which are aimed at developing the community only in ways that serve to support partnership structures (Banks and Shenton 2001).

The increased complexity of governance can also be viewed through the lens of 'governmentality', the Foucauldian concept, which draws attention to the idea that government goes beyond making policy and implementing it, to include the creation of 'governable subjects' suitable for the form of government (Newman 2005). That is, shaping the mentality of the governed so that they can play the roles expected of them; hence capacity building programmes in both the East and the West. Pishchikova (Chapter 3) in particular points to the debates within Western support agencies about the suitability of local subjects for democratic government.

While it is clear that any form of government requires subjects who can be governed, to see the new governance purely as a way of creating 'active citizens' as new governable subjects is an unduly structuralist approach which denies any agency to citizens, their organizations or their social movements. This theoretical pacification is at odds with discourses of civil society. The history of civil society activity demonstrates that active citizens were not created in Western Europe by the likes of the British Government's 'Active Citizenship Unit' nor was civic activism in Eastern Europe invented by foreign donors. What is clear is that they are attempts to manage civil societies. Neither civil societies, nor their relationships with states and governance structures have been innocent of power. Indeed civil activity is necessarily competitive and it is argued that power differentials are increasing (Keane 2003). New governance spaces, whether local or global, are places where a range of powers are exercised. Whether the political opportunities they represent for civil society are opening up cannot be categorically denied in advance, especially if they are compared with the closed and technocratic forms of government that preceded them. However, it is important to remember that, particularly in times of transition, the political opportunity structure can be volatile as Salmenniemi (Chapter 2) demonstrates in respect of Russia, where 'managed democracy' clearly constitutes a closing down of opportunities for civil society.

Civil society for or against the state?

As Kim observed in Chapter 11, an important distinction has been drawn between two images of civil society (Foley and Edwards 1996; Edwards and Foley 2001). The first is that of civil society as the social oil of the state system (as in the dominant view of social capital as proposed by Putnam, and widely taken up in policy circles). The contrasting view is of civil society as the coun-terweight to the state, which is more akin to the role assigned to civil society in the social movements literature (Melucci 1989, 1996; Chesters and Welsh 2005). A tempting solution to this problem is to say that it depends on the nature of the state – that in, say, Apartheid South Africa civil society occupied an oppo-sitional role, but that in established democracies civil society plays a more sup-portive role. Yet, it is a constant and nagging question in community politics and in almost any social movement milieu in advanced democracies as to whether civil society is most effective when engaged with state agencies in governance, or as a challenge to states and state forms from the outside? While that is a polit-ical and empirical question, it is clear at a theoretical level that these two are not mutually exclusive. Social movements at global and local levels frequently work in alliances between radical outsiders, whose contentious repertoire can shift the terms of debate, and those on the inside, who use more conventional repertoires, but are able to capitalize on these radical interventions (Purdue *et al.* 2004). In contemporary Britain, new governance spaces appear at the local level to incor-porate civil society into cooperation with the local state. Policy actors in central government portray the role of civil society representation very much as oiling the wheels of local governance, providing much needed feedback loops and legitimacy (Purdue 2001; Chesters and Welsh 2005; Taylor 2006). However, it is clear that many local community activists see themselves precisely as a coun-terweight to government policy and practice and approach the governance struc-ture with views and agendas that do not fit well with a placid acceptance of state authority (Purdue 2005). Leaving aside debates over the effectiveness of civil society participation in governance structures, it is clear that civil society is not restricted to supporting the state, and can simultaneously act as a counterweight to state policy and power. This is evident from successive protest cycles, appear-ing most recently in the dramatic form of the global anti-Iraq War protests explored by Verhulst and Walgrave in Chapter 8.

Multi-level movements: global, local, national

Social movements are complex networks which operate simultaneously at varying geographic scales. Local neighbourhoods are often the physical places in which movements cluster, but they also mobilize through virtual spaces and are mediated by a whole series of macro- and micro-level processes. The 'paradox of space and place' (Harvey 1993) is that despite global communica-tion systems, which appear to make proximity unimportant for social interaction and political and economic organization, the most global industries (e.g. finance) do in fact cluster in particular places (e.g. New York or London). Instead of globalization creating undifferentiated space, place retains its importance. This paradox of space and place permeates social movements and civil societies in their contemporary forms. Indeed local 'community' has come to take a dis-tinctly social movement form of identification (O'Doherty *et al.* 1999) as a sym-bolic mobilizing point against the accumulation of global power (Harvey 1993).

Yet even the most avowedly localist of movements utilize global communications technologies to connect up with other local actors around the world, as in the case of Local Exchange Trading Schemes (LETS), which invent local currencies to create mutual benefits through trading skills locally (O'Doherty *et al.* 1999). On the other end of the scale social movements mobilizing on global issues and utilizing global ideas are rooted in specific neighbourhoods and face-to-face networks. Haunss and Leach (Chapter 5) have shown the local dimension of a movement concerned with global issues in their use of the concept of 'scene' to indicate the networks arranged around particular venues in particular neighbourhoods, in particular cities.

Global governance structures have become a focus of social movement and civil society activity – summits, world trade negotiations, as well as numerous slightly less well known international regimes regulating whaling, trade in endangered species, ozone depletion, carbon emissions and so on, not to mention housing and homelessness, population growth and gender relations. Movement activists who attend these events frequently bypass their own governments and ally themselves with others in wider international alliances (Purdue 2000). While these were given a brief showing by Boudourides and Botetzagias (Chapter 7), the single biggest global mobilization reported in this book focused on the global hegemon (USA) as a decidedly ambivalent player in global governance. The central point of the two chapters dealing directly with global mobilization, or mobilization on global issues, was the continuing significance of the nation state as shaping the political opportunity structure (POS) for the movements in their territory. Anti-war protestors found themselves either siding with or against their own national government and political elites, depending on the decisions made at a national level as European governments split over the Iraq War. Thus some of the protests were primarily aimed at their own national governments, while others were part of a global civil society mobilization against the hegemon and its allies.

The continuing significance of the national in global-oriented movements includes the influence of national traditions, political opportunity structures, protest cycles and ideological cleavages. Boudourides and Botetzagias point to the cleavage between political blocks expressed at a national level in their research into mobilizations in Greece, which they argue manifests through competitive 'anti-participation' based on rival networks. Competition is a feature of civil society not only between movements, but within them, and ideological cleavages at the national level remain an enduring issue even in the most global movements. Where national policy is the principal target, national government shapes the POS as Cinalli (Chapter 6) again points out in relation to issues such as asylum and unemployment policy, in spite of European integration.

Social capital and trust

Social capital links notions of associational density, inter-personal trust, trust in public institutions and the cultivation of civic virtues of participation and discussion of public issues. As a heuristic mechanism we have introduced the now familiar distinction between bonding, bridging and linking social capital. Bonding consists of dense ties within a group and therefore corresponds to issues such as 'community cohesion' and social movement identity. Bridging refers to the 'strength of weak ties', i.e. the value of connections between groups within wider civil society. Linking capital concerns the ability of civil society actors/organizations to link to institutions in order to acquire access to resources and influence decisions in their favour. The emerging governance structures are a channel for linking. Bridging capital requires spanning established cleavages between different communities, movements or political blocks. A consistent finding across the third section of the book is that bonding capital is more likely to exist and easier to promote than bridging capital. This may well be through the social learning process of becoming increasingly co-operative by repeated involvement with co-operative ventures, as explained by Curini (Chapter 9), or the defensive social structures described by Vázquez García (Chapter 10), or the social movement structures Talpin (Chapter 12) explores in conflict with the state in Argentina, or the problems Kim (Chapter 11) identifies in translating membership of voluntary associations into political participation in South Korea. Linking capital, which involves trust and engagement with the state, poses its own problems, not least in establishing the trustworthiness of state institutions. Social movements in the same country can be successful in accumulating differing mixes of these types of social capital according to their political opportunities and strategies. Cinalli (Chapter 6) demonstrates this in relation to the pro-asylum movement in Britain, which was able to accumulate bonding capital internally as well as bridging across to other civil society organizations. The pro-unemployment movement on the other hand, had strong links into governance, but was much weaker in developing bridging connections with civil society organizations, and lacked a strong supply of bonding capital unifying and grounding the movement.

An important contribution to the social capital debate can be made by work on the nature of trust. While there are debates over the bases on which trust develops, and the importance of power in relation to trust (Hardy *et al.* 1998), these types of social capital also correspond to trust directed at different types of object. Linking capital clearly involves more trust in institutions, whereas bonding is mainly about inter-personal trust of like-minded or familiar people. Bridging involves trust of others who are different in some significant ways. This means building horizontal links with wider civil society, outside of familiar communities or movements. Trust is thought to grow from three different bases: shared values, confidence in the predictability of the performance of the other and shared language. The latter implies that disagreement and difference is possible as part of the tie between parties (Lane 1998). While all three types of trust are present in some combination within all three types of social capital, values are clearly central to bonding capital and the most secure basis for social bonds in tighter communities and more narrowly defined movements. The predictability of performance is more important in establishing confidence in state institutions central to linking capital. Similarly, confidence in the effectiveness of political actors and processes is the basis of public trust in the state and political system, which Kim refers to as 'political capital' (Chapter 11). Shared language plays a role in both of these, but is most significant in bridging capital, where links are made with others in separate communities with their own values, but lacking the public agency roles of resource distribution and formal accountability. The formal value of reciprocity often connected to social capital is part of the language of civil society. Shared language is the most precarious of the three bases of trust and bridging is potentially the weakest form of social capital. Yet bridging is the type of capital that is most closely associated with civil societies as such. Where bonding looks inward to closer communities of interest, and linking focuses on connecting to external resources, bridging capital is the point at which competing elements in civil societies form bonds, however loose.

In Woolcock's (1998) model of social capital, two of his types of social capital – integration (bonding capital) and linkage (linking capital) – overlap with the bonding, bridging, linking triad, but he adds an extra dimension in that social capital is a capacity of governing agents as well as civil society. Thus his further categories of social capital concern the capacities of states: 'organizational integrity', the capacity of state actors to deliver promises and generate trustworthiness; and 'synergy', their capacity to act with other agents (e.g. in partnerships). These two types of institutional social capital relate to the functions of government and governance respectively. Authors concerning themselves with recent democracies, such as Kim (Chapter 11) with South Korea and Taiwan, and Salmenniemi (Chapter 2) with Russia, point precisely to problems with corruption in politics and the lack of the ability or willingness of state actors to engage with civil society on equal and trustworthy terms. However, Western agencies also come under fire from Pishchikova (Chapter 3), as do British local government and regeneration agencies from Diamond (Chapter 4), for a similar lack of institutional social capital. Indeed Woolcock's model, supported by several of the contributors to this volume, is very powerful in countering the suggestion that building social capital from the ground up through associational life can guarantee political legitimacy, trust and participation independently of state action to ensure trustworthiness.

Conclusion

This book has explored three dimensions of civil societies – according to the kinds of ties which characterize them, the scales on which they operate and their interaction with state forms. Social capital forms distinct clusters among the like-minded, more open, but fragile connections between dissimilar citizens and forges links to state and business. There is a shifting balance between these forms. Social movements appear to mobilize at different scales, but the local, global and national all interact. Political transitions and shifts to new forms of governances have opened up new political opportunities, but also new issues and challenges, which will dominate may vary from case to case. One of the implications of this shifting boundary between state and civil society is that civil society has (at least) two faces, one engaging the state, the other keeping a distance from its power. We hope that this volume will stimulate further work in this direction.

References

Banks, S. and Shenton, F. (2001) Regenerating Neighbourhoods: a Critical Look at the Role of Capacity Building, *Local Economy*, 16 (4): 286–298.

Chesters, G. and Welsh, I. (2005) *Complexity and Social Movements: Multitudes at the Edge of Chaos*, London: Routledge.

Edwards, B. and Foley, M. (2001) Civil Society and Social Capital: a Primer, in B. Edwards, M. Foley, and M. Diani (eds) *Beyond Tocqueville: civil society and the social capital debate in comparative perspective*, Hanover, NH: University Press of New England.

Foley, M. and Edwards, B. (1996) The Paradox of Civil Society, *Journal of Democracy*, 7 (3): 38–52.

Hardy, C., Phillips, N. and Lawrence, T. (1998) Distinguishing Trust and Power in Interorganisational Relations: Forms and Facades of Trust, in C. Lane and R. Bachman (eds) *Trust Within and Between Organisations: Conceptual Issues and Empirical Applications*, Oxford: Oxford University Press, pp. 64–87.

Harvey, D. (1993) From Space to Place and Back Again: Reflections on the Condition of Postmodernity, in J. Bird, B. Curtis, T. Putnam, G. Robertson and L. Tickner (eds) *Mapping the Futures: Local Cultures, Global Changes*, London: Routledge, pp. 3–29.

Hodgson, L. (2004) Manufactured Civil Society: Counting the Cost, *Critical Social Policy*, 24 (2): 139–164.

Keane, J. (2003) *Global Civil Society*, Cambridge: Cambridge University Press.

Lane, C. (1998) Introduction: Theories and Issues in the Study of Trust, in C. Lane and R. Bachman (eds) *Trust Within and Between Organisations: Conceptual Issues and Empirical Applications*, Oxford: Oxford University Press, pp. 1–30.

Lowndes, M. and Skelcher, C. (1998) The Dynamics of Multi-organisational Partnerships: an Analysis of Changing Modes of governance, *Public Administration*, 76: 313–333.

Melucci, A. (1989) *Nomads of the Present: Social Movements and Individual Needs in Contemporary Society*, London: Hutchinson Radius.

Melucci, A. (1996) *Challenging the Codes: Collective Action in the Information Age*, Cambridge: Cambridge University Press.

Newman, J. (2005) Participative Governance and the Remaking of the Public Sphere, in J. Newman (ed.) *Remaking Governance: Peoples, Politics and the Public Sphere*, Bristol: Policy Press, pp. 119–138.

O'Doherty, R., Purdue, D., Jowers, P. and Dürrschmidt, J. (1999) Local Exchange and Trading Schemes: a Useful Strand of Community Economic Development Policy? *Environment and Planning A*, 31: 1639–1653.

Purdue, D. (2000) *Anti-Genetix: The Emergence of a Global Movement against GM Food*, London: Ashgate.

Purdue, D. (2001) Neighbourhood Governance: Leadership, Trust and Social Capital, *Urban Studies*, 38 (12): 2211–2224.

Purdue, D. (2005) Defensiveness and Trust: Group Emotions in Community Networks and Partnerships, Paper to be presented at *ECPR Conference*, Budapest, September.

Purdue, D., Diani, M. and Lindsay, I. (2004) Civic Networks in Bristol and Glasgow, *Community Development Journal*, 39 (3): 277–288.

Taylor, M. (2006) Communities in Partnership: Developing a Strategic Voice, *Social Policy and Society*, 5 (2): 269–279.

Woolcock, M. (1998) Social Capital and Economic Development: Towards a Theoretical Synthesis and Policy Framework, *Theory and Society*, 27: 151–208.

Index

Local Strategic Partnerships (LSPs) 6, 54, 55, 59, 220–1
López-Pintor, R. 168
LSPs *see* Local Strategic Partnerships

managed democracy 5, 25, 27
Marshall Plan, new 36–7
Medical Foundation for the Care of Victims of Torture 98
Melucci, A. 7
methodologies 13–15, 91–2, 110–13
Middle East conflict protests 115–17
militancy 77
monitor channel 147–8
Morales, L. 181
movement militancy frame 77–8
movement scenes *see* scenes
multilevel model 154–5, 222–3

Nastia (Russian activist) 19
National Coalition for Anti-Deportation Campaign (NCADC) 99
National Council for One Parent Families (OPF) 102
Nationality, Immigration and Asylum Act 2002 104
National Unemployed Centres Combine (CC) 95, 96–7
NCADC *see* National Coalition for Anti-Deportation Campaign
NDC *see* New Deal for Communities
Neighbourhood Renewal Strategy (NRS) 54, 55, 57
neoliberalism 25, 57
network analysis 90–2
networks: horizontal 89; social 72–3; vertical 89
New Deal 101, 102, 104
New Deal for Communities (NDC) 54
New Labour 104–6
'new' local governance 53–8
New Partnerships Initiative (NPI) 40, 41–2
new social movement protesters 129
new social movements theory 6–7
newspaper data 114
'NGO empowerment' 41–2
NGOs 4, 43, 48
non-profit organizations 24
Norris, P. 169
NPI *see* New Partnerships Initiative
NRS *see* Neighbourhood Renewal Strategy

OPF *see* National Council for One Parent Families

organizational structure: Autonomen 76–7
Oxfam 92, 93–4, 98, 99

parochialism 204
participation 46, 111–13, 117–18, 119, 185–7
participatory democracy 207
patriarchy 78
peace activism 6, 8
peace movement 125–6
Pérez-Díaz, V. 168, 181
personalization: public relations 29–30
police surveillance 30–1
political capital 195–7
political citizenship 20
political groups 24
political identity 196
political opportunity structure (POS) 5, 7, 71, 104
political participation 185–7
political parties: and civic groups 30; Spain 172–3; Ukraine 44; unemployment and asylum policies 105
political power 23
political trust: and social capital 189–95
Polletta, Francesca 217
POS *see* political opportunity structure
poverty 45
power: of civil societies 221; political 28; state 5, 30–2
power imbalance 63
pro-asylum field 92–4, 97–106
pro-beneficiary movements: asylum 88–9, 92–4, 97–106; horizontal networks 92–100; networks 88; and New Labour policies 104–6; unemployment 88–9, 94–5, 96–7, 100–6
professionalization 21–2
Progressive Socialist Party of Ukraine 44
protest cycles 7
protest events 111, 114–22
pro-unemployed field 94–5, 96–7, 100–6
public interest groups 4
Pursiainen, C. 24
Putin, Vladimir 19, 25, 31
Putin administration 30
Putin era 5
Putnam, Robert D. 72, 148, 186, 188, 203

Race Relations Acts 102–3
radical environmental movements 8
RC *see* Refugee Council
reforms: local government 54–5
Refugee Council (RC) 92, 94, 97, 98, 99, 103

Lightning Source UK Ltd.
Milton Keynes UK
28 July 2010

157541UK00001B/31/P